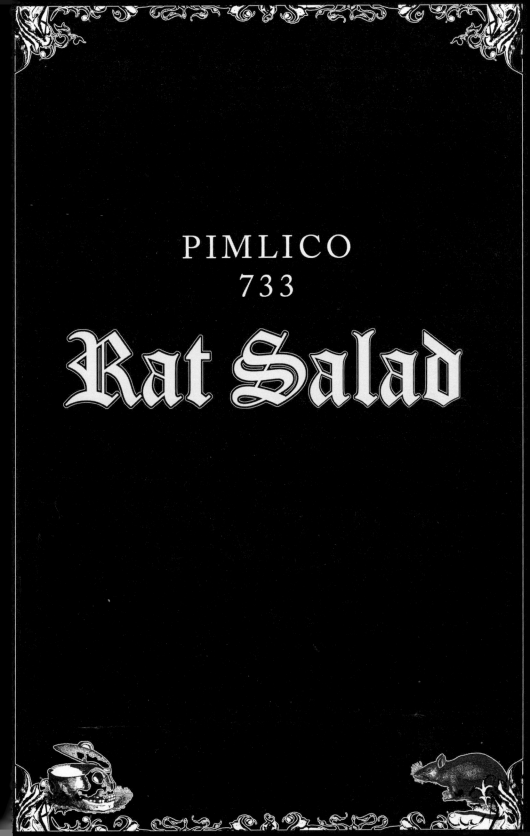

PIMLICO

733

Rat Salad

Rat Salad

BLACK SABBATH

THE CLASSIC YEARS

1969 † 1975

PIMLICO

Paul Wilkinson

Published by Pimlico 2006

2 4 6 8 10 9 7 5 3 1

Copyright © Paul Wilkinson 2006

First published in Great Britain by
Pimlico 2006

Pimlico
Random House, 20 Vauxhall Bridge Road,
London SW1V 2SA

Random House Australia (Pty) Limited
20 Alfred Street, Milson's Point, Sydney,
New South Wales 2061, Australia

Random House New Zealand Limited
18 Poland Road, Glenfield,
Auckland 10, New Zealand

Random House (Pty) Limited
Isle of Houghton, Corner of Boundary Road & Carse O'Gowrie,
Houghton 2198, South Africa

The Random House Group Limited Reg, No. 954009
www.randomhouse.co.uk

A CIP catalogue record for this book
is available from the British Library

ISBN 9781844139247 (from January 2007)
ISBN 1844139247

Papers used by Random House are natural,
recyclable products made from wood grown in sustainable forests;
the manufacturing processes conform to the environmental
regulations of the country of origin

Text design by Matt Broughton

Printed and bound in Great Britain by Scotprint

Contents

Acknowledgements   vii

A Note on Sources   ix

Foreword   1

1.   Wicked World / 1967–69   12
2.   What Is This . . . ? / 1969   26
3.   *Black Sabbath*   36
4.   War Machine Keeps Turning / 1970   56
5.   *Paranoid*   68
6.   Sweet Life / 1971   90
7.   *Master of Reality*   102
8.   Going through Changes / 1972   122
9.   *Vol. 4*   134
10.   Looking for Today / 1973   156
11.   *Sabbath Bloody Sabbath*   166
12.   Killing Yourself to Live / 1974–75   188
13.   *Sabotage*   202

Afterword: Thrill of It All   222

Glossary   230

Credits   237

Index of Songs   238

Acknowledgements

My sincere thanks go to a number of people who have helped me out by enduring early drafts of this book and offering their advice. In particular, I thank Eugene Ludlow, Stephen Barnett, Jon Cooke, and Tim and Rob Crump. I envisage a day when we can all get together over a crate of brown ale and let what's left of our hair down while we turn the clocks back.

I thank the charming Dan Hyams at Regent Sounds and the delightful Shona Robertson of Castle Hillbillies for help with the photographs. David Godwin, Rowan Cope, Sarah Savitt and everybody at DGA, thanks for all your support and advice – always so affably proffered – and for taking this project on.

Will Sulkin, Jörg Hensgen, David Milner and Ros Porter at Random House, thank you for your tireless enthusiasm and for making me feel so very welcome.

I'd like to thank my parents, June and Keith Wilkinson, for allowing me to believe whilst growing up that listening to Black Sabbath was just unacceptable enough to constitute healthy teenage rebellion. It is thanks to them that I never felt it necessary to vandalise a bus stop.

Finally, my biggest thank you goes to Jane, my keenest fan and harshest critic. Thank you for your love and support and for putting up with my funny ways.

A Note on Sources

Wherever practical so to do, I have noted my sources in footnotes. There are a number of sources I have referred to on several occasions. For these I have adopted a kind of shorthand: Mike Stark's *Black Sabbath: An Oral History* (part of the *For the Record* series, edited by Dave Marsh, Avon Books, 1998) is simply represented as Stark; Steven Rosen's *Black Sabbath* (MPG Books, 2001; originally published as *Wheels of Confusion* in 1996) is referenced as Rosen; David Tangye and Graham Wright's *How Black Was Our Sabbath: An Unauthorized View from the Crew* (Sidgwick & Jackson, 2004) is identified as Tangye and Wright; Chris Welch's *Black Sabbath* (Proteus Books, 1982) is listed as Welch; Robert V. Conte and C. J. Henderson's rather slim *Black Sabbath: The Ozzy Osbourne Years* (Studio Chikara Books, 2000) I have noted as Conte and Henderson; and Joe Siegler's thorough and user-friendly website, www.black-sabbath.com – from which my records of the band's early touring itinerary have been fleshed out – is otherwise referred to as Siegler. The page numbers I have cited in reference to these texts and others refer to the editions quoted above.

For general rock history information, I have dipped into *The Rolling Stone Encyclopedia of Rock & Roll* (third edition) edited by Holly George-Warren and Patricia Romanowski (Rolling Stone Press, 2001), *The Complete NME Album Charts* edited by Roger Osborne, Michael Gray and Barry Lazell (Boxtree, 1993), *40 Years of NME Charts* edited by Dafydd Rees, Barry Lazell and Roger Osborne (Boxtree, 1992) and various other dog-eared texts bought at car-boot sales and the like and now littered around the six cubic metres of space laughably described as my study.

As far as the non-musical detail is concerned, I am indebted to Martin Gilbert and volume three of his prodigious and highly readable *A History of the Twentieth Century* (HarperCollins, 1999), together with numerous other sources too disparate or embarrassing to mention. The bits about me have been painfully recollected through several expensive sessions with my Freudian analyst; either that or I've just made them up.

Foreword

I'd been thinking about writing this book for six years, but I'd always managed to come up with an excuse for not doing so. Either I didn't have the time, or there wasn't a market for it, or I wasn't sure I could actually write it, or my computer wasn't working properly. There was always something. And then I suddenly got very sure about things, quit work for six months and gave it a go.

This is not really a biography of Black Sabbath; that's been done already. Not as well or as thoroughly as it might have been, perhaps, but it's been done nonetheless. Sure, there's lots of biographical detail in this book – I've certainly managed to get in all the important bits – but this is more a story of music than of men. It's that way because I want it to be that way. Although it's hard (and probably pointless) to detach the men from the music they created, the music has always been my primary focus – and I've tried to talk about it intelligently. Obviously, I'm a fan of Sabbath's music, and, at times, this must trespass into the words I've committed to print. However, I'm guessing that you're a fan, too. So, if I wax on enthusiastically for three or four hundred words on the merits of, say, a thirty-eight-second curio like 'Embryo', I hope you'll bear with me. I've taken pains to make the ride as smooth as possible: I've avoided the adolescent clichés normally associated with Sabbath-orientated literature, and, despite my fan status, I have tried to aim for moderation wherever I thought it prudent. This might disappoint some fourteen-year-old Americans who are accustomed to reading articles strewn with phrases like 'really rockin', 'awesome riff' and the like, but this book is

not so much aimed at them. It's more for the grown-ups who were there at the time and who lived through it. Rock music actually seemed to mean something then. There were no computer games, video or DVD; there was never anything on television – music was all we had. And – whilst knowing I court dismissal on the grounds of sounding like a boring old fart – the music really *was* so much better. There is no cogent counter-argument to this. Rock music was born, screaming and kicking, in 1956 when Carl Perkins and Elvis Presley fused gospel, roots and boogie-woogie; in Britain, it came into the world in a characteristically more civilised manner with Lonnie Donegan acting as midwife. After a couple of years of retching and hollering, it lived the remainder of its infancy in quiet acquiescence. At six or seven, when it threw forth The Beatles, The Stones and Dylan, it started to display its character and exert its independence: for the first time, it was capable of forming complete sentences, and it could walk to school all by itself. When it hit its teenage years it was unstoppable. Rock was then at its apogee: big, proud, full of itself on the one hand; quiet, introspective and foamingly eloquent on the other. Turning twenty-one, it had its big, last-ditch bacchanal – punk – and has since settled down to a life of industrious mediocrity. Music today is not more vital, inventive or relevant; that is merely the line we are spun by those with a vested interest in its marketing.

The truth is that, unlike today, music in the late sixties and early seventies emanated from a creative movement independent of its parent, corporate ownership. In those days, records were made to shift consciousnesses and opinions, not units. Music was crafted with toil and skill, rock music particularly so, and it offered an escape from the environment, a place for either contemplation or communal revelry. Now, music *is* the environment. It is everywhere: it is used to sell everything from toilet tissue to politicians, nappies to pensions. Its manifold genres and sub-genres multiply, divide, expand and fragment with all the inexorable energy and devious reinvention of a virus. The scope of music has exploded, and its component vicissitudes have crystallised in the igneous effluvia of rock's own great meltdown.

Nothing shocks us anymore. Music has become so populated by sex, hatred and violence – these things have become so expected of modern music – that its latter-day purveyors are termed 'retro' should they choose to avoid them. Music has not only become an industry, it has assumed the mass-produced anonymity of a product. Its artists, merely spokespeople for their parent corporations, have all the lustre of factory workers, with little of consequence to say and no means of expressing it with any lucidity. There is no underground, and there is no real rebellion, because everybody wants to get rich and no one wants to die trying. No one is interested in art anymore; it's all about careers. Rock's great independence, its firebrand obstreperousness, has been consumed by the need to make a buck, and individual rock stars have become battery chickens fed on the excrement of their own publicity.

Music itself has become a hurtling juggernaut so fast, so wide and so all-encompassing that the fleetest of feet and the most ascetic of lifestyles can't avoid it. It has its own TV stations; it blasts out of speeding cars and leaks out of incontinent Walkmans and iPods, and the vast majority of it is crap. Of course, a lot of late sixties/early seventies' music was crap too (for every Leonard Cohen, there was, most unfortunately, a Gilbert O'Sullivan), and not everything that The Stones, The Who, Dylan or David Bowie put out in the seventies equalled *Sticky Fingers*, *Who's Next*, *Blood on the Tracks* or *Hunky Dory*. But there was a reassuring predominance of truly excellent music created then, as any nostalgic browse through the relevant pages of an album chart encyclopaedia will substantiate, and the good-to-crap ratio was a lot more in our favour. Music then was intelligent even when it was unintelligible. So when Uriah Heep or Caravan were singing about rainbow demons or weeing in the garden, there was always the compositional opulence of, say, a D major ninth followed by a G minor sixth that somehow kept you a believer. It was a time when the 'eight' in 'middle eight' was more likely to refer to minutes than bars, and when it was absolutely impermissible to repeat a chorus and 'commercial' (the term is distinctly pejorative) even to have one in your song. In short, it elevated and championed everything which modern music seeks to subjugate: art, intelligence, individuality

and excellence. When it failed – and some of it *did* fail – it did so both heroically and unashamedly and ended up looking spectacularly ridiculous. There's no way you can blame any of its failures on either apathy or lack of invention (well, not until 1974, anyway), and this contrasts markedly with so much of today's vapid output.

It would be difficult to discuss – positively and at any great length – the creative or compositional quality of today's music. With Sabbath's early output, however, there is no such difficulty. Nevertheless, it's hard to talk about music intelligently without resorting to a number of trade terms. If you're not a musician, you might have difficulty with words and phrases like 'arpeggio' and 'suspended fourth' – not to mention D major ninth and G minor sixth above. Wherever I've used such terms, I've put explanatory words in a Glossary, located towards the back of the book. In not avoiding the technical niceties of musical nomenclature, I am assuring that I don't dumb down for the ones of us who do know our crotchets from our quavers, and – bit of a bold assertion, this – I'm providing a fuller appreciation of the music under discussion. So there's no need to put this book back on the shelf if you think your musical knowledge is not up to scratch; on the contrary, if you read this book, you might end up knowing a lot more about the subject – assuming your interest holds out as far as the Glossary.

None of the members of Black Sabbath has contributed to this book. This is not because I've asked them and they have refused; it is rather that I consider them to have done their bit already. In a six-year period, those four individuals produced six truly exceptional albums, about which remarkably little of consequence has been written. Sure, you do come across the occasional retrospective, but these tend to be wrongly centred in my opinion: they do little to address the musical content of these records and merely concentrate on Sabbath's output as some sort of primordial grunge gene pool. In contrast, this effort reviews their legacy in its own right – not merely as the now sacrosanct ancestry of Nirvana, Marilyn Manson and the ever-increasing tide of NuMetal bands currently featuring in such organs as *Kerrang!*, *Metal Hammer* and their like. Along the way, I've tirelessly set out the case for Sabbath: what made

them so great, so – and this word has been so abused, you'll have to try and remember what it really means – *unique*. I've looked at the music note by note, bar by fascinating bar; when something unusual happens, I tell you about it. By the end of the book, we have some idea of what makes Sabbath's songs so different and immediately recognisable. Another reason I have made no effort to contact the individuals concerned over the biographical element in this book is because – and I don't mean this to be in any way critical – I can't be sure that their memories are absolutely accurate. Where I have come across differing versions of the same event, and I have considered that the various versions are worthy of note, I have noted them. Furthermore, much as I would dearly love to tune up with Tony and have him teach me his weird stuff, I can't allow such proximity to colour the tone of this book. I love Sabbath, but some of their stuff doesn't work; I want to retain sufficient distance to say that without feeling I have necessarily betrayed anyone. And, although I certainly have criticisms, I have no wish to belittle the achievements of perhaps the most inventive – and arguably the most important – heavy rock band ever. Nor am I of a mind to place further obstacles in the way of the members' continued attempts at reunion; so I've absolutely no desire to rake over old coals, denigrate individuals by focusing on their weaknesses or in any way strive for contentiousness when simplicity and concord seem altogether more appropriate.

Another thing you won't find in this book is any concerted analysis of Black Sabbath's album releases from 1976 on. I am aware that, for many people, Sabbath ceased to be when Ozzy Osbourne left, but I do not include myself amongst that set. For what it's worth, I think the first two post-Osbourne albums (with Dio singing) and the Tony Martin trio of *Eternal Idol*, *Headless Cross* and *Tyr* have much to recommend them. It took me some time to get round to listening to them during my estrangement from music in the eighties, but they are, however, beyond the scope of this book – as are the comparatively lacklustre Ozzy-era efforts *Technical Ecstasy* and *Never Say Die*. Were I to go into detail about every Black Sabbath release, this book would not fit so easily in your pocket, and it would be more expensive to buy. Besides which, the first six albums

are widely recognised as forming a single body of work – and I am more than content to treat them as such.

Because this book isn't really a biography as such – as I've said, I've concentrated more on the music – I've not tried all that hard to fill in the gaps in the story. That there *are* gaps isn't surprising: the state the band members were in for much of the seventies doesn't easily lend itself to lucid retrospection. Because I've not resorted to guesswork to fatten the story out for you, I'm especially certain that what I *have* written is accurate. You certainly won't be coming across such screaming howlers as

> … while the guitarist was plunking around on some chords, the rest of the band heard the ideas, found inspiration and turned the song, ultimately, into 'Changes' (the track on which Rick Wakeman appeared).*

Well, that's about it then. I hope you enjoy the book. Thanks for buying it.

In September 1974, I was twelve years old and just starting my second year at secondary school. I seem to remember that I was quite keen on football at the time, but not on very much else. During lesson breaks at school, I and a dozen or so others would vigorously pursue a tennis ball around the school playground – attacking it violently with our feet – until the bell would ring out, and we were summoned back to the tedious business of learning. Such was our decorousness, and so different were the times then, that some of us would even dust off our uniform trousers and straighten our ties before reaching the classrooms. For some reason, this pleases me in retrospect.

---

* Rosen (p. 79). Wakeman *didn't* appear on Sabbath's 'Changes' (and would probably not welcome the assertion that he did) – nor, indeed, anything from its parent album, *Vol. 4*; he did, however, play piano on David Bowie's 'Changes'.

Of course, school was a bore: thirty-five-minute classes dragged for ostensible hours; seventy-minute ones seemed like minor eternities. Although the licensed butchery that passed for woodwork and the mind-numbing hours of colouring-in for art were bad enough, it was the surreal eclecticism of modern languages that proved the most difficult, and ultimately fruitless, to endure. To this day, I can still remember the tedious goings-on of Hans und Lieselotte – not forgetting their ubiquitous pet Lumpi der Hund – and the inglorious habitudes of the anaemic famille Marsaud – depicted in ghostly white visages and invariably dressed in khaki – and I have to wonder, why do I still know this, and what possible good has it served me? I once lost my passport in Berlin, and, although my German wasn't anywhere near good enough to make this known to the local constabulary, I was, at least, able to tell them that my name was Hans, I worked in a bank which I travelled to by tram, I had a sister named Lieselotte, and that the castle was only three kilometres from here.

But school was worth it on account of the aeons of playtime available to the indolent scholar. And there's a certain camaraderie you come across with your teammates when you've been on the wrong end of a 10–0 drubbing in a fifteen-minute lesson break. It transcends the ordinary levels of adolescent friendship; it is something approximating the communal spirit you find in air-raid shelters and hospitals: tacit understanding, shared fear and shame, and, added to the cocktail, a little British embarrassment at having broken out into a sweat over nothing.

And it was during these athletic, if inexpert, recreations that I was fortunate enough to become friendly with Rob Crump. Rob was my age and was renowned for looking and acting a bit weird. He had an irritating nervous habit of drumming his fingers violently against desktops, his teeth biting down onto his lower lip as if in the process of expelling some particularly colourful fricative. All the while, his eyes would twinkle as if to say *I know something you don't* – and so he'd get hit quite a bit. His hair was unkempt, and it possessed the strange faculty of extending further horizontally than it did vertically. This fascinated me at the time, and I would often wonder whether it managed this feat through some

quirk of its own curious biochemical composition or an eccentricity of static electricity – or whether he merely sprayed it with Silvikrin. While the rest of us were etching 'Showaddywaddy' onto our pencil cases, Rob harboured more exotic tastes in music, benefiting, as he did, from having an older brother who was sufficiently well off to buy albums regularly. This was an expensive business in those days: albums were around three quid in 1974; that's about twenty-five pounds in today's money. You couldn't just roll along to your local store and come out with an armful (like you can today with CDs – if you're like me and totally irresponsible).

Rob had invited me over to his house one Saturday that September. I can't remember now how I felt about the invitation – whether I looked forward to the visit, whether anything particular had been planned for the day – but I do remember, and I remember this very vividly, that the sky that day was impossibly blue, and the air was infused with the faint, cold throb of autumn. The golds and browns of the trees shone like new shoe-leather against the sky, the surrounding hills like giant piles of honey. I remember feeling quite blithely happy as I walked the two-and-a-half miles to his house along the quiet country roads so familiar to me in my childhood.

At some point after my reaching Rob's, we repaired to his older brother's room to survey his spectacular record collection. Not that I had very much interest. I mean, I wanted to get to know this culture, this other world of long hair and moustaches, nonsensical band names and inscrutable lyrics, I just didn't think I'd ever really embrace it. You see, you have to realise that my musical interests in those days were really rather limited. I had bought The Osmonds' 'Crazy Horses' single with my own pocket money the previous autumn, and my parents had bought me The Beatles' 'Red Album' the following Christmas, and I'd also quite liked a song I'd heard on the radio the previous year that went, or so I thought, 'I wanna be a lettuce',* but – honestly now – I really preferred the schmaltzy orchestral stuff that went with the adverts on

---

* Alice Cooper's 'Elected'.

TV. I make mention of this merely in order to assert the unimpeach-ability of my credentials.

So it was with no great interest, then, that I watched Rob withdraw *Sabbath Bloody Sabbath* from its pristine sleeve. The artwork looked quite flash, I thought, as he gently manoeuvred the resplendent disc onto the turntable, but I didn't really expect to like it.

And that's really where my love affair with Black Sabbath began – right there in that tiny, congested bedroom in the sumptuous, fat belly of the Peak District.

Thank you, Rob.

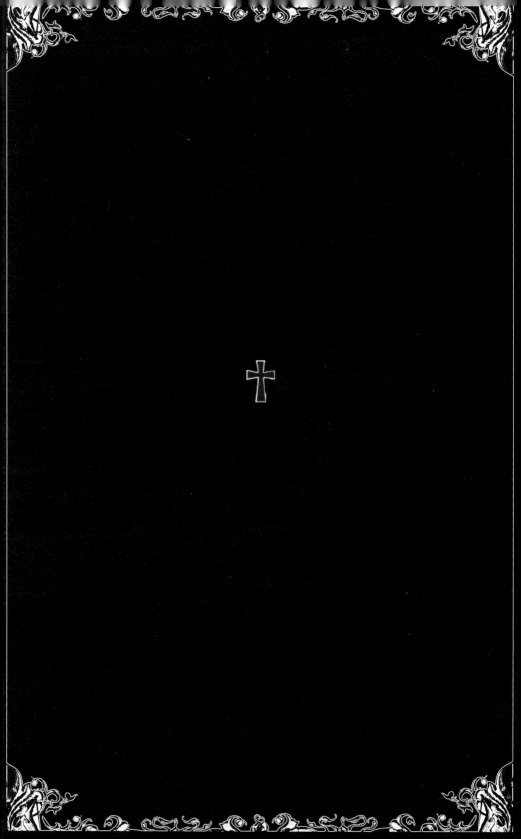

Chapter One
Wicked World / 1967–69

✝

It's 1967 and America is both at peace and at war. On 14 January, Golden Gate Park in California hosts the 'Human Be-In': The Grateful Dead, Jefferson Airplane and Quicksilver Messenger Service – the three leading exponents of the burgeoning San Francisco scene – together with counterculture gurus Allen Ginsberg and Timothy Leary and over 30,000 self-proclaimed hippies, enjoy free tea and oranges whilst propagating the message of universal love. Martin Luther King urges black Americans to take to the streets in an organised campaign of civil disobedience. In Vietnam, meanwhile, a combined force of 32,000 American and South Vietnamese set out to destroy the communist stronghold in the Mekong Delta, south-west of Saigon. In the last two years, the number of American dead in Vietnam has exceeded 15,000. Peace and war. In Washington, President Johnson's portrait is publicly displayed above the words WAR CRIMINAL; Che Guevara is killed; the Boston Strangler is sentenced to life imprisonment after pleading guilty to thirteen murders; China explodes its first hydrogen bomb, part and parcel of its ongoing Cultural Revolution.

The Beatles release *Sgt. Pepper*, a Technicolor northern-suburban romp depicting a fast-disappearing England. Italian film-maker Michelangelo Antonioni's *Blow-Up* continues to screen on the art-house circuit, its languid surrealism portraying an England we all want to buy into yet know we could never afford.

Over three days in June, 50,000 attend Monterey International Pop Festival* – the biggest and best of the various outdoor sixties' festivals.

---

* Probably most famous for Hendrix's immolation of his Fender, Monterey Pop (as it became known) sounded the death knell for saccharine sixties acts such as The Mamas & The Papas, The Association and Johnny Rivers and, not to put too fine a point on it, 'pop' itself. Out of the crucible that was Monterey came the hard-edged chiaroscuro of rock – a true counterculture not supported and made respectable by Top Forty radio stations – which proved a foundation for the musical eccentricities of the seventies. Often seen as merely a dry run for the more famous Woodstock festival two years later, Monterey was perhaps the definitive sixties event.

The event is singularly responsible for creating global stars out of Janis Joplin, Jimi Hendrix, Otis Redding and The Who,* and guides pop through its metamorphosis, out of which it emerges as rock.

A fascist military coup in Greece ushers in the regime of the Greek Colonels, whilst French president, confirmed egomaniac and troublemaker, Charles de Gaulle, speaks out against British entry into the EEC. The BBC rethinks its radio service; as a result, British kids have their first onshore 'pop' station: Radio One.

On 3 December, Dr Christiaan Barnard, the South African pioneer of heart surgery, performs the first heart transplant on a human being. It is acclaimed as a major breakthrough – despite the fact that the patient doesn't even live to see Christmas.

As we move into 1968, most of the seventy-eight million television sets in the United States are turned on and tuned in to Vietnam. Highlights are being broadcast home to a troubled nation divided in its support of the war. On 31 January, the North Vietnamese Army launches what will become known as the Tet Offensive – a sweeping initiative, involving 70,000 Viet Cong, which takes the war out of the jungles and into the towns and cities of South Vietnam. Within a few hours, twenty-four major battles are underway. Saigon, the South Vietnamese capital, is overrun, and American Embassy invaded, by the NVA. Around fifty million viewers, stateside, are watching it all on TV. The following day, as Saigon passes back into the hands of American and South Vietnamese forces, televisions show the Saigon chief of police, General Nguyen Ngoc Loan, calmly executing a Viet Cong prisoner with a single revolver shot to the head. Reality TV.

Kubrick's *2001: A Space Odyssey* and Roger Vadim's *Barbarella* make space chic; James Earl Ray and Sirhan Sirhan bring us back to Earth with

---

Despite the conspicuous presence of armed police and 50,000 fans – many of whom were indulging in Monterey Purple, a specially concocted variant of LSD – there were no arrests and no reports of trouble.

* Redding was to die later in the year when his plane crashed into a Wisconsin lake; Joplin and Hendrix lasted until 1970; The Who lost drummer Keith Moon in 1978 and bassist John Entwistle in 2002. Paul Butterfield, Mike Bloomfield, Laura Nyro, Skip Spence from Moby Grape, Al Jackson from the MGs, Mama Cass and Papa John Phillips, and Bob Hite, Alan Wilson and Henry Vestine from Canned Heat – all of whom performed at Monterey Pop – have also since died.

two bumps: Martin Luther King, genius and architect of peaceful persuasion, is shot dead in Memphis, and Robert Kennedy follows two months later in Los Angeles. The Soviet Union sends tanks into Czechoslovakia, and everybody holds their breath. All around the world, anxious governments and police forces are trying to deal with increasing student unrest: there are riots in Holland, France, America, Japan . . . Mexico has both student riots *and* the Olympics. African-American athletes punching the Black Power salute from the winners' podium send shockwaves through America's bloated white underbelly.

Whereas The Beatles' *Magical Mystery Tour* EP, released the previous Christmas, had seen the band trying to prolong the civic psychedelia initiated by *Sgt. Pepper*, it is The Stones who have their fingers on the world's now quickening pulse: 'Sympathy For The Devil' and 'Street Fighting Man', with their references to dead Kennedys, risings in the street and revolution, mirroring the turbulence of the times.

The Pope officially prohibits the use of artificial contraception amongst Catholics. Subsequently, the UK government legalises abortion. Post hoc ergo propter hoc.

Nigeria and Biafra are at bloody loggerheads, the latter having asserted its independence from the former. Britain offers famine relief to both, whilst secretly supplying arms to Nigeria.

While Cliff Richard sings 'Congratulations', Roman Polanski's *Rosemary's Baby*, Michael Reeves' *Witchfinder General** and George Romero's *Night of the Living Dead* hit the high-street Odeons. Valerie Solanis, would-be actress and member of SCUM,* shoots and wounds Andy Warhol. The Summer of Love was last year's thing. The Beatles get with it again, join the Revolution and release the 'White Album' for Christmas. Charles Manson writes a letter to Santa.

Back in Vietnam, American soldiers devastate the South Vietnamese village of My Lai. More than a hundred villagers – none of them soldiers and a great proportion of them women and children – are butchered in an act of pointless, gung-ho brutality.

* Titled *The Conqueror Worm* in the US.
* The Society for Cutting Up Men. Cripes.

So we limp edgily into 1969. Three days before Nixon is inaugurated as 37th President of the United States, Czech student Jan Palach publicly burns himself to death in Wenceslas Square, Prague, in protest at the continued Soviet presence in Czechoslovakia. Despite significant US troop withdrawals from Vietnam, and Nixon's 'Peace with Honor' pledges, hostilities rage on and plastic-wrapped bodies continue being returned to sender.

Ah, the good old days.

Madeleine Morgan takes me one lunchtime into the girls' toilets at school and kisses me on the lips. It lasts for so long I begin to think it's some kind of dental procedure. Uncertain of what to do with my hands, I thrust them as far into my pockets as they will go. They remain there, tightly compressed into rigid fists as she goes about her business. She's seven years old – where did she learn to do that? As a result, I do badly on the spelling test afterwards (she kept looking at me funny and I couldn't really concentrate).

August 1969. We're on a ferry, battling our way southwards through an unseasonably inhospitable English Channel. As the ferry dips and rocks, ploughing an awkward furrow through the frothing waters, four young men, dog-tired and bug-eyed and little more than lads really, are wrestling to keep hold of their drinks as they slip and slide across the Formica tops of the tables bolted to the floor of the ship's bar. Sea spray hits the windows like blood in a slasher movie, as the troubled craft, pitching this way and that, edges its way further from the comfort of England and deeper into one of the world's most notorious maritime black spots. It won't be a short crossing at this rate, and the four individuals are fortifying themselves with regular, inelegant lurches to the duty-free bar.

Four more pints clonk onto the table; four hands reach out quickly in order to save further liquid from spilling onto the already sticky floor. Above the table, a steady fug of cigarette smoke hangs like a nimbus,

the ashtrays are full and the air is punctured by the soft, nasal laughter of the four men, beer froth now settling like cake icing upon their upper lips.

They're talking about music. We shouldn't be surprised: these four men are musicians. They're a second-rate, four-piece rock-blues band from Birmingham, and, at the moment, they're calling themselves Earth. Let's have a look at them.

The oldest of the group is guitarist Tony Iommi; he is six months on from his twenty-first birthday. His longer-than-shoulder-length hair, tail-fin moustache and soft, doleful eyes give him the appearance of a benevolent spaniel. Then there is drummer Bill Ward, a close friend of Iommi's. His longer-than-shoulder-length hair, tail-fin moustache and bright, inquisitive eyes give him the appearance of a playful spaniel. These two had played together in groups called The Rest and Mythology before they came to be in Earth.

The singer's name is John 'Ozzy' Osbourne, and, with his longer-than-shoulder-length hair, lack of moustache and deep, penetrative eyes, he manages to look nothing like a spaniel at all. A convicted burglar and sometime worker in a slaughterhouse, and a school year behind Iommi and Ward, Osbourne is a close friend of the fourth member of this quartet, bassist Terence 'Geezer' Butler. Butler, with his longer-than-shoulder-length hair, tail-fin moustache and don't-hit-me eyes, has the appearance of a spaniel that has just crapped on your carpet and is expecting the worst. These two had played together in the short-lived The Rare Breed before throwing their hand in with Iommi and Ward. When the four first got together, sixteen months previously, they called themselves Polka Tulk* and later changed their name to Earth.*

Since then, it's been a bit of a struggle. Holding down paying jobs during the day whilst playing in the evenings has been proving difficult. Osbourne's periodic forays into burglary have been nothing short of

---

* The name Polka Tulk derived from either a tin of talcum powder belonging to one of Osbourne's sisters or a local Indian clothing establishment; both versions have been well and copiously documented.
* Various embellishments on these names have been recorded: Polka Tulk Blues Band, Earth Blues Company and Earth Blues Band being but three.

disastrous: on one occasion, his detection and subsequent prosecution and conviction are facilitated by the fact that he had sported gloves so worn out that he had left thumbprints at the scene of the crime. A short period in Winson Green prison had followed, during which time he started what was to become a lengthy obsession by boldly tattooing the word OZZY on the knuckles of his left hand.

Ward has been busily gigging with a variety of bands for the last six years. Originally inspired by the post-war big-band sound, and adopting Gene Krupa and Buddy Rich in particular as heroes, Ward's baptism into rock and roll began in 1958 with Elvis Presley's 'Jailhouse Rock'. Teaming up with Iommi as early as 1963, Ward has been assimilating the explosive scatter-bomb techniques of Keith Moon and the thunderous, syncopated backbeat rhythms of drinking buddy John Bonham into his methodology.

Butler, meanwhile, not long out of school, has developed an interest in the popular occult fiction of Denis Wheatley, Hammer Horror films and, more seriously, the megalomaniac writings of the English überwitch and self-proclaimed 'Great Beast', Aleister Crowley. A confirmed vegan since the age of eight, Butler, stoically tolerant of his reluctantly adopted soubriquet 'Geezer', began playing guitar when he was eleven, after his brother bought him an acoustic for his birthday. Like so many of his contemporaries, he only became seriously interested in music when he heard The Beatles. He began growing his trademark moustache at age seventeen, after being introduced to the music of Frank Zappa and the Mothers of Invention. Switching to bass later on, after realising that he couldn't compete with Iommi on guitar, Butler has developed a unique style: replicating Iommi's parts on bass – a habit which comes naturally to a guitar player – he exploits the gaps with some imaginative fill playing influenced by his admiration for Cream's Jack Bruce.

A keen fan of Hank Marvin & The Shadows, Iommi, who has held down a variety of jobs whilst trying to pursue his musical career, had once worked on a cutting machine at a sheet-metal factory. On his last day in the job, just three years earlier, an accident had left him without the tips to two of the fingers on his right hand. If you're a right-handed

guitar player, it is not such a big deal, assuming you use a pick: the pick can effectively be held between the thumb and any other finger; if, however, you play guitar left-handed, then such an injury will significantly reduce the amount of activity possible on the fretboard of the guitar. Iommi is left-handed.

What happens to Iommi between the accident and this ferry journey is not only a courageous and inspirational tale, it is also a particularly significant element in the Black Sabbath story.

Originally tutored on the accordion and later taking up drums before settling on guitar, Iommi has been accustomed to changing instruments according to whim and circumstance, and this must have been going through his head whilst he was trying to recuperate and focus on his future. For a time, Iommi's outlook is so bleak that he resigns himself to a career outside music.

But then something truly wonderful happens.

A friend of Iommi's presents him with a Django Reinhardt album. Reinhardt, the Belgian jazz guitar player, only had two fingers on his fretting hand but still managed to produce work of stunning virtuosity. Although Iommi doesn't at first like the music Reinhardt has recorded, he nevertheless marvels at his dexterity:

> He was the main inspiration, without a doubt . . . I was taken
> aback that he could do it with such a disability.*

Revitalised by this discovery, Iommi determines to come up with a way that he can continue playing the guitar. In a flash of kitchen-sink inspiration of thrift-driven ingenuity, his first step is to fashion plastic 'thimbles' from a washing-up bottle. These he then slips onto the ends of his affected fingers. This takes him half the way there: although these basic prosthetics enable him to hold down the strings, there is still too much residual pain in his injured fingers to make continued playing possible. There is pain because the strings, with the standard tuning, offer

---

* Iommi, speaking to Helen Dalley for *Total Guitar* magazine, 2000.

19

too much resistance to his fingers: they are simply too tight.

So he loosens them. On stringed instruments, three things determine pitch – that is, how high or low a given string will sound: the gauge or thickness of the string, its tension and its length. By reducing the tension on the strings to accommodate the tenderness of his fingers, Iommi was also lowering the pitch of each of those strings. And in order for him to be able to follow Iommi's playing in rehearsal, Geezer Butler had to detune his bass. In effect, this, as they say in the business, gives them more bottom: it makes their sound even heavier.

The music our boys are playing at this time is largely blues-inflected twelve-bar rock.* There are probably two reasons for this: blues is big at the moment and is attracting a reasonably appreciative audience, and blues is easy to play – badly, that is – so a lot of groups are starting off playing blues to develop an understanding both of music and of each other. This is the time of the great British blues explosion; you can't walk more than half a mile in any direction without bumping into a blues band. John Mayall, Fleetwood Mac, The Yardbirds, Alexis Korner, Cream . . . these are just a few of the names that will survive through the years; there are countless others at this moment plying their trade up and down the country who will shortly after slip into musical oblivion.

And that is the real danger here. No one knows exactly how long the blues boom is going to last. So, realising that it might prove difficult for the band to assert any kind of individual identity amongst so much blues-inflected music, their manager, Jim Simpson, encourages the boys to incorporate some jazz chops. Simpson, himself a big jazz fan and something of a fixer in the Birmingham club scene, is also proving instrumental in getting the band regular gigs in the West Midlands, as well as putting together a short but eventful tour of Scandinavia and Germany and a subsequent return to the infamous Star Club in Hamburg's notorious Reeperbahn district for a week-long residency. That's where they're bound for now, on that ferry.

---

* Butler recalled the band's rehearsing eighteen twelve-bar blues numbers (Willie Dixon, Howlin' Wolf, Lightnin' Hopkins, Muddy Waters, that kind of thing) on its first rehearsal day; Butler speaking to John Stix for *Guitar for the Practicing Musician*, May 1994.

The previous month, Iommi had had the chance of hitting the big time. After having lost Mick Abrahams, who went on to form Blodwyn Pig, Jethro Tull had been looking for a guitarist. Iommi had landed the job just in time to appear with Tull on The Rolling Stones' *Rock & Roll Circus* film,* where he mimed unconvincingly – and with little evident enthusiasm – to a rendition of 'A Song For Jeffrey'. Within a month, however, Iommi had left Tull and joined his mates back in Birmingham. Freeze-frame:

Pretty big decision this. Look at the facts: Earth had no record contract and no record company interest. They were playing the Transit-van circuit in Britain and, as we know, were booked in for a residency at the Star Club. Now, everyone has to start somewhere, and the Star Club was a pretty good place to start,* but it was still a long way from being there. Tull, on the other hand, had made it: their first album, *This Was*, had spent time in the charts over the autumn and had peaked at number five; their next album, *Stand Up*, was to spend six weeks at the top. Tull were huge, in fact: in *Melody Maker*'s annual poll of 1969, they were only kept from the top of the best band category by The Beatles. More significantly perhaps, Earth were *supporting* Tull when Ian Anderson, singer and flautist for the latter, approached Iommi and offered him the job of guitarist.

So why then did he quit Tull?✣ Why give up the steady paycheck, and the (almost) assured renown, and go back to struggling Earth? Sentimentality? Fear of the big time?

> It just wasn't right, so I left. At first, I thought [Jethro Tull] were great, but I didn't much go for having a leader in the band, which was Ian Anderson's way. When I came back from

---

* Shot on 10 December 1968, and subsequently played down by The Stones (until recently) as they were bested by just about everyone else on the bill, particularly The Who.
* We all know that The Beatles – among many others – did their stint there. It has since been reported that Black Sabbath broke The Beatles' attendance records at the club – a quite remarkable achievement, since they were nowhere near as good, as handsome or as integrated as The Beatles.
✣ Tangye and Wright (p. 16) recount that Iommi had second thoughts after deciding to quit Tull and tried to negotiate a return. However, in the meantime, Tull had recruited Martin Barre, and, after the Stones' *Rock & Roll Circus* footage had been shot, Iommi's services were no longer required.

Tull, I came back with a new attitude altogether. They taught me that, to get on, you've got to work for it . . . Somebody's got to be a leader of sorts . . . I was put in the spot of leader, really.*

Interesting: when Iommi joined Tull he didn't like the idea of there being a leader; in fact, he left on account of it. When he rejoined Earth, however, he not only recognised that there had to be a leader in the band, he selflessly appointed himself to the position. But let's all be grateful that he did: there is no doubt that, without him, Earth would have dried up, and there would have been no Sabbath, and can you really imagine him hacking his way through 'Aqualung' and 'Songs From The Wood'? Thought not. Earmark the page though: the issue of Iommi as the *de facto* leader of Black Sabbath comes up again in this narrative.

So, Iommi has returned to the fold and taken on the responsibility for whipping Earth into shape. The first step is to consolidate rehearsal time and exercise a discipline in performance. The best way to do this is by getting out there and playing. The next thing to crop up on the agenda is the band's name. That's what our boys are talking about on the ferry now.

The consensus is that it's not really strong enough to represent the kind of music they're playing. There's another problem, too: they had recently been booked to play at a dinner dance, an engagement which they kept, only to discover that they had been mistaken for *another* band called Earth.* The mistake didn't come to light until the lads turned up for the gig to be met with plaudits for their recent record release, an achievement that was still some way down the line for them. To make matters worse, this other Earth wore suits and ties and gained a following by playing lounge pop on the cabaret and wedding circuits, a far cry from the music our boys were striving to put together. I'm not

* Iommi in Rosen (p. 37).
* An understandable confusion. Incidentally, Bruce Springsteen was in a blues-based, Cream-style trio called Earth in 1967. It's too much to expect that he spent time touring the West Midlands pubs and clubs.

talking about the twelve-bar repertoire now; I'm talking about the new music the band were working on.

> We were waiting to go into a rehearsal in Birmingham one day and, across the road, there was a cinema and there was a horror movie on . . . and Tony said, 'Innit funny, man, that people pay money to see a movie that scares the shit out of them? Why don't we try to put that to music – like an evil kind of music?' And that's really the way it started, and we wrote the song 'Black Sabbath', and, on the ferry going to Germany to do some work in Hamburg, we said, 'Why don't we call the name of the band Black Sabbath?' Geezer thought of the name Black Sabbath.*

And with Butler's satanic preoccupations steadily insinuating themselves into the band's music, we have all four cornerstones of what was to become the Sabbath phenomenon in place: the devilish lyrics, the commitment to creating scary music, the dropped-tone guitars producing sounds of unimagined heaviness and, finally, the name. All we need now is for someone to give them a recording contract.

---

*Osbourne, speaking in the video *Don't Blame Me: The Tales of Ozzy Osbourne,* Sony Music Entertainment, 1991. Although the band named themselves after their own composition, it must be noted that *Black Sabbath* was the English title of a 1963 (not 1935, as you may have read elsewhere) horror film by the Italian director, Mario Bava. The blurb for the film, originally entitled *I Tre Volti Della Paura* (trans. *The Three Faces of Fear*), read, 'This is the night of the nightmare . . . when a headless corpse rides the cold night wind . . .'. In other words, Butler didn't so much think of the name 'Black Sabbath' as co-opt it. Although the name change was agreed on 9 August, the band didn't perform as Black Sabbath until they had returned to England later that month.

Chapter Two

What Is This . . . ? / 1969

†

As 1969 continues, a newly sworn-in President Nixon declares that America must never again be drawn into a war on Asian soil* – a promise that displays as little prescience as it does serious intention. Before the details of the My Lai massacre are laid before the world's public, Nixon withdraws 25,000 combat troops from Vietnam. This does little to assuage the war protesters, who, by that October, are massing in their millions on the streets of America.

Attention is momentarily deflected from the Asian conflict, and some national pride restored, in July, when America succeeds in landing two men on the moon. Losing out on the prime objective of the space race, the Soviet Union has to settle for second prize: a hamper consisting of the first docking of, and subsequent crew transferral from, two manned spacecraft, and the landing of a satellite on Venus.

As Senator Edward Kennedy gets a two-month suspended sentence for killing Mary Jo Kopechne at Chappaquiddick, Dennis Hopper's *Easy Rider* and Lindsay Anderson's *If . . .* posit an amoral nonchalance and vain rebelliousness that are to be crystallised at Altamont before the year is out.

The summer sees tensions in Northern Ireland between Catholics and Protestants erupt into violence. In the largely Protestant city of Londonderry, orchestrated acts of Protestant aggression and provocation finally elicit a response from the burgeoning Catholic minority. In a measure intended initially as providing protection for the beleaguered Catholic community, British prime minister Harold Wilson sends troops to the troubled province – an act that is immediately regarded as treacherous by the Protestant Loyalists.

---

* The Declaration of Guam, January 1969.

On the mainland, as capital punishment is permanently abolished, renegade Tory MP Enoch Powell, a year on from his infamous 'Rivers of Blood' speech, publicly calls for the repatriation of all black immigrants.

On a muggy August night, failed singer-songwriter Charles Manson sends his lapdog acolytes trick-or-treating at two houses in Beverly Hills. In what Manson maintains is merely his interpretation of the subliminal agenda of The Beatles' 'White Album', a total of 169 stab wounds are inflicted, seven people die – including the pregnant Sharon Tate, wife of film director Roman Polanski – and the slogans DEATH TO PIGS, RISE and HEALTHER (*sic*) SKELTER are daubed onto walls and fridges in the lifeblood of the seven victims. Although the neighbours are largely oblivious, a nearby camper hears a shout of 'Oh, God, no! Please . . . God, no!' as it rips through the night.

The theatrical sex-revue *Oh! Calcutta!* – capitalising on theatregoers' acceptance of nudity garnered two years earlier with *Hair* (it's okay as long as it's tribal) – premieres in New York. Upstate, the counterculture's no less theatrical production, Woodstock – featuring, amongst others, Janis Joplin, Jimi Hendrix, Ten Years After, Crosby, Stills, Nash & Young and half a million audience participators – plays for one performance only in the open air.

Kurt Vonnegut's *Slaughterhouse-Five*, a dispassionate, cross-temporal and almost dreamlike recollection of the Allied bombing of Dresden in 1945, sits alongside Richard Attenborough's *Oh! What a Lovely War*, a film that elevates armed conflict to a level of absurdity concomitant with the goings-on in Vietnam. In stark contrast, the first in vitro fertilisation of a human egg is achieved in the English university city of Cambridge.

As the US launches the first jumbo jets on commercial flights, England and France test-drive Concorde, a multi-million-pound project that will bring supersonic flight within the reach of the spectacularly rich. Not to be outdone, the US sends up space probes, bringing the first close-up pictures of Mars back to Earth.

After plague is discovered amongst sheep grazing adjacent to a nerve gas testing site in Utah, and Presidential Advisor on Urban Affairs Daniel Moynihan warns that Earth has 'less than a 50–50 chance of surviving until 1980', the US takes its first steps to ban the insecticide DDT. Meanwhile, it continues to strafe the Vietnamese countryside and its people with Agent Orange and napalm.

The innocence of the sixties dies screaming at the stake.

Contracted to perform up to seven sets a day – largely to a clientele more intent on inebriation, chemically induced oblivion and getting off with the local hookers – Sabbath's week at Hamburg's Star Club is nothing if not arduous. With an increasingly original repertoire, still augmented by twelve-bar standards and some lengthy improvisations, the audiences are proving hard to win over. This is not so much because the band is uninteresting; rather it is the audiences who are proving almost wilfully nonchalant. Osbourne:

> [I] had the feeling that they didn't care what we were doing on stage as long as something was going on. If we stopped or anything, they used to go mad.*

As Earth, they had enjoyed appreciative, if small, houses wherever they had played in England. Their stint as support for Jethro Tull had put them before somewhat larger crowds; again, they had been listened to, thoughtfully evaluated and generously applauded. But it's different here: this is, very definitely, an away fixture. The number of sets the band are contracted to play each day compounds the problem. As Iommi put it:

> After we had done three shows, we began to run out of material, so we used to play songs over and over again or just make a terrible mess of something we never really knew how to play

---

* Quoted in Alan Clayson's *Hamburg: The Cradle of British Rock* (p. 149), Sanctuary Publishing, 1997.

. . . It got so bad we ended up devoting entire sets to solos. We got Bill to do a [half-hour] drum solo . . . I used to do complete sets on my own . . . we even managed to get Geezer doing a whole set soloing on bass. I don't think anybody noticed, to be honest.*

In an attempt to prise the audience's attention away from the abundance of bacchanalian distractions on offer, the group goes to more extreme lengths to focus it upon themselves. The amps are turned to louder settings, the musicianship becomes more outlandish and Osbourne even goes to the trouble of daubing purple paint on his body in order to provoke a reaction. In the end, the Hamburg engagement becomes a war of attrition; a war from which Sabbath eventually emerge, if not exactly victorious, at least unscathed.

Pleased with their limited success, the lads return to England. On 22 August, the band – still under the name of Earth – cuts a demo under the supervision of future David Bowie and Elton John producer Gus Dudgeon. The resultant disc will feature the two songs 'The Rebel' (featuring a guitar phrase not unlike the melody in The Hollies' 'Bus Stop') and, dedicated to Simpson, 'A Song For Jim' (a piano-based blues-rock number).* Both efforts will bear real traces of Simpson's guidance, in the form of Ward's natural jazz and swing-beat playing and Iommi's derivations from the Reinhardt and Joe Pass catalogue. Although still without a recording contract, the band is working sedulously at expunging the old twelve-bar material from its repertoire. This is being replaced by darker, original material, that better reflects the band's growing fascination with the occult (this dalliance having now spread from Butler to the rest of the band) and their commitment to producing work of a more brooding, sinister nature.

Due in no small part to near-constant gigging around the country, Sabbath are building an ardent fan base. The band is entertaining

---

* Ibid., p.154. Also quoted in Welch (p. 18).
* You can hear brief excerpts from both of these songs on the DVD and video *The Black Sabbath Story: Volume One*, Sanctuary Records, 1991, reissued in 2002.

audiences with lengthy, bottom-gear compositions, only briefly punctuated by some faster, slicker solo improvisations from Iommi. More significantly, they are getting tighter on stage: whereas Ward had noted that the Hamburg concerts were undisciplined and unpredictable, the demands of a more discerning British audience are engendering a hitherto unknown order and discipline to the band's performances.

As the year wears on, and the band continues to get better and more popular, impatience starts building from within. Although thankful for the popularity they have amassed on the tour circuit, there is still not a lot of money coming in. The situation is so desperate that Iommi's mother, who owns and runs a grocery-cum-hardware store, has constantly to provide sandwiches and cigarettes for the foursome. Additionally, the band members are beginning to sense the frustrations of not being able to lay their work out on vinyl.

Osbourne, whose father has contributed financially towards the setting up of his son's career in the music business, is growing particularly anxious to bring the meat home:

> My father said to me, 'There's two things I had in mind for you: either prison or something special.' I love my father; I always wanted to achieve something for my father, because I always felt that I let him down.*

Coming from an environment where he was one of six siblings living in a two-bedroomed house in Aston, Birmingham, Osbourne is especially intent on breaking out of the grip of poverty. Keen to help the family out financially as well as establish his own independence, Osbourne has tried and failed to hold down a succession of jobs: in addition to his working in an abattoir, he has had a number of other jobs, including plumber's mate, tool-maker and one alongside his mother in the Lucas factory, manufacturing car horns on an assembly line.

But Osbourne isn't the only one who is growing restless: Butler is

---

* Ozzy Osbourne, speaking in the video *Don't Blame Me: The Tales of Ozzy Osbourne*, Sony Music Entertainment, 1991.

getting bored with his job in a local company's accounts department, and Iommi's disability manifests itself into a reluctance to take on any kind of manual work.

Eager to take that next step, the boys articulate their impatience for a recording contract to their manager, Jim Simpson. Simpson redoubles his efforts and, after receiving over a dozen rejections from various record companies, secures financing from Tony Hall – independent entrepreneur, ex-Radio Luxembourg DJ and friend of Simpson – for two days of recording in Trident Studios, off Wardour Street in London's Soho.* Much has been made in previously published Sabbath literature about the cramped surroundings of the studio and the limited nature of its installed technology. However, Trident Studios – although small – was certainly one of the better-equipped studios in Britain at that time. It was, in fact, the only British studio to boast its own eight-track and, because of this, had an edge over many of its competitors. The Beatles had even used it earlier that year to record some tracks for the *Abbey Road* album, in preference to using the more familiar Abbey Road studios.*

At this point, there is still no recording contract in the bag; the venture merely assures the boys have a chance of putting together something more polished with which to solicit record company interest. For the band, despite the paucity of time and money available to them for the project, this is an unbelievable opportunity:

> In those days, you didn't have the luxury of being able to take a long time . . . to take a day in the studio was a long time for us. We thought, 'Great! We've got a day to record the album.' ✝

---

* Conte and Henderson (p. 15) and Welch (p. 32) maintain it was Regent Sound studio, not Trident; Rosen makes no mention of the studio concerned; Ward admits to having forgotten (Marsh, p. 6). However, as Barry Sheffield – co-owner and manager of Trident – is credited as engineer on the album, it can be safely assumed that the recording took place at Trident. Mojo Books publication *The Mojo Collection: The Ultimate Music Companion* (ed. Jim Irvin, 2000) also plumps for Trident.

* The previous year they had also used it to put down the finale of 'Hey Jude' and to record the 'White Album' tracks 'Savoy Truffle', 'Martha My Dear', 'I'm So Tired' and 'Dear Prudence'.

✝ Iommi, speaking to John Stix for *Guitar for the Practicing Musician*, May 1994.

It was either do it, or forget it . . . We had a chance to make an album. It was what we [had] worked for.*

We played our asses off. We recorded onto a little eight-track machine. That was all we had to work with . . . *

Let's just hit the pause button for a moment.

As I said in the Foreword, I never really intended this book to be a biography of Black Sabbath. What's always interested me about Sabbath is the music – specifically, their recorded legacy stretching from the debut album, upon the doorstep of which we now find ourselves in this narrative, and their 1975 release, *Sabotage*, the last album to retain all the elements of Sabbathness and the last truly great album the four were ever to produce.

I've put together this biographical narrative merely to establish some sort of prologue to the music. This is essential if we're going to understand some of the songs: how backstreet poverty and industrial grime coloured the first album; fresh self-confidence, the second; a desire to dig deeper, the third; excessive drug use the fourth, and so on. Then there's all the historical stuff about Vietnam and what have you – I'm bringing this in because that gives the music context. We need to know what was going on in the world if we're to understand Sabbath's part in it. And although both these things are important – the biographical minutiae and the international events, the microcosmic and the macrocosmic – the music is really the focus and what I really want to talk about. So, hereon in, that's mainly what you'll be reading. I'll still be giving you updates from the news desk, and naturally I'll let you know if something happens to one of our boys along the way.

Oh – and then there's me and my story. I have to figure out how much of a damn you might give about Madeleine Morgan and the way she kissed me in the school toilets on that cold January afternoon in 1969. I mean, this stuff matters to me, but it might not be all that important

* Butler, ibid.
* Ward, speaking to Jeb Wright for *Classic Rock* magazine, June 2002.

to you. Do you need, or even want, to know that her lips tasted like cherries and that I had to stand on tiptoes in order to get the full benefit? For what it's worth, she tasted of liquorice.

Where are you now, Madeleine? And why did you have to go? Did you know that you were the first girl to kiss me, and that I would always remember you because you were the first? And do you know that I think about you still? Even now, when I am supposed to be writing about Black Sabbath, and my hands are cold because the heating's packed in again. And how odd that, in some inversion of Marcel Proust's most famous pastry moment – the small Viennese cake that actually shares your name – the mere recollection of things past should bring the taste of you back to my lips.

Once again, I digress. After recording the album, Sabbath play a gig at London's Marquee club, where they had appeared a number of times earlier in the year; make a nostalgic but nevertheless tiresome trip to Carlisle, where Iommi and Ward, in particular, had played so many times in pre-Sabbath days; and perform twice in their hometown of Birmingham. In February, a week before the debut album is finally released, the band appears with Tea and Symphony, Quintessence, Pink Floyd and others on a mixed bill at Cardiff Arts Centre – their biggest gig so far. But things are about to get much, much bigger.

Chapter Three

Black Sabbath

✝

We're not a progressive rock band, we're a heavy pop group and we don't mind the word pop . . . It's just that some pop groups are deeper than others. I think we're medium.*

Given just two days at Trident Studios to produce the album, and only £600 to spend in the process, the music for this record was laid down in a single day, whilst the second allotted day was put aside for editing and mixing down the sound.* Rodger Bain handled production duties, as he was to do for the following two albums, and he must be accorded at least some of the credit not only for the finished release but also for what later became recognisable as the Black Sabbath 'sound'.

Phillips' subsidiary label Fontana showed interest and, in January, put out a single from the resultant recordings: 'Evil Woman / Wicked World'. The band was not happy at having to record 'Evil Woman'. As Ward was later to recall:

> It was at a time when, to sell a record, you gotta do this, you gotta do that . . . and so we bought into it. I didn't want to do the song. I didn't like the song . . . [We] did it because we thought, at the time, 'Well, I guess this is what you have to do to make a hit record.' Nobody was happy with that.✝

It flopped anyway, and the band was then shunted to Phillips' 'progressive' offshoot, Vertigo. At that time in a position where its

---

* Butler speaking to *Disc and Music Echo*, 1970, in a real *Spinal Tap* moment.
* Conte and Henderson (p. 15) have it that the band occupied the studio for twelve hours during a three-day period. Either way, it is a remarkably short space of time.
✝ Ward in Stark (p. 10).

roster needed building, Vertigo committed itself to releasing the album. Sabbath was in business, and, on Friday 13 February 1970, its first album hit the stores.

I'm holding it in my hands now;* sadly, not the original Vertigo pressing but the WWA reissue from 1973, which I bought as a twelve-year-old for £2.99 in Bradley's Records, Sheffield. Let's just talk a little about the album's packaging before we get on to the music. Of course, it's no doubt very nostalgic of me, but in those days an album's cover was something you could really rhapsodise over. If you'll forgive a brief digression, I'd like to rhapsodise now a little. It won't take long and it's very general. Here goes.

Throughout most of the sixties, the convention in album cover design was figurative and nominal: in other words, an album's cover had predominantly to portray the image and the name of the recording artist(s) involved. This was a natural legacy from the fifties, where recording artists were groomed to within an inch of their lives for album cover photographs: the idea being that the desirability and seductiveness of the image was directly proportional to its prospective sales. In other words, cover art, such as it was in those days, was intended to glamorise and market the artist – and this was equally true for both male and female recording stars.

There was a slight shift away from this in the later part of the sixties as bands – as opposed to individual artists – started to make up a larger share of record sales. Although record companies were still mindful of appearance, the posed formality of photographic cover art was relaxed somewhat in favour of images which were no doubt seen as being more playfully illustrative and natural. Throughout the late sixties, groups started to exert a greater influence over cover art, and the creative decisions were wrested away from record companies' promotion teams (although, of course, they still retained a powerful veto). Either through enduring vanity or an adherence to custom, it was still the case that the

---

* Figuratively speaking: I can't type and hold the damned thing at the same time – it's propped up in front of me.

artists themselves were visually depicted on the cover. The exceptions were very rare:* The Beatles were depicted on all of their records, so too The Rolling Stones,* The Who,† Dylan and the burgeoning roster of contemporary singer-songwriters. It wasn't really until the seventies kicked in that the practice of facial absenteeism became at all conspicuous in rock album covers, and it wasn't until then that the composition of cover art was recognised as an art form itself, as distinct from mere gimmickry or a promotional tool.

During the course of the seventies, cover art became more and more elaborate: artists such as Roger Dean created sleeves of striking originality,§ and companies like Hipgnosis peddled a Magritte-like absurdism.♦ Some of these creations have stood the test of time better than others; some were pretty awful even then – King Crimson's nauseating cover for *In the Court of the Crimson King* being particularly notable. Some sleeve art took vanity to new extremes: think of the pompous self-importance reflected in Deep Purple's *In Rock* and the inside cover of Zeppelin's second album; it's difficult to tell whether any irony was intended.

Punk was purposefully and determinedly iconoclastic: not just musically but also in terms of image and cover art. Just as the abstruseness of progressive rock was overthrown by the searing, reactionary simplicity of barre-chord thrashing, so was the notion of album packaging reduced to its barest necessities – it was the demise of the gatefold. Whereas the great 'arty' covers from the progressive period could transport you away from the music, or along with it, to some perceived state of otherness, the arresting immediacy of punk cover art was more grounding: music's own no-frills value line; it does – or is – what it says on the cover.

With the coming of the eighties, there came a renaissance in vanity –

---

* Pink Floyd springs to mind, so too The Small Faces' *Ogden's Nut Gone Flake* (June 1968), but nothing much else does.

* On *Beggars Banquet* (1968) the Stones were relegated to the inside of the gatefold.

† Their faces are there on the 1969 release *Tommy*; you just have to look hard. *Live at Leeds* (1970) was their first not to portray their facial images.

§ Predominantly (although not exclusively) the fantastical sleeves for Yes and Uriah Heep albums.

♦ Floyd's *Wish You Were Here*; Zeppelin's *Presence*, for example.

and this was, once again, reflected in the cover art of the period. We're now beyond the timeframe of this book, so I'm not going to say a lot about the eighties. Just this really: whereas the donning of make-up and silly clothes during the seventies 'glam' period is somehow endearing in retrospect – you get the impression they were only ever doing it for a *laugh* – in the eighties, it was deadly serious: think how miserable they all looked but, oh, how beautiful. In its way, this cosmetically promoted narcissism was more self-serving and offensive than the worst of the seventies' excesses.

Originally issued in a gatefold sleeve, *Black Sabbath*'s front and back cover* together show a photograph of a rather desolate and isolated rural landscape. There is a mill building that stands aback a pool of still water. A youngish, sallow and slightly green-looking woman occupies the middle distance, caught grasping a cloak about her,* presumably to beat off the chill. The tableau is presided over by a solitary black crow (actually, it could be a rook – either way, it's part of the crow family)✝ that stands atop a gnarled and disfigured tree trunk. The grainy overexposed photo, shot at Mapledurham in Oxfordshire by Marcus Keef, is not only beautiful in itself – capturing, as it does, a sort of Christina Rossetti-like bleak midwinteriness, albeit without the snow on snow – it also sits sympathetically alongside the music contained within, and it must vie for position as Sabbath's best album sleeve together with 1973's *Sabbath Bloody Sabbath*.

The inside sleeve is rather poor by comparison. The legend 'Black Sabbath', represented in a most unsuitable pop-art/rococo font,✣ is emblazoned adjacent to an upside-down cross framing the track listing, band personnel and production credits. The band is said to have recoiled

---

* 'We approved the cover, but it wasn't our design.' Butler speaking to the *Birmingham Post* in March 1970. Welch (p. 28).
* Tangye and Wright maintain the woman in question was holding a black cat (p. 36). They may be right.
✝ *Corvidae*: the rook being *Corvus frugilegus*, and the carrion crow *Corvus corone corone*. However, regardless of which of these two species the bird is, you simply can't get past the fact that its cooperative presence on the cover is down to the fact that it's been killed, stuffed and just nailed there.
✣ Ward later used this design on the skin of his bass drum.

at the inclusion of the inverted cross – put in at Vertigo's insistence, presumably to capture satanist interest – but couldn't act quickly enough to prevent it. It is unlikely, however, that the band would have had such control over the album cover art at this early stage in its career.

Also contained within the framework of the cross, there is a poem. Precise authorship of this poem has yet to be pinned down. It's almost certainly the case that the band had nothing to do with it; Osbourne, in fact, claims never to have read it. I'm reproducing it here, however, because I'd like to talk a little about it. The punctuation of the poem is a little eccentric in places, and there's a subject–verb disagreement near the end, but I've left these idiosyncrasies as they are. You don't muck about with poetry. Here it is:

Still falls the rain, the veils of darkness shroud the blackened trees, which, contorted by some unseen violence, shed their tired leaves and bend their boughs toward a grey earth of severed bird wings, among the grasses, poppies bleed before a gesticulating death, and young rabbits, born dead in traps, stand motionless, as though guarding the silence that surrounds and threatens to engulf all those that would listen. Mute birds, tired of repeating yesterday's terrors, huddle together in the recesses of dark corners, heads turned from the dead, black swan that floats upturned in a small pool in the hollow. There emerges from this pool a faint sensual mist, that traces its way upwards to caress the chipped feet of the headless martyr's statue, whose only achievement was to die too soon, and who couldn't wait to lose.
The cataract of darkness form fully, the long black night begins, yet still, by the lake a young girl waits, unseeing she believes herself unseen, she smiles, faintly at the distant tolling bell, and the still falling rain.

Frankly, although I'm no poet, I think it could have done without the 'severed bird wings' bit, which takes it a little over the top. However, it's

nicely bookended and, obviously, it ties in with the cover, but there's something else I'd like to say about this poem – and, I'm sorry, but it's going to incur another fleeting digression.

Edith Sitwell (1887–1964), later Dame Edith Sitwell, was an English poet. She was raised (in that lonely, unhappy and frustrated way that poets are) in a large family home in rural Derbyshire. Coming to poetry as she was leaving adolescence, she gradually developed a style that ran against the limp quietism of Georgian verse prevalent at the time. By 1923, she had collaborated with composer William Walton to produce *Façade*, a work that, for those times, was as shocking as it was unprecedented. Subsequently, her fantastical lamentations transmuted to indignant wrath as she published a series of poems and prose works, both before and during the Second World War, which denounced the evil in society and the horrific cruelty of war in particular.

One of her poems begins, 'Still falls the Rain'* and continues with lines such as, 'In the Field of Blood where the small hopes breed and the human brain/Nurtures its greed' and, ' . . . the sad uncomprehending dark . . . the tears of the hunted hare'.*

Coincidence? I reckon not. But the thought of Osbourne hunkered up with his copy of Sitwell during a tea break at the slaughterhouse beggars belief. Perhaps I do him an injustice: we all need a little light relief. *'Oi, Sharon! Clean that f***ing dogshit up – and where's my* Oxford Anthology of English Verse?'

Unlike many of their predecessors and contemporaries, none of the members of Sabbath attended art school. Art schools, in those days, were not so much academies for the studying of fine art as opportunities for school leavers not inclined toward university education to postpone their entry into the job market for anything up to three years. Amongst others, members of The Beatles, The Stones, The Kinks, The Who, Pink Floyd

---

* 'Still Falls the Rain', subtitled 'The Raids', 1940. *Night and Dawn* (1942).

* I'm just quoting bits of it here. If you want to read it all, you'll have to track it down for yourselves. Incidentally, you might also like to have a look at lines 377–99 of T. S. Eliot's 'The Wasteland' (1922), which contain references to a woman with long black hair, tolling bells, faint moonlight, tumbled graves, thunder, lightning and rain.

and Led Zeppelin attended art school, which provided them with sufficient luxury of circumstance to pursue their musical ambitions. Indeed, it was whilst at art school that many of the sixties/seventies rock alumni first entertained the idea of pursuing music as a career.

There is a significance to this which influences the early Sabbath repertoire. Forgoing a politically motivated and artistically stimulating art school education gifted much of Sabbath's initial output with a brutal anti-literate immediacy. On the first album, there are but five words – 'disappears' in 'The Wizard', 'tomorrow' and 'awoken' in 'Behind The Wall Of Sleep', and 'forever' and the old chestnut 'Lucifer' on 'N.I.B.' – which exceed two syllables. Furthermore, the lyrics are scanned without exception into fierce, unremitting rhyming couplets – hammer blows of unpolished, homespun philistinism – which gives such messages as there are in the lyrics an arresting, almost palpable, urgency.

In Britain, a hard-won fanbase accrued through almost two years of constant touring ensures that the album makes the charts. In fact, it peaks at an unbelievable number eight on 25 April of that year – a fair achievement considering the band has no recording pedigree.

While claims that this album single-handedly invented the heavy metal genre are as exaggerated as they are unwelcome, it is certainly true that nothing – before or since – sounded like the music on this record. Sure, the sound is rough, and that probably owes more to the strictures of its recording economy than any conscious stylistic intent; and sure, the sound is bleak and other-worldly, like it was coming at you from out of some hellish dream; but the most noticeable thing about the album is that it is just so, for want of a better term, scary.

Denied the then luxurious opportunity of spending time in pre- and post-production, the band simply set up and played its live set. These were the nascent, experimental days of stereo sound, and, typically for those times, the channelling is very extreme in places, giving the record a sense of argument or discourse between the competing instruments.

1) Black Sabbath

The song that gave the group its name, the lead-off track on the debut album, probably goes further in asserting a group's presence into the rock and roll marketplace than any other – certainly when looked at in comparison with debuts from other acts of the time. Led Zeppelin's first album, for example, which had been released the year earlier, was wary enough to start off with 'Good Times Bad Times', virtually a pop song, and then worked through the acoustic, folk-based balladry of 'Babe I'm Gonna Leave You' and the traditional blues of 'You Shook Me', before we got anything that represented any kind of statement of intent: 'Dazed And Confused'. Deep Purple, whose first album, *Shades of Deep Purple*, predated Zeppelin's by almost a year, started off their debut with a Cream-like* blues-psych instrumental 'And The Address' – a number that might have been equally at home on an acid-jazz sampler. We'd heard this sort of stuff before. But 'Black Sabbath', from its famous rain-and-thunderstorm beginning, recalling both the cover art and the poem we've already discussed, through to its cataclysmic, reverb-drenched conclusion six minutes later, is pure drama.

The lyric, written by Osbourne himself, recounts a ghoulish apparition Butler experienced a year or so earlier, in which a figure, dressed entirely in black, appeared at the foot of his bed. The predominant musical theme, a tritone* in the key of G, the idea for which Butler and Iommi have since maintained came to them both simultaneously, sounds like the very gates of Hell opening up. Ward's drumming rumbles ominously throughout these passages – in a style I'm going to call 'noir-tribal' – and gives the slow, ponderous accompaniment an unsettling and pendulous momentum.

The vocal is delivered in a pained, throaty, almost strangulated moan, and at 3:58 and 5:11 there are the chilling cries of, 'Oh, no! No! Please,

---

* Deep Purple guitarist Ritchie Blackmore actually plays a variation from Cream's 'Sunshine Of Your Love', released on the album *Disraeli Gears* the preceding year, on this track. Iommi snuck his Cream tribute into the track 'Warning' – see subsequent entry.
* The interval is not replicated in the vocal melody to 'Black Sabbath', although the offending C sharp is sung as the final syllable of each line.

God, help me!' and, 'No! No! Please, no!' that, strangely reminiscent of the sounds heard escaping the Polanski house the year previously, sound as heartfelt as they do forlorn.

At 4:36,* the song ups its tempo considerably into a galloping riff of four triplets indicative of some pursuer on horseback. Two lines later, we discover that the pursuer is (indeed) Satan, the Dark Lord himself, up to no good, no doubt. Such discovery does little in assuaging the sense of dread that has been building inexorably throughout the song.

That the song is frightening, there is no doubt. However, it engenders this disturbing, claustrophobic terror in the listener not from the lyrics – a sort of late-night compendium of Hammer Horror out-takes – but from the massive, sonic structure of the song's composition and its imaginative and wholehearted rendition by the band. This latter, exemplified by, first, catatonic, zombie-like possession and, by way of conclusion, frenzied, bug-eyed terror, is so bewitchingly overwhelming that it leaves you both drained and jittery. Like a perfectly filmed special effect of calmly executed visceral grisliness, you know the blood isn't real, but your senses are screaming, nevertheless.

Reckoned by *Mojo* magazine* to be in the top fifty pieces of music that 'changed the world', the track is a truly terrifying experience, and, as I said earlier, there can be no mightier or more meaningful debut found anywhere.

2) The Wizard

Telling the story of some benign sorcerer who passes through the town handing out spells and generally making everything tickety-boo, 'The Wizard' builds from an eerie – no, damnit, outright *spooky* – solo harmonica introduction (half train whistle, half 'Jet Song'✝ and – yes –

---

* Earlier versions of this song feature a third verse along the lines of the first two and merely an instrumental rendering of the faster section. Later versions comprised all three 'slow' verses and lyrics over the final, faster verse. Wisely, the third 'slow' verse was dropped at the time of recording.
* Issue 120, p. 88.
✝ From Leonard Bernstein's *West Side Story*.

that *is* Osbourne blowing it) to a full instrumental recapitulation. The guitar and bass accompaniment during the verse, a sort of accentuated dagger-stabbing of A power chords, somewhat prefigures the verse riff found on the later 'War Pigs'.

Although the general feel of 'The Wizard' is upbeat, there is nevertheless a constant sense of threat running throughout the song. The lyrical extracts 'Never talking – just keeps walking' and 'Casting his shadow' offer strong indications of a sullen ambivalence and nebulous influence at odds with his 'funny clothes' and 'tinkling bell'. In fact, the title character is more *High Plains Drifter* than medieval mystic – fitting in with the general belief that this song is merely homage to the band's drug dealer – and there is the distinct feeling that, upon his leaving, it is relief more than anything else that has left the townspeople 'feeling so fine'. It's clear that Osbourne is relishing the lyric – according it a raspy St-John-the-Baptist-style proclamatory quality – and this commitment is well matched by the enthusiastic playing of Butler, Iommi and, especially, Bill Ward.

Although 'The Wizard' can't under any circumstances be considered a Sabbath classic, it nevertheless retains a unique charm in their early canon. It remained a periodic favourite of Osbourne's after he went solo and occasionally featured in his early live solo sets. Propelled infectiously by Ward's explosive counter-rhythms and decelerating fills, the song can be seen now as something of a museum piece, exhibiting Sabbath's early forays in search of a definitive style.

3) Behind The Wall Of Sleep

Mixing less than glamorous references to hallucinogenic drugs with images of death and, possibly, transfiguration, 'Behind The Wall Of Sleep' bears all the indications of being written from Butler's morbidly preoccupied imaginings. After a brief introduction in waltz-time, alternating between the subdominant and the mediant, the song employs a call-and-response motif, determined by Iommi's A minor guitar phrase and Osbourne's vocals, the latter sounding almost like incantations. The

double-tracked and slightly unsynchronised vocal lines are set at the furthest extremes of the stereo picture – an effect best heard through headphones – and this lends Osbourne's voice an unsettling omnipresence, a Big Brother-type authoritarianism appropriate to both the song's grim subject matter and the wary exhortations of its second-person narrative.

The song modulates a full tone up to B minor at 1:29 for the middle section; the effect of this typically clever jump providing both a variation and a lift, before it slips back to A minor for the final verse. In so doing, the track lays out something of a template for many following Sabbath compositions: the single-tone modulation is to be found in, amongst others, 'Fairies Wear Boots', 'Sweet Leaf' and 'After Forever'.

The lyric is dark, very dark, and, with its correlation of drugs and death, can be seen as a precursor to 'Hand Of Doom', which was to follow later in the year on the album *Paranoid*.

4) N.I.B.

Prefaced by a bass solo from Butler, the main riff with its preposterously accentuated opening spondee kicks in at 0:41, a giant mastodon of a thing in E minor which you just know they're enjoying playing. A second before, at 0:40, you can hear Butler jacking up the volume knob on his bass in readiness for the sforzando powerhouse explosion about to follow. I mean you can actually *hear* him doing that. Not that we should be surprised, of course: the songs constituting this album were recorded entirely live. The band simply set up, plugged in and played. One take, two takes, that's it: that's the song done.

The exuberant but nonetheless menacing irresistibility of the main motif is lightened at 1:57 with a more sedate and restrained descending figure, which runs for an unusual length of thirteen bars, before collapsing once more under the relentless wheels of the juggernaut riff.

The lyric, another Butler composition, concerns the romantic adventures of our old pal Satan and his endeavours at persuading an Earth girl to fall in love with him. Somewhat vicariously, the listener is

allowed to eavesdrop on Satan's courtship skills – a process that, however well intentioned, shows clear signs of uncharacteristic desperation. Here we see the Dark Overlord minding his p's and q's as he pleads for the hand of his bride; there's none of the wing-beating rape and abduction we've come to expect from this habitual recidivist. Changing his name to the more girl-friendly 'Lucifer', and with promises that she won't regret leaving behind the life she had before they met, he succeeds; yup, he actually gets the girl. Amazing.

What's even more amazing, however, is that the old fellah ends up being a good guy after all. The bowing and scraping, the humbling emasculation of a desperate guy out to get his girl, all that wasn't just diabolic subterfuge, it was real love – love that, in all its intrinsic worthiness, has the power to vanquish evil, even in its darkest form. Or at least that's the interpretation accorded the song by Butler, its lyricist. This was obviously lost on future Sabbath singer Ronnie James Dio, however, who imbued many of the song's more declamatory lyrical statements with such ridiculous comic-book melodrama that it changed the whole character of the song into one in which, once again, evil was in the ascendant.*

Featuring an especially melodious (in parts, double-tracked) solo from Iommi (2:53), which is repeated towards the end of the song in a slightly adapted form, this song is truly a *tour de force*. At times almost tender, it's an energising piece that, for all its ersatz romanticism, leaves the listener feeling sorry that it's over.

The name 'N.I.B.' (long thought to stand for 'Nativity In Black', for some reason) merely referred to the 'nib-like' beard Bill Ward was sporting at the time.

5) Evil Woman (Don't Play Your Games With Me)

Initially a minor US hit for the American band Crow,* this is, without doubt, the weakest song on the album – and by some measure. One

* As heard on the 1983 post-Ozzy release *Live Evil*.
* Songwriting credited to Wiegand.

of two cover versions on the album, 'Evil Woman' bounces along at the tempo of a campfire singalong in G minor and has about as much passion.

Starting off with an uncredited horn fanfare promising soul-food exoticism and descending with an arresting shudder into the verse riff, the song quickly palls thereafter. The brassy exertions are never reprised, the light of promise soon fades, and the song immediately assumes a ponderous and repetitive Aeolian character relying heavily on its chorus to save it from banality. Unfortunately, the chorus only accentuates the song's arid limitations.

'Evil Woman' may have sounded pleasing enough at the time, and the general feel of it as a danceable swing-boogie was to prove commercially popular just a few weeks down the line when Norman Greenbaum took the similar 'Spirit In The Sky' to number one in the singles chart in April of that year. However, there's just not enough going on here. It's all a bit tired, poppy and vacuous – particularly when coming after the rampant zeal of 'N.I.B.'. Based on the familiar I/IV/V* format, and with an ostensibly all-join-in-type chorus, the song is reproduced in a rather pedestrian, going-through-the-motions manner by the band, although the interplay between Ward's drums and Butler's bass is engaging enough.

The lyric, although not written by Sabbath of course, ties in loosely with the band's *raison d'être*, bestowing, as it does, a variety of undesirable characteristics on a particularly gruesome-sounding female; however, Osbourne's sardonic delivery of the line 'Don't you wish that you could see me dead?' is one of only a few he invests with any kind of feeling.

The song was pushed out as a single (b/w 'Wicked World') both on the Fontana label (January 1970) and by Vertigo (March 1970). Neither issue charted.

* Shorthand for a compositional format, first popularised by Johann Sebastian Bach, that utilises the chordal progression from the tonic to the subdominant, back to the tonic, then to the dominant, and finally back to the tonic. This covers virtually all of the old rock and roll repertoire by fifties stalwarts Little Richard, Chuck Berry and the like and almost the whole of Status Quo's recorded legacy from 1973 through to 1977. Punk, also, was to rely heavily on its anthemic simplicity, and The Beatles, too, were enthusiastic advocates of the form.

6) Sleeping Village

'Sleeping Village', by contrast, is an overlooked masterpiece. Originally entitled 'Devil's Island',* it begins with a brooding adagio on guitar, joined almost immediately by a not altogether unsympathetic Jew's harp (yes, you read that right). The first part of the song is a brief, dark pastorale, similar to Free's 'Over The Green Hills' from their 1968 release *Tons of Sobs*.

Iommi's picked E minor arpeggio, given an air of suspense and melancholy by an added second, is augmented by a breathy, perhaps slightly overstated, eclogue from Osbourne. In a scant four lines, the singer borrows from the palette of J.M.W. Turner to describe a rich, early morning sun rising to the sound of cawing poultry and a gentle wind rustling through the trees.

For years (in fact, until really quite recently), that's where I thought the song ended. The sudden eruption at 0:53, which unexpectedly heaps musical chaos onto what was otherwise a perfectly idyllic georgic paean, I always assumed belonged to the following track, 'Warning'. In a way, it sort of belongs there: the outbreak of which I speak, and which is blisteringly expectorated by Iommi's guitar, modulates to the key of D minor at 1:38 (the same key as 'Warning', and a full tone lower than the initial key of 'Sleeping Village').

It's almost as if, in 'Sleeping Village', Sabbath have painted this slightly sombre, but nevertheless beautiful, image of dawn breaking over some forgotten hamlet, recalling Goldsmith's 'The Deserted Village',* only then to destroy it completely by the sudden searing violence of the ensuing ensemble playing: a sort of acrimonious and temper-fuelled ripping of the canvas.

Brought to an end by some sustained guitar feedback at a rather

---

* Tangye and Wright recount that the song was thus titled when it was aired on John Peel's *Top Gear* radio broadcast of 29 November 1969.
* Oliver Goldsmith (1728-74), Irish poet, playwright and novelist: after frittering away his student loan at the gambling tables, he busked around Europe for a while with his flute. Perhaps best known for his drama, *She Stoops To Conquer*, he published 'The Deserted Village', widely regarded as his premier work of poetry, in 1770.

premature 3:46, the explosive turmoil of 'Sleeping Village''s coda melts, yes *melts*, into the opening blues of 'Warning', which follows.

7) Warning

Originally the last song on the album, the sprawling blues workout of Aynsley Dunbar's 'Warning'* is the second cover version on the album; it was also the last cover version Sabbath were ever to record. Largely given over to Iommi's detuned* guitar (the passage from 3:22 through to 9:03 is entirely instrumental), the ten minutes-plus of 'Warning' was boiled down from a much longer version laid down on the first (and, most likely, *only*) day of recording in the studio.

Although dominated by Iommi's by turns crunching and incisive playing, the song succeeds best when it stays within the rumbling blues typified by the verse structure. Again based around the I/IV/V format, the song features a menacing bass figure which, if played at volume, will seriously test the woofers of any speaker system, and an outstandingly powerful vocal from Osbourne. Alternating between fierce pride and self-deprecation, Osbourne laments his experiences with another awkward bit of skirt – the broodier half-sister of Evil Woman, perhaps – the separation from whom has left him with 'iron in [his] heart and sorrow [in his] voice'. And you can hear it, too: nowhere more so than on the make-do chorus line, 'I was born without you, baby, but my feelings were a little bit too strong' – the acrimonious delivery of which leaving you in no doubt that the break-up was her fault all along.

At 3:22, Iommi's extended solo begins – and a right mixed bag it is, too. Edited down from an original length of eighteen minutes,† Iommi calls upon a variety of styles and techniques to give the passage its jerky, fractured momentum. At 4:33, there is a brief quote from Cream's

* Originally credited on the album to Dunbar alone, the title now lists Dunbar, Dmochowski, Hickling and Moreshead as writers.

* Down a full tone to D. This is the only track on this album to feature detuned guitar. Although Iommi's fingers were still sensitive, he had started using lighter-gauged strings, which helped significantly.

† As recalled by Butler, speaking to John Stix for *Guitar for the Practicing Musician*, May 1994.

'Spoonful', fuelling criticism in one contemporary music paper that Iommi's style was too similar to Clapton's for the former to be of any real significance in rock's scheme of things. Done more or less as a single take, the solo would have been a faithful representation of his stage suites at the time. The double-tracked fragment (6:15–6:55) should never be listened to at volume whilst wearing headphones; trust me: it will split your head open. Although less experimental than, say, Jimmy Page's protracted workouts on live renditions of 'Dazed And Confused' or anything that Hendrix had committed to vinyl, Iommi's work here is creditable enough: it is certainly more bearable than Page's more oblique peregrinations. The solo, in its manifold and diverse composition, also elucidates the manner of Iommi's entrance into the role of rock guitarist. His style, then, as now, truly unique, is an alchemical hybrid of blues, jazz and folk, steeped in brooding minor keys and given bizarre left-field twists by tonal juxtaposition and exotic, rarely heard intervals. Despite a fluff at 7:40, Iommi brings together successfully a number of contrasting musical styles into what ends up being an entertaining enough divertimento, perhaps recalling happier times in this most disastrous romantic affair.

At 8:11 a monstrous riff kicks in, and, with the rest of the band in tow, we are taken through a powerful, grinding rallentando back to the main theme, which Osbourne brings to a close with a growling vocal with which his larynx only just manages to cope.

8) Wicked World

Making its first appearance as the B-side of both Fontana's and Vertigo's single releases of 'Evil Woman', 'Wicked World' did not feature on original UK releases of the album. It did appear (in place of 'Evil Woman') on corresponding US releases, but, in Britain, it remained a forgotten curio from the early period, not reproduced on album-length vinyl until the Christmas 1975 compilation, *We Sold Our Soul for Rock 'n' Roll*.

One of the first original songs written by Black Sabbath – perhaps, even, the very first – 'Wicked World' (which now features on all CD reissues of the *Black Sabbath* album, thus its inclusion here) belongs to the period in Sabbath's history where they were still immersed in the blues and jazz influences wielded by then-manager Jim Simpson. Ward's 'sighing' hi-hat work in this number, reminiscent of Count Basie's drummer, Jo Jones, is a direct influence.* Similar in a way to 'Warning' – the song breaks down into a series of melancholy guitar arpeggios midway through (these were executed by Iommi whose guitar was suffering from a faulty pick-up) – the song is constructed from pentatonic blues raw material in E and is sung in a gravelly, almost choleric, manner by Osbourne.

Referring in turn to war, political mismanagement, the space race and ill-health, this is more of a protest song than some febrile dystopian vision. However strong the temptation may have been to engender some sort of facile optimism in the lyric – something along the lines of 'Come on, people, let's all live in peace' – it was resisted, leaving the listener with this feeling of abject despondency: nothing can be done about this, and nothing ever will be. It was to feature in an expanded and extemporised format in the unofficial 1980 release *Live at Last*.* Although the original version's inclusion on contemporary pressings of the album is a welcome bonus, the sound quality is too poor to showcase the song's undoubted merits.

---

* Simpson was fond of 'indoctrinating the young musicians with old Basie records'. Welch (p. 17).
* An album comprising material of much earlier vintage, put out by NEMS (who then owned the Ozzy-era Sabbath catalogue) to 'satisfy' public demand for a Sabbath live album featuring Osbourne. *Live at Last* has now been extended, remixed and reissued as *Past Lives* (2002). A curate's egg of a collection, you can hear Osbourne rupturing his blood vessels during his rendition of 'Megalomania'.

Chapter Four
War Machine Keeps Turning / 1970

†

As 1970 dawns, and family entertainer Rolf Harris sits atop the singles chart with his 'Two Little Boys', it is revealed that doctors in England are writing almost five million prescriptions a year for Librium. Additionally, a further seven million are being written for Valium and Mogadon.

In April, Nixon announces that 150,000 troops will be withdrawn from Vietnam before the end of the year. This is the first mooted troop withdrawal of any numeric significance, and there is brief cause for hope amongst the war protestors, before Nixon snuffs out the candle by declaring his intention to bomb nearby Cambodia. Four American students partaking in a demonstration against the war are shot dead at Kent State University campus in Akron, Ohio, after the Governor of Ohio, James Rhodes, orders the National Guard to open fire.

In Washington, Congress vetoes Nixon's Cambodian pledge, although it does give the go-ahead to bomb the Ho Chi Minh trail. Hollywood, meanwhile, is still trying to figure out whether war is cool or not. Although Robert Altman's *M*A*S*H* and Mike Nichols' *Catch-22* are both aimed at the anti-war vote, it is Franklin Schaffner's *Patton* that cleans up at the Oscars:* Francis Ford Coppola's screenplay, portraying the aggressive US general as an object of sympathy, helping to keep middle-America's sensitivities about Vietnam at bay.

Michael Wadleigh's documentary *Woodstock*, which chronicled the peace and love celebrated festival-style the previous year, sits awkwardly alongside Albert Maysles' *Gimme Shelter*, a film of The Rolling Stones' performance at Altamont, where Hell's Angels, contracted to provide 'security', brutally clubbed and stabbed a fan

---

* *Patton* won seven Oscars, including those for Best Picture, Best Director, Best Actor and Best Original Screenplay. Ring Lardner Jr's adaptation of Richard Hooker's novel earned him the Best Adapted Screenplay for *M*A*S*H*.

to death. And, yes, you do get to see this in the movie. Jagger further cements his celluloid status by starring in Tony Richardson's hilarious *Ned Kelly* and Nicolas Roeg's dense melodrama of drug-induced hallucination, *Performance*: wherein, to the chagrin and consternation of Keith Richards, he enacts a steamy sex scene with Richards' lover of the time, Anita Pallenberg.

As the Equal Pay Act makes it illegal for conditions of employment in Britain to be predicated on the basis of gender, political feminism resurfaces through the publication of Germaine Greer's *The Female Eunuch* and Kate Millett's *Sexual Politics*. The world of literature is inundated with birds: Richard Bach's *Jonathan Livingston Seagull* contrasting with Ted Hughes' stark *Crow* poems, and Barry Hines' *A Kestrel for a Knave* receiving an effective screen treatment from Ken Loach.

As Apollo 13 suffers a near-fatal setback on its aborted shoot for the moon, French and British doctors implant the first nuclear-powered pacemakers into three patients suffering from 'heart block'. Someone pays $50,000 for one of Warhol's soup tins.

Santana release *Abraxas*, and Miles Davis produces *Bitches Brew*. Both albums explore the connections between jazz and rock, albeit they approach that common ground from opposite perspectives. Van Morrison's *Moondance* and Traffic's *John Barleycorn Must Die* are both released and show distinct traces of having been influenced by Dylan's *The Basement Tapes*, available on bootleg the previous year and espousing a concurrent return to homespun, rootsy arrangements with a debunking of psychedelia's exploratory journeyings. The Stooges' *Fun House* and MC5's *Back in the USA*, meanwhile, threaten to whelp in a punk scene still in gestation. Simon and Garfunkel's *Bridge Over Troubled Water*, James Taylor's *Sweet Baby James* and Carole King's *Tapestry* are all released, establishing a popularity for singer-songwriters that is to continue well into the decade. Jimi Hendrix and Janis Joplin check in to the Big Hotel; both are just twenty-seven years of age.

A uniquely talented Brazil team cruises to a 4-1 victory against Italy in the World Cup final in Mexico City; football will never look this good again. I say this without the slightest fear of ever being proved wrong.

Pope Paul VI, a year away from receiving a namecheck in Sabbath's 'After Forever', declares priestly celibacy to be a cornerstone of the Catholic Church and survives an assassination attack in the Philippines.

In Britain, Harold Wilson's Labour government cedes power to a rampant, grinning Edward Heath and the Conservatives, in a June election in which Labour voters are too apathetic to partake. One Margaret Hilda Thatcher is appointed Secretary of State for Education, and, after she's nicked our school milk, she starts grooming herself for even greater infamy.

British troops fire rubber bullets for the first time in Belfast, following earlier violence in both Londonderry and Armagh; real bullets are flying all over the place in Biafra, as it continues to maintain its independence from Nigeria.

Charles Manson and four of his 'family' stand trial for the Tate/Labianca killings; The Beatles disintegrate amidst acrimonious financial squabbles while McCartney sings 'Let It Be', a quasi-religious plea of characteristically saccharine ripeness.

There are 700,000 left homeless and 30,000 dead following an earthquake in Peru. In East Pakistan, a country we now know as Bangladesh, half a million perish in large-scale floods. The US surreptitiously dumps sixty-six tons of nerve gas three hundred miles off the Florida coast, and the American government recalls a million cans of tuna contaminated by mercury.

As the final touches are put to the World Trade Center, Arab terrorists hijack three European jets bound for New York . . .

I don't remember much about this time. In 1971, I had my head split open by a roofing slate thrown at me by a local gang rival. There was some sort of territorial dispute, I seem to remember: we were apparently on their patch. You know how it is. Whilst I was addressing my troops from a position behind a gorse bush, their premier slate-slinger launched a beauty. It was simply my misfortune that I stood up and broke cover at precisely the wrong moment. The sound of the impact was sickening.

My comrades dropped back for safer cover, and, under the flag of truce, I was left to make my way blearily home. By the time I got there, I was a real mess: in an attempt to fix the blow, I had been frantically rubbing the heel of my hand against the cut, but this had merely opened the wound up and stimulated the flow of blood. And, with my carrying home a large bough of gorse (for reasons that now escape me), my arrival must have resembled a sort of 'worst of' compilation of Shakespeare's *Macbeth*. There was the usual parental alarm and confusion; I am inundated with questions I'm in no fit state to answer, before being bundled into the car and driven to the nearest hospital, twelve miles away. I don't make it – I pass out on the journey. Next thing I can recall is lying face up on a hospital trolley, white ceiling tiles with dots on hurtling by, the clatter of feet, people whose voices I don't recognise talking in rushed, out-of-breath tones, that hospital smell and a sick feeling in my stomach. They dope me, shave off my hair, do the life-saving op. I'm going to be okay. I'm going to look pretty ridiculous for a while, but I'm going to live.

Trouble is, loads of stuff that was in my head – all short-term memory stuff – that's gone, and it never came back. So, much of 1970 is a blank. I do remember the World Cup though: the physical poetry of the Brazilian team; Banks' miraculous save from Pelé's header; the worry over whether Bobby Moore would have to go to jail or not. The greatest World Cup final ever (yes, better even than '66), and Brazil got to keep the Rimet trophy. 'That's it!' Kenneth Wolstenholme declared at the final whistle, 'Brazil have won the cup!' Yeah, I remember that. I was no longer George Best in the playground – I was Carlos Alberto.

The members of Sabbath have every reason to feel optimistic over the release of their first album. Indeed, most things are rosy: with more money than they've ever had before – and an album they can actually wave about in people's faces – they are on a high. This is an immensely proud moment in the lives of Ward and Osbourne, who, for differing reasons, are both keen to show off their accomplishments to their respec-

tive fathers. Ward's father, critically ill at the time, is expressing concern over the drummer's exertions with the band,* whereas Osbourne's just wants something to happen for his son.

In March they make a triumphant return to London's famous Marquee. They are moving up the billing order and are debuting new songs in their stage sets. It's all going wonderfully – and the best is yet to come.

However, despite the pervading sense of happiness and accomplishment (some unfavourable reviews notwithstanding), there's still a niggling concern. With Sabbath contracted to perform small venues* arranged in advance of the album's success – and, more importantly, in having to play them for derisorily small fees – disgruntlement with the band's management is beginning to grow from within. The resentment is no doubt compounded by an arduous and illogical touring schedule: during April, the band play London on the 16th, travel 250 miles to Plymouth on the 17th, back to London on the 18th, make another 250-mile journey northwards to Darlington on the 19th, back again to London on the 20th, Birmingham on the 21st, Watford on the 22nd, north again 300 miles to Newcastle on the 23rd and back down to Crawley, another 300 miles, on the 24th.✝ Nine days on without a break. It can't have been much fun travelling two thousand miles in a beat-up Transit van with only a skeletal motorway infrastructure in place.

Ultimately, with tempers understandably a little frayed, original mentor Jim Simpson is ousted in a bloodless, yet nevertheless acrimonious, takeover that puts Patrick Meehan and Wilf Pine,⚹ late of the Don Arden (Sharon Osbourne's father) school of business management, at the helm. Although it has subsequently been reported that Simpson's financial dealings with the band had been less than straightforwardly honest,✝ the more likely scenario is that, as a manager of a major musical

---

* Ward in Rosen (p. 45).
* The band, with an album already in the top fifty, played Bletchley Youth Centre on 8 March. Siegler.
✝ Siegler.
⚹ Pine later threw in his lot with Meehan and rejoined Arden. He was later to testify by affidavit against both Meehan and Black Sabbath.
✝ 'Simpson had secretly decided to keep his clients' fortune for himself.' Conte and Henderson (p. 17).

concern, he was now out of his depth; there is also the wide consensus that he was simply not aggressive enough on the band's behalf. Meehan, on the other hand, a loquacious and impetuous go-getter with an eye on the quick buck, who was handling Black Widow, a more minor concern than Sabbath, was offering much greater financial returns for his clients.*

A US tour scheduled for July to promote the album (which is selling well there, despite the band being both unknown and unheard in America) is prudently postponed in the aftermath of the Manson trial.* In Britain, the press heaps derision both on the band's first release and on its performance skills in general. In spite of this (or possibly on account of it), sales of the first album continue strongly: the album enjoys an unbroken sojourn of five months in the charts.

To boot, its release meets with – and fuels – some controversy, not least on account of the inclusion of the inverted cross on the inside cover. Indeed, it is this – and the attendant popular misconception that the band members are satanists – that leads to their involvement (such as it is) with the purveyors of the Black Arts:

> We got involved with all sorts of people. Alex Sanders, who was the head witch here in England, used to come to the show . . . and wanted us to go to his little meetings. All sorts of different stuff used to happen.✝

But nothing ever comes of it. In fact, after Sabbath decline an invitation to celebrate Walpurgis✣ at Stonehenge in May of that year, a spell is

* *Into the Void: Ozzy Osbourne and Black Sabbath*, ed. Barney Hoskyns, Omnibus Press, 2004 contains a hilarious portrait of Meehan ('Everybody Hertz: A Journey with Sabbath's Manager') written by Chris Charlesworth that throws some light on his managerial traits. Jim Simpson's case is best put in Welch.
* Welch maintains, probably with justification, that the tour was called off because the necessary contracts hadn't been secured.
✝ Iommi, speaking in the video/DVD *The Black Sabbath Story: Volume One*, Sanctuary Records, 1991/2002.
✣ The Witches' Sabbath – come out from behind that sofa. You may wish to know that Alex Sanders finally succumbed to lung cancer (or, as he himself might have put it, transcended his body into a new incarnation) on Walpurgis night, 30 April 1988.

placed on the band, sending them off into a blind panic. Butler was later to recall that they sought solace from a white witch who reversed the spell.* In order for the antidote to succeed, however, the band had to wear crucifixes. It was Osbourne who volunteered his father's services for the task – Iommi wasn't having anything further to do with metalworking – and, by the time of their next release, the accessories are being conspicuously sported.

There is little let-up in the work schedule during the spring, as Sabbath's continuous touring sees them playing over forty gigs in April and May alone, including engagements in France and Germany as well as the less glamorous Redcar and Leamington Spa. Despite playing seventeen concerts in June, including a week of commitments in Germany, the band somehow manages to find time that month to cut its second album. The basic tracks are laid down over just five days,* this time at London's Regent Sound studio on Denmark Street using the studio's recently acquired 24-track machine.⚜

Before the post-production work is carried out on the album at Island Studios on 12 July, the record company Vertigo makes it known that *War Pigs* – at that time the album's title – is a no-no. Worried that the strong anti-military message conveyed by the title would prejudice sales in a much-divided America, Vertigo demands the band think again. By this time, the artwork⚜ for the album has been commissioned and signed off. Sabbath reluctantly title the album *Paranoid*, the name of a throwaway number they have hurriedly conceived to fill out the album, which has been earmarked for possible single release, and which has also been going down well at live performances during late June and the early part of July.

---

* Tangye and Wright maintain it was Sanders himself who reversed the hex and advised the band to wear crucifixes.
* 16–20 June. The following day they are appearing with Colosseum, Family, Humble Pie, Gentle Giant, Uriah Heep and others at the 'Big Gig Festival' in Hamburg.
⚜ Twenty-four-track machines were the very latest in technology, and Regent Sound was one of the first British studios to acquire one. Regent Sound, like Trident, had been used by The Beatles, who recorded 'Fixing A Hole' there in February 1967; The Rolling Stones had also used Regent to record their second album in 1964.
⚜ Don't worry: we'll be discussing this in more detail shortly.

The latter part of July, which was to have been taken up with the now-postponed US tour, taking in San Francisco, Los Angeles, Chicago and New York, to promote the first album, is spent amidst a fug of hashish and alcohol; the band, with the second album in the bag and only a couple of gigs in London and Dunstable to honour in a three-week period, kick back and enjoy their first (and last) real break away from things for some time.

In June, Deep Purple had released *In Rock*, their first real rock album and a million miles from the preceding *Concerto for Group and Orchestra* – an indulgently conceived and lavishly executed spectacular recorded at the Royal Albert Hall. The following month, troubled supergroup Free had brought out *Fire and Water*: both great albums, both resounding with 'bottom', neither of them, however, quite preparing you for what was about to come limping and groaning out of the Vertigo crypt that September.

I remember there was mashed potato every day. Mashed potato and maybe peas, a stone-faced orderly pushing some massive bain-marie, and dessert was always, and I mean without exception, jelly and ice cream – ice cream covered in Smarties. And after lunch, the doctors and nurses would come round and, well, play doctors and nurses. The doctors would push and prod my head, determined, or so it seemed, to halt any regrowth of skin tissue. The nurses would all smile and say how brave I was, and that I'd soon be going and how they'd all miss me, and I'd smile back and say, you know. And this little drama would be enacted maybe twice a day. It was okay.

Then one day a doctor found an infection. He'd taken the bandages off to check the stitches, see how everything was shaping up, and there it was. I can't describe it to you: it was on the top of my head. I couldn't see it, but there it was – an infection. I think he even gave it a name. It's not a major infection, he says, and it'll go right enough, but you may have to stay a while longer. So I get these new pills, penicillin. They're

bigger than the red ones I'm getting, and they're harder to swallow, but I'm brave (they said so) and I force them down.

Next few days I'm slipping in and out of consciousness. I've developed a fever, and my skin has burst out in a rash. It appears I'm allergic to penicillin, and I'm moved into isolation. My parents have to wear space suits when they come and visit me – the nurses and doctors, too. I feel like a freak. My throat and head have swelled up, the pressure's playing on my stitches, everything just hurts so damned much. More pills, blackouts, bad dreams, needles the size of pool cues, bogeymen coming out of the walls, the room littered with get well soon cards and chrysanthemums – drug-induced paranoia in a florist's shop.

Fade out.

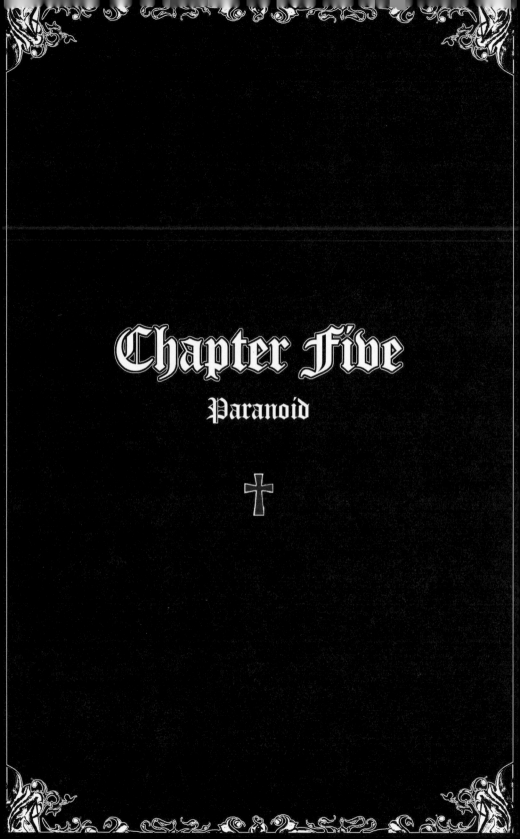

Chapter Five

Paranoid

†

Having spent the few months since the release of the debut album in good spirits, regardless of the onerous burden of near-constant touring, the band, enjoying a period of tremendous synergy, finds the music for *Paranoid* just falling together, almost by itself. Although there is evidence to suggest that 'War Pigs', 'Rat Salad' and 'Fairies Wear Boots' might have dated back to the time of *Black Sabbath*, the majority of the album's material is new – i.e. weeks old rather than months old – and is being honed on the road. Building on the perceived strengths of the debut, and again working with the estimable talents of Rodger Bain as producer, the band consolidate the leaden riffery of *Black Sabbath* and use it as a structural template for the new album. Moving further away from their blues roots whilst still maintaining a foot in the camp, the album shows a tightness in execution only hinted at in 'N.I.B.' on the previous release.

Released on 18 September, the album knocks Simon and Garfunkel's *Bridge Over Troubled Water* off the 'top spot' (if you'll forgive a little seventies DJ argot). The latter had been number one for twenty-five out of the previous thirty-four weeks.* I tell you this because statistics, as we know, are important. Before I get on to discussing the individual tracks in detail, it interested me to discover that 'War Pigs', 'Paranoid', 'Planet Caravan', the end bit of 'Iron Man' and 'Electric Funeral' are all in the key of E: in other words, the first five tracks of the album all have some sort of compositional 'home'. I don't know whether this was intentional or whether it was merely the result of the sequencing, but it does lend a sort of quasi-symphonic identity to the album. It interested me, at any rate; I just thought I'd share it with you.

---

* The Beatles' *Let it Be* had enjoyed six weeks at the top (although not consecutively) between June and August, and The Moody Blues' *A Question of Balance* had three weeks at the top in September before *Bridge Over Troubled Water* resumed its number one status.

That the band managed to come up with so many good songs in such a short space of time warrants particular mention. Remember that this record was recorded only five months after the first album was released, and bearing in mind that this intervening period saw the band performing almost to the point of exhaustion, it's nothing short of miraculous that this album proved to be as good – and original – as it is. Led Zeppelin's second album, by contrast, although produced in an equally short-time period, includes what amount to three cover versions* – as well as a good deal of general mucking about – and must, if used as some sort of comparison, be seen as a much lesser achievement. Additionally, the songs on *Paranoid* have proved the most durable and clamoured-over of the Sabbath catalogue, five of the eight featuring on the 1998 *Reunion* live album.* The fact that 'War Pigs', 'Paranoid', 'Fairies Wear Boots' and 'Iron Man' are such obvious crowd-pleasers may distract us from their intrinsic merits as pieces of work; it's worth noting that these songs are great not just because they *sound* great (and they're what we want to hear) but because there is some considerable artistry about their construction. We'll get onto this later.

As already mentioned, the album was originally to have been titled *War Pigs,*⚕ hence the cover, but was changed to *Paranoid* at some point between the commissioning of the sleeve art and the record's release. Although it has been mooted that the album's change of name was instigated by the success of the 'Paranoid' single,⚜ this is not true. The single was not released until August 1970 and did not chart until

---

* Zeppelin's initial reluctance to acknowledge the sources of some of their songs ensured that 'Whole Lotta Love' and 'Bring It On Home' were marked down as originals; 'The Lemon Song' was appropriately credited to Chester Burnett (Howlin' Wolf), from whose 'Killing Floor' the song was lifted.

* 'Planet Caravan', 'Hand Of Doom' and 'Rat Salad' being the only ones left off the album.

⚕ Would you believe, whilst leafing through the Rolling Stone publication *Decades of Rock & Roll*, I came across an interview *Rolling Stone* did with Osbourne, and it says, honestly it does, that this album was originally to have been titled 'War Pinks'. Now, I'm not sure what went wrong here: maybe the interviewer misheard Osbourne; maybe he was making some sort of cheap jibe, but there it is. To make matters worse, after boldly asserting this nonsense, the interviewer then goes on to say (something along the lines of) 'that explains the guy dressed up in pink on the cover'.

⚜ Most notably by Geoff Barton writing for *Sounds* magazine, 24 January 1976.

26 September (eight days *after* the album was released). Furthermore, it did not achieve Top Ten status until 10 October. Besides, the Island Studios recording log, dated 12 July, clearly shows the album title as being *Paranoid*.

The front cover, depicting a bearded man in hosiery and wielding some sort of sabre, is highly ridiculous. It was designed with the original album title in mind but, quite honestly, it seems just as inappropriate for that. Assuming for a moment that this ludicrous character is a War Pig of some sort, are we to be frightened of him? Are we to steal a glance at the cover and, shuddering with tremulous fear, think, 'What an evil bastard this guy is'? I mean, is this how War Pigs dress? Crash helmet right out of *C.H.I.P.S.*, shield (yup) purloined from the local am-dram production of *Camelot*, yellow rugby-style shirt (emblazoned with a pink beauty-queen-type sash – no doubt held in place with a satanic safety-pin), lurid pink pedal-pushers and – as some sort of sartorial *coup de grâce* – blue underpants, worn Superman-style over his trousers. Not even Bill Ward dressed that badly in the seventies.*

In contrast, the inside photograph is rather lovely: it is a bled-out, black and white shot of the band, making them look like a less stylish Crosby, Stills, Nash & Young. Iommi and Butler go for that cowboy/rocker look,* Osbourne adopts a sort of pixie/rocker thing and Ward sports his favourite 'star' shirt,✚ presumably in an attempt to embody the wizard/rocker look. Fat leather belts were clearly de rigueur at the time: not only are Iommi, Butler and Osbourne all sporting them, they are wearing them, like gun-belts, over their shirts and trousers. Osbourne, standing adrift from the other three members, boasts a very commanding presence: his attitude is one of superiority, characterised by the tilted-back head and the distinct I'm-looking-down-my-nose-at-you expression; his hands-on-hips stance is arrogant; the only vulnerability

---

* The cover of *Sabotage* notwithstanding.

* The film *Butch Cassidy and the Sundance Kid* came out in 1969 and further bolstered the popularity of this particular fashion trend.

✚ You see Ward wearing this same shirt in film footage of the band's live performances of this period. One hopes it saw the inside of a washing machine in-between times.

suggested by the large crucifix he wears (a talisman rather than a badge of office) and a fragile verge-of-tears look in his eyes. It is the image of Osbourne which dominates the inside cover, not so much because he has the entire right panel to himself (the other three share the left panel) but because he conveys such dramatic intention. Equal parts menace and frailty, this iconic representation of Osbourne is hard to square with the comical grotesquery of his subsequent incarnations.

1) War Pigs

Although many see events such as Altamont and the disintegration of The Beatles as bringing about the end of the sixties, ideologically, the decade ended much earlier. The May riots in 1968, the acceleration of the Vietnam conflict, the pervading sense of confrontation generally: these are events more typical of the following decade, when earnestness and intensity, political commitment and polarisation – rather than whimsicality and the notion of abstinence encouraged by 'dropping out' – provided the focus of 'informed' political thinking. This song – and this album generally – marked Sabbath's entry into the political forum of the sixties/seventies crossover. It was to prove only a brief flirtation: by the time of *Vol. 4*, a mere two years later – global popularity achieved and egos inflated through a surfeit of cocaine – the band were to slink back into lyrical introspection, mental disquiet and personal angst.

The transformation from 'Walpurgis' (the original manifestation of this song, a version of which appears on Osbourne's *The Ozzman Cometh* recording)* to 'War Pigs' was undertaken because main lyricist Butler was tiring of the association Black Sabbath had developed with the occult, as a result of the packaging, sound and lyrical tenor of the first album. Indeed, such was the band's displeasure at being ceaselessly diagnosed as occultists, they went public with their grievance, resulting in *Disc and Music Echo*'s front-page splash in October, FANS WE DON'T WANT.

---

* This is a 1997 compilation of the best of his solo work. The track is listed as 'War Pigs' and is taken from 'Ozzy's 1970 Basement Tapes'. If you haven't heard this, it's worth doing so; the lyrics are delivered in a far throatier way, redolent of Osbourne's singing on the *Black Sabbath* album.

The precise timing of the name change we can place at some point between 26 June and 12 July 1970.* In the rewritten version, the characterisation of these warmongers as pigs – War Pigs is a fortuitous corruption of Walpurgis – intensifies the obscenity of the subject matter by colouring it with the bloody hues of capitalism. There is no explicit reference in the song to anthropomorphised, suit-bursting, cigar-smoking, porcine aggressors – as there is in The Beatles' less considered predecessor 'Piggies', but the connection is nevertheless unavoidable. This ensures the song has relevance today, when human slaughter and land rape are part and parcel of corporate empire building, and wars are fought over oil reserves, telecommunications franchises and fast-food chains.

There are some lyrical similarities between the two incarnations of the song: 'Walpurgis' – a veritable *grimoire* of an affair – starts with witches gathering for a black mass, and those of you amused by the rhyming of 'masses' and 'masses', 'destruction' and 'construction' on the latter version, will almost certainly be tickled pink by the coupling of 'ruin' and 'evil doin'' and 'sinners' and 'dead rats' innards' on the former.

'War Pigs' will rightly stand as one of Black Sabbath's greatest achievements, mixing, as it does, some spectacularly intricate and weighty guitar work with passages of surprising, and enduring, melody. The opening passage, lasting just under a minute, describes perfectly an urban landscape laid to ruin by some terrible, anonymous power. The air-raid siren, which cuts in midway through this passage, alerts us to further destruction on the way. We then begin to realise that, amongst the dead and dying, there are still people very much alive here. As the siren weaves in and out of the two-chord motif of Iommi's guitar and the blustering, mortar-like drumming of Ward, Butler's bass describes the sound of panicked footfalls, desperately seeking shelter from an onslaught too terrible to describe; so we cut to those generals assembled in their masses and are thus transported behind the scenes, as it were, to the people

* A live bootleg recording from Freie Universität, Berlin, dated 26 June 1970, has the song in its original version; the Island Studios recording log, dated 12 July, has it down as 'War Pigs'.

responsible for this unspeakable evil. Apart from a couple of the song's lines, in which smouldering corpses and battlefield detritus are thrown before us, we never revisit the shocking scenes of carnage in the trochaic tetrameter of the lyric — it is left to the music to do that for us — but, instead, with those images burned in our minds, we look long and hard at the War Pigs themselves.

Okay, Benjamin Britten's *War Requiem* it ain't, but this is, nevertheless, a very potent and damning blast against politicians and the military alike: not just because it confronts the listener with a terrifying aural depiction of war, but because, in the lyric 'treating people just like pawns in chess', we are reminded that there is no tragedy quite as lamentable as the self-inflicted one. And when Osbourne delivers his desperate Kyrie at 1:45 (and again at 5:22), you really get the impression he's saying 'Lord, is there anything you can *do* about this?'

Osbourne's repeated invocations finally elicit a response from God in the concluding verse. Here, after the world has been laid waste, Osbourne sings of the Day of Judgement, bringing to mind corresponding images of the weighing of souls and other such pre-Reformation dogma. God's belated intercession in this metaphysical court martial assures the humiliating capitulation of the warmongers as, at 5:07, we learn how these War Pigs are now begging for forgiveness. The real villain of the piece, however, Satan — assuming, as he does in Milton's *Paradise Lost*, the role of architect of mass destruction and all-round bad egg — sneaks off to fight another day.

By the time Iommi's sublime solo arrives (6:34), we've been told the whole story, and we're waiting for the credits to start rolling. Ward's alternating shuffle and rock rhythms remind us that all is still chaos, but,

---

* John Milton (1608–74): English poet. *Paradise Lost*, by far his most important and famous work, and concerning a battle royal between God and Satan — much as 'War Pigs' does (both God and Satan are invoked throughout the piece) — contains the lines, 'The infernal serpent; he it was whose guile / Stirred up with envy and revenge, deceived / The mother of mankind, what time his pride / Had cast him out from heaven, with all his host / Of rebel angels, by whose aid, aspiring / To set himself in glory above his peers, / He trusted to have equalled the most high / If he opposed, and, with ambitious aim / Against the throne and monarchy of God / Raised impious war in heaven and battle proud / With vain attempt. Him the almighty power / Hurled headlong flaming from the ethereal sky / With hideous ruin and combustion down / To bottomless perdition, there to dwell / In adamantine chains and penal fire, / Who durst defy the omnipotent to arms.' (Book 1; 34–49)

as Iommi's solo starts, we might be forgiven for thinking that we are now rising above it all on a military chopper and leaving it behind, so simple and elegiac are its tones. However, nine bars in, we realise that we are being elevated only so we can survey the scene in its gross atrociousness. The curious speeded-up finale suggests total meltdown: not even the machines are working now, everything's gone wrong, this is the end.

Despite the terrible and unprecedented nature of the Vietnam War itself and, just as significantly, its lasting aftermath in both Vietnam and America, it must be conceded that, by its very happening, it provided contemporary songwriters with much-needed subject material. There were only so many songs that could be written about flowers and LSD and wanting to hold your baby's hand, and, if songwriting was to survive as a credible and worthy expression of the cultural youth ethos, it had to move on. Vietnam gave songwriters something they could push against. Stylistically, there were three reactive approaches. The first, and most overt, of these was typified by songs such as Country Joe and The Fish's 'Feel-Like-I'm-Fixin'-to-Die Rag': half interrogative protest song ('What are we fighting for?'), half ironic black comedy ('Yippee! We're all gonna die!'). An equally scathing but less satirical variation on this first approach was taken in, for example, Tim Buckley's 'No Man Can Find The War', Buffy St Marie's 'Universal Soldier' and, towering over all else in this canon, Dylan's terrifying 'Masters Of War'.

In songs such as these, the treatment of the subject matter, war, was direct and unconcealed. The second approach was lyrically more subtle: Kenny Rogers and the First Edition's 'Ruby Don't Take Your Love To Town', referenced the conflict incidentally;* the principal subject matter was not the war itself, but the knowledge that a war was being – or had been – fought, and that attempts had to be made to assimilate this into the everyday lives of ordinary individuals. The final interpolation of the war in song was epitomised by The Doors' 'The End', Hendrix's brief but celebrated rendition of 'The Star-Spangled Banner' and The Nice's

---

* Rogers sings from the perspective of a paraplegic veteran, struggling to hold on to a woman he is now physically incapable of satisfying, and thus brings the legacy of Vietnam into the domestic theatre.

interpretation of Leonard Bernstein's 'America', a tune from *West Side Story*. Here, there were no lyrical references to the conflict, but it was clear, just from listening to the instrumentation, that the war (and the concurrent perception of America as an unjust and arbitrary power) had nevertheless informed the music.

'War Pigs' stands as a powerful, if ultimately only partly considered, polemic of the reactionary sub-genre typified by the first of the above three examples. The assertion of Miltonic metaphysics in preference to the era-defining idiosyncrasies of Country Joe's and Tim Buckley's contributions, and its lack of any specific historical or geographical context, render it a song for all time: for whenever and wherever man sees it fit to take up arms against fellow man.*

2) Paranoid

Reportedly knocked together in twenty minutes, as a last-minute album 'filler', there is no question that 'Paranoid' is Black Sabbath's most famous song. Invariably featured in live performances (regardless of the prevailing line-up), and often found on 'heavy metal' and 'seventies rock' compilations – as well as being covered countless times by other performers – it is nothing if not ubiquitous. Not only ubiquitous: in choosing to play it at the 2002 Queen's Golden Jubilee Party, Osbourne and Iommi even ensured the song garnered royal approval. However, it is odd that this song is commonly held as being archetypal Black Sabbath; it is, in fact, far from being so.

For one thing, its length (2:46) is more typical of a sixties chart hit than the more protracted track-lengths expected of rock artists at that time. Its pace, too, was uncustomary. Osbourne's keening vocal, starting a minor third above Iommi's guitar, was a stylistic departure in as much as it hammered out the melody in a swinging four stresses to the bar manner, rather than the longer note values or bluesy pentatonal melismas

---

* The claim that 'War Pigs' is inextricable from Vietnam – the conflict that undoubtedly inspired it – is rubbished by the presence of air-raid sirens (archetypically and uniquely Second World War) in the opening section.

more normally associated with his singing. The lyric, too, with Osbourne declaring that he's left his woman as she couldn't ease his troubled mind, is a curious inversion of the more traditional 'My baby left me', typical of the blues and rock idiom.*

Butler, the song's lyricist, fondly recounts that, when he came up with both the song title and its lyric, none of the other band members knew what 'paranoid' meant. He himself wasn't all that sure. It was, he recalled, merely a vogue word at the time.* Notwithstanding, the lyric, with its prevailing aura of psychosocial estrangement, anxiety and compulsion, is fortuitously appropriate. There was considerable concern over the final couplet, in which, many thought, Osbourne was seemingly encouraging the suggestible listener to end his life. This appeared as an interesting move sideways from The Who's 'My Generation', with its famous 'Hope I die before I get old'. But, of course, that's not what Osbourne sang, this being one of the seventies' most notorious mondegreens:✝ it was to *enjoy* one's life, not end it. So it was all a big fuss about nothing.

The main riff, recently voted the best guitar riff ever⸸ (an accolade that, however gratifying, Iommi would probably not concur with), is a simple figure alternating between E and D, with a punctuating G – D – E – G change that feels like the sudden and forceful application of a footbrake – the resuming E/D figure then resembling an equally vigorous acceleration. The combined effect of this start/stop/start arrangement is one of absolute, raving, sociopathic madness: a wildly careering White Van Man overdosed on amphetamines and vodka chasers – and he's

---

* Two points here: first, 'Paranoid' is not a love song (the topic of the severed relationship recounted in the first line is not subsequently revisited; it is merely listed as one of a number of symptomatic ailments which characterise the singer's dissociated paranoid state); second, love was not a subject Sabbath would frequently resort to lyrically – the notion of Sabbath as a ballad band is not one that sits comfortably in my imagination.

* From the video/DVD *The Black Sabbath Story: Volume One*, Sanctuary Records, 1991/2002 .

✝ Worthy of more than the mere footnote they get here, mondegreens are misheard lyrics, the most famous, perhaps, being Hendrix's 'Scuse me while I kiss this guy' ('Scuse me while I kiss the sky') from 'Purple Haze'. The term was coined by author Sylvia Wright in 1954. As a child she had heard the lyric to the Scottish ballad 'The Bonnie Earl of Murray' as, 'Ye highlands and ye lowlands / O, where hae you been? / Thou hae slain the Earl Of Murray / And Lady Mondegreen'; the correct lyric ending, 'And laid him on the green'.

⸸ *Kerrang!* magazine readers' poll.

coming your way.*

Butler had reservations about the song: speaking in 1998, he recalled:

> When we did 'Paranoid', I said to Tony, 'It's too much like Zeppelin; we can't do that!' I thought that it was 'Communication Breakdown'.*

And although Butler had a point, the majority opinion held sway. But although it's easy to regard this song as a simple, perhaps derivative, throwaway number, it is not without its merits — and Iommi's solo in particular is worthy of mention. The kind of solo that Eddie Van Halen or Steve Vai could play just using their toes, what it lacks in technical artistry it more than compensates for in luscious, elevating sinuousness. And, without wishing to denigrate Iommi in any way, that was really his trademark. Like Carlos Santana, Iommi has a gift for melody; he has guitar solos you can actually hum, and they still sound like tunes. Although the structural rigidity of 'Paranoid' does not allow for any lengthy instrumental digressions, Iommi's outbreak at 1:23 provides a sense of crazed mania to the song, perfectly balancing the depressive apprehension of the lyric.

Twice charting as a single release — it made number four on 17 October 1970 (Deep Purple's 'Black Night' was at number two), and number fourteen, ten years later when it was rather pointlessly re-released, on 27 September 1980 — the track is probably singularly responsible for giving Sabbath the 'dumb rockers' tag the remainder of their output so demonstrably confutes.

---

* I was going to use the word behemoth somewhere in that sentence. Then I suddenly realised that behemoth is one of the many terms now clichéd in its use as a descriptive noun to describe guitar riffs. So I didn't. But I did look it up in a dictionary. It seems that behemoth, which is an Old Testament word occurring in 'The Book of Job' (40:15), probably means hippopotamus. Now, hands up if you knew that.
* Butler speaking to Mick Wall for *Classic Rock* magazine, January 1999.

3) Planet Caravan

The third track on the album, the third to be in the key of E and the third to be based around the minor key tonic/subtonic shift of E and D, 'Planet Caravan' – despite its structural similarities to the two foregoing pieces – manages to maintain a quite independent identity on the album. The prosaic – and, by now, familiar – E/D interchange is cleverly disguised by 'jazzy' chordal ornamentations (Em9 and D6sus4) in a nevertheless repetitive piece that somehow manages to sustain the interest of the listener for four-and-a-half minutes or so. That it does so is due in no small part to the delicate understated playing of Ward, Butler and Iommi and a treated vocal from Osbourne which lends the piece its ethereal other-worldliness.

The lyric, which, it has to be said, is barely discernible through the panoply of effects, is a view from space of a disintegrating Earth – a raging splendour evident in its death throes, a final, terrible beauty as witnessed from the window of a rapidly fleeing spacecraft. Incorporating a multiple-rhyme scheme and deploying colourful (literally)* images of astrophysical and terrestrial phenomena, the song can firmly be placed amongst others of the then nascent space-rock idiom; which, arguably starting from a desire to elevate psychedelia to a 'cosmic' level,* and given a significant shot in the arm by the moon landing in July 1969, was developing through artists such as David Bowie;✝ The Grateful Dead;✱ Crosby, Stills, Nash & Young;✦ and Hawkwind,⁑ and an explosion of

---

* 'Black night', 'silver trees', 'purple blaze', 'sapphire haze', 'silver [again] starlight' 'crimson eye'.
* Early examples of 'space-inspired' rock include Pink Floyd's 'Astronomy Domine' and 'Interstellar Overdrive' (both from 1967's *Piper at the Gates of Dawn*), Hendrix's 'Third Stone From The Sun' (from the same year's *Are You Experienced?*) and the musical *Hair* (debuting off-Broadway the following year).
✝ 'Space Oddity' charted in October, 1969.
✱ Their 1970 release *Live/Dead* featured lengthy extemporisations typical of the genre.
✦ Not, perhaps, 'space rock' per se, but CSN's 'Wooden Ships' (1969) and Young's 'After The Goldrush' (1970) both explored the notion of atomic meltdown and the possibility of subsequent cosmic relocation.
⁑ 1970 saw the release of Hawkwind's first album.

interest in both Holst's *Planets* suite and Richard Strauss's *Also Sprach Zarathustra.**

Iommi's solo, which pips in at 2:30 and takes us through to the close of the song, is a delightful Joe Pass-inspired contribution which veers, at times, dangerously close to lounge-jazz without ever quite getting there. Played with genuine sensitivity and feeling over an extemporised bass-line from Butler, some deft hand-played percussion by Ward and a delicate 8/8 limping waltz time signature,* the solo conjures an image of disappearing perspective (like the Tardis graphics in the title sequence of *Dr Who*): Earth is staying resolutely in centre shot, but its significance — as we encroach further into the gaping and infinite unknown — recedes steadily to an eventual cosmic vanishing point.

A lovely piece, usually omitted from subsequent *Best Of* and *Greatest Hits* packages, 'Planet Caravan' has not dated a jot, has much to offer and deserves to be heard again and again.

4) Iron Man

Adopting a technique much practised by The Beatles,† 'Iron Man' cleverly begins with a repeated key-disguising guitar slur from F sharp to E — suggesting either a further continuation of the key of E which has so far been the only key on the album or, once again, the minor key tonic/subtonic shift — this time in the key of F sharp — featured in all the preceding numbers. When the riff proper does kick in, it does so in the key of B minor — the sudden leap reminiscent of some giant thing being stirred into action (appropriately enough).

Iommi has, of course, often been hailed as the greatest ever composer of guitar riffs, and there is certainly a good deal that can be said in support of this claim; that he would, with seemingly prodigal abandon,

---

* Featured in Kubrick's 1968 film *2001: A Space Odyssey* and as the 'theme tune' for the American space programme. A condensed version of the *Introduction* from this Strauss tone poem made it to number thirty in the UK singles chart in August 1969 – a month after the first moon landing.
* Broken down into two part-measures of 3/8 followed by a part-measure of 2/8.
† I'm thinking predominantly of 'I Want To Hold Your Hand', but there's also 'Tell Me Why', 'I'm Happy Just To Dance With You' and 'Hold Me Tight' amongst others.

squander four or five grade-A riffs on the one song (where two or three would have sufficed) attests to his prodigious compositional talent. The main riff in 'Iron Man', which strikes us initially as a stupefying, gonzoid affair with little finesse, possesses a prosodic quality in keeping with the lyrical tenor of the song. The idea of the Iron Man as some tragic creation, whose only sin was to be bolted together by man and who is bound to a life of destructive servitude and alienation – a futurist *Frankenstein*, if you will – is well reflected in the catastrophic tones of the song's rendition. The lurching shift from the minor tonic through the mediant to the subdominant (the initial five notes of the main riff) suggests the first lumbering steps of the character of the song's title: menacing, robust and robotic, capable of immense destruction. The quavering between the submediant and the dominant, which immediately follows, is indicative of weakness: the great iron giant stumbling, showing both frailty and vulnerability. The fourth bar of the riff embodies recovery and resolution: he cannot yet fall, there is work to be done, he must carry on.

The second riff, starting at 1:14 (exemplifying what I mean by Iommi's open-handed generosity with composition – this riff could well have been used as the basis for a further composition), with its semitonal runs between the tonic and the subtonic, is a musical pan-shot similar in effect to the development of the solo in 'War Pigs': we are now viewing the embattled hulk as it cleaves its way through the post-apocalyptic landscape, before Ward's simple fill takes us back to the character's laboured but seemingly unstoppable momentum in close-up. A third riff at 2:04, again employing semitone runs, is suggestive of sudden crisis – a system malfunction, perhaps, or an operational breakdown – a temporary blip that the resumption of the main riff (2:22) suggests is not terminal. But then it happens again at 2:53, and an ensuing chromatic descent (3:11) informs us that, this time, there is something seriously wrong. Iommi's solo then provides us with the robotic equivalent of a collapsed *in extremis* flashback: on the verge of destruction, the hapless automaton's life flashes before its eyes.

But, of course, it doesn't die; its tragedy is that it is left to carry on.

We are told of this lyrically at 4:19, where its doomed deathlessness is grimly proclaimed. When we then come to a reprise of the guitar slur used at the beginning of the track all the signs are pointing to an imminent but uncertain conclusion: a fade to white, an audience left to contemplate the nebulous terror of an unseen dénouement. We do get closure – the end does eventually come – but only after the guitar slur takes us into yet another riff (this is the coda in E referred to at the start of this chapter) and a further solo. The end is, in short, just as dramatic as the beginning: the damned thing's gone mad; it won't stop; what the hell are we to do?

5) Electric Funeral

A luxuriant wah-wah guitar introduction again in E, and again making use of the panicked uncertainty of quavered interchanges between the dominant and the submediant (and also the supertonic and the mediant), firmly establishes that we are still in the post-apocalyptic frame of reference we inhabited in 'Iron Man'. In fact, the image of slave robots leading captives to their graves suggests that we haven't really moved on at all. Chronologically predating 'Iron Man' in terms of its description of atomic meltdown, 'Electric Funeral' casts a wider shot at a burned-down panorama. The central character of this song is not a War Pig, neither is it some sort of robotic nemesis, and neither is it you or me; it is the planet itself – its recumbent majesty scrutinised in both sweeping strokes and minute detailing.

As such, it shares a lyrical basis with the preceding 'Planet Caravan'; however, whilst in the former the livid hues of terrestrial meltdown are viewed from afar with pronounced emotional detachment – and are phrased in terms of incongruous spectral beauty – here the listener is inescapably restrained within the apocalyptic arena, and the images are both brutal and terrifying.

The main motif (the riff which prefaces the verse) is heavy and ponderous. Like the predominant riff in 'Iron Man', it embodies an inexorable sense of threat, and – with its undeniable aura of instability –

its perverse energy is imaginatively mixed with the eponymously funereal sloth of its pacing. Contrastingly, the compositional structure of the middle section, kicking in at 2:25, is purposefully rushed and chaotic; the searing vividness of the images and the accompanying music cry 'Run!' – but every possible avenue has been blocked.

The verse motif, featuring a semitonal slide from the fifth to the fourth – bizarrely redolent of Verdi's* 'Dies Irae' from his *Requiem*, only replacing Verdi's explosive apocalypse with a simmering conflagration – is quintessential Sabbath: if ever there were a riff that embodied the plainsong harmony of Iommi's guitar and Osbourne's wailing vocal, this would be it.

There is the slight suggestion that, at 4:53, the song is somewhat overcooked. The three riffs are all strong, interesting affairs, but there is a distinct lack of additional colour and the compositional palette lacks the finer tints and shades that may have provided that. Specifically, the song misses an instrumental coda – an opportunity for the listener to assimilate the weight of the lyrical images and a platform for the ceremonial loss to be mourned. Undoubtedly, had the band had longer than five days in which to record the whole album, then this song might have benefited from more scrupulous attention. As it is, 'Electric Funeral' is a good, workmanlike piece that fulfils its role as a side-two opener adequately if not spectacularly.

6) Hand Of Doom

Along with 'War Pigs' and 'Fairies Wear Boots', 'Hand Of Doom' is one of three major songs on *Paranoid* that together form a sort of blues-rock power triptych. Of these, only 'War Pigs' escapes the personalised,

---

*Giuseppe Verdi (1813–1901): an Italian composer most noted for his operas (*Rigoletto*, *Il Trovatore*, *La Traviata*, *Aïda* and many others). His *Requiem* – which he dedicated to Alessandro Manzoni (1785–1873), Milanese nobleman, poet and novelist, and later senator – was published during a lull in his operatic output and signalled the beginning of a tentative and gradual resumption of his Catholic faith. Verdi himself later became a deputy in the 1860 Italian parliament, but he quickly renounced his political duties, which were not to his taste, and concentrated on tending his garden and living the wholesome agrarian life.

hallucinocentric world of drug use: 'Hand Of Doom' and 'Fairies' showing respectively the introspective, cloistered, bedsit hell and the delusional, alfresco mania of chemical brain-shaping.

The song is too earnest to function merely as a self-referential, finger-wagging critique of the band's spiralling substance abuse. It is, instead, a story told from the inside: the only thing to escape the claustrophobic environment of the self-imposed junkie sanctum being the story itself; the protagonist, like so many dirty needles, is caught spent and dis-carded on the fag-burned carpet.

It's difficult to believe how Osbourne's sardonic and caustic exhorta-tions – very much in evidence throughout the song's lyric – could have been taken as anything other than admonitory sarcasm, but they were. In telling the story of a Vietnam veteran who seeks escape from the remembered horrors of war in shooting heroin, the song drew attention to itself as advocating the merits of the drug as a psychopathological diversion,* a momentary respite from psychiatric trauma. Although, of course, it's not so much a diversion as it is an exit. We know he's going to die right from the off; more to the point, *he* knows he's going to die, too.* The snide delivery of the lyric – which is palpably unsympathetic and cautionary – militates against the song being merely some sort of louche suicide ode: every line brings pain – and only pain. There is no retrospection, no anticipation of the release which death might bring. There is no regret, no 'Tell Laura I Love Her', no glamour. There is – *only* – pain. The ineluctability of this character's death elevates the notional preciousness of life itself. That life, even when it's this hopeless, is at once both sacred and redeemable: even if it isn't a sin to throw it away, it must at least be conceded a waste. The song derives its tragedy status not through any detailed characterisation of its protago-nist – this is not Dylan's epic narrative 'Ballad Of Hollis Brown' – and

---

* John Prine's 1971 debut album featured the song 'Sam Stone', which, in detailing the experiences of a drug-addicted Vietnam veteran, shared a lyrical similarity to 'Hand Of Doom'. However, whereas Prine's effort was guilty of drifting toward the sentimental, Sabbath's was both plainly spo-ken and stark; neither did 'Hand Of Doom' possess the lyrical nonchalance and musical frivolity of Neil Young's 'The Needle And The Damage Done' (also 1971).
* The fourth line is quite clear on this.

neither through a succession of illuminating snapshots of his predicament – neither is it The Beatles' painterly 'Eleanor Rigby' – but in its observation that killing and dying are but opposite sides of a nowadays valueless coin.

The song begins with Butler's bass, describing, in a simple but articulate manner, the clandestine secrecy of dubious goings-on behind locked doors: the D minor figure suggesting a quiet, furtive process with its initial seven notes; the prefiguring of impending and inevitable tragedy enforced by the semitonal ascent of the following four. This figure is replicated an octave higher by Iommi: suggesting a composition – at least in the early stages – that was largely extempory. Ward's clonking and clattering* – suggestive of some fatalistic voodooism, perhaps – gives the song a fractured momentum which reinforces the inevitability of the final outcome, eventually revealed lyrically in Osbourne's rudimentary Aeolian melody.

The riff is too good not to exploit further: after a few bars of quiet menace, it explodes into a power chord recapitulation before slinking back into its original form. At 2:05, the song changes pace suddenly; at which point, we deduce that the lethal dose has been injected. Iommi's guitar and Butler's bass, locked onto a disturbing C, sound like some pneumatic drill rigged to function as an alarm clock. This gives way to a rapid barrelhouse figure at 2:19 – crazy and unstable and a million miles from its New Orleans roots – before a four-chord ascent, in what is now the temporary home key of C minor, depicts the heroin taking hold.

At 3:38, the poison has brought on euphoria. As the song's subject is held in the drug's thrall, Butler and Iommi play a heart-racing figure, suggestive of capillary overload and exploding blood vessels. That this perilous rapture is but temporary, we know to be true already: nothing that lives this fast can last that long. Butler maintains a hold on the pumping C figure whilst Iommi produces a dreamlike solo with appropriately psychedelic overtones.

As Iommi's solo finishes, the hard braking action of the three-chord

---

* This is good work; I'm not being negatively critical.

C – B flat – G (4:52-4:58) – the body hitting the floor – prefaces a reprise of the original motif. Osbourne's screaming hysterics at 6:43 herald the next departure of the Styx ferry.

7) Rat Salad

When I was about thirteen, my little sister and I would play a game that involved depicting song and album titles graphically. The one would have to guess what the other had drawn. We'd play it for hours. Years later, Pictionary came out and made a few more people millionaires. I mean, I'm not trying to say that we invented the game – it had been around for years – it just amazes me that someone can claim a copyright on it. Anyway, whenever we used to play this game, 'Rat Salad' would always come up. It got to the point where one of us would only have to start drawing whiskers on the paper for the other to say – in crowing triumph, naturally – *Rat Salad!* After a few hours of this sibling intimacy, she'd beat me up with a hairdrier and things would return to normal.

Often overlooked on account of its misdiagnosis as a drum solo, 'Rat Salad' is an engaging piece of work. Led Zeppelin had earlier indulged Bonham on *II* with 'Moby Dick': a funky riff followed by a stupefyingly dull pattering from a normally energetic drummer. Sabbath may have seized the opportunity for a riposte (Ward and Bonham were close friends and drinking partners, and the bands themselves were well acquainted with one another), and, be this the case, I'd say they won out.[*] For one thing, Ward doesn't extend our patience beyond its natural limits – his unaccompanied middle section lasts less than a minute – and his drumming, however rudimentary, is never less than entertaining. What makes Ward's work all the more remarkable here is that it is executed on a small kit. In something of a storyteller's style, he holds back the rumbling drama of the tom-toms until he has established some sort of exposition with the snare and a hard-working foot on the bass drum.

---

[*] There can be little doubt that Bonzo was the better drummer, but I've never known anyone – and I'm including drummers of my acquaintance in this assertion – who can actually listen to 'Moby Dick' without losing the will to live – or, at least, hitting the 'skip' button.

Iommi's guitar figure, a perfunctory jog in G minor, is performed with confidence and panache. At times sounding like his guitar work on the following year's *Master of Reality*, the riff is an intelligent fusion of blues licks and jazz phrasing and was doubtless used as the basis of an instrumental on account of its unsuitability for vocal embellishment.

8) Fairies Wear Boots

Widely reported as being an angry retaliation against the skinhead thugs who set on the band and caused Iommi to injure his arm,* 'Fairies Wear Boots' is, surprisingly when this is taken into consideration, mischievous and playful. A palinode to the diametrically attitudinal 'Hand Of Doom', 'Fairies' is a joyous satyric drama, saturated in its own hedonism, and over twenty years ahead of Oasis' 'Cigarettes And Alcohol', the only other song with which it can be even remotely compared.

Beginning with a muted guitar figure in G, the song modulates after only fourteen seconds to the key of A. Here it reposes for all of twelve seconds before modulating a further tone to B. It hangs around in B for twenty-some seconds and then – and this is just so *witty* – it nudges itself up into C sharp. We're now as far away from the initial key of G as it's possible to get, and, when listening to the song, you do have to wonder how it will progress from this rather isolated and faraway location. Had Bach written it, it might have repeated the process of tonal modulation through D sharp and F back to G: this would, no doubt, have satisfied the mathematical proclivities with which his compositional technique has been retrospectively accorded. But we know Bach didn't write 'Fairies Wear Boots': if he had done, he'd never have landed that cushy number at Leipzig (although it would have done wonders for his apoplexy).

Resisting the temptation to prolong its tonal progression through the chromatic scale, the song bravely – nay, *recklessly* – plunges from its C sharp roosting post back into a tonally ambiguous E – D – B – A

---

* An incident reported to have taken place that June in Newcastle. Welch (p. 32).

(1:03– 1:13) and thence, after a precipitous fill from Ward, back into the home key of G at 1:16. And it works splendidly. Bach wouldn't have had the balls to try that. From hereon in, the song has a rollicking good time. Iommi's clumsily energetic riff – redolent of drunken wrestlers dancing naked in a forest clearing at twilight – fortifies the song and inures the work against any possible charges of earnestness. This teasing friskiness and lack of any real conviction is further bolstered by an inchoate and juvenile lyric which sounds largely improvised: after having spotted the eponymous fairies dancing with the dwarfs one *night* (which gave him a *fright*), Osbourne sings of visiting the doctor, who – as doctors will – tells him that he's rather overdone it with all the smoking and tripping. The final 'Yeah!', so full of sneering pride and self-satisfaction, epitomises the ethos of the song: this is me, I love me, you love me, pass the hash pipe.

Simply put, this is Sabbath having a good time. And if you'd just written and recorded the *Paranoid* album, you'd probably want a bit of fun, too, and 'Fairies Wear Boots' brings the album to an uncharacteristically joyous, if nevertheless reprehensible, close. There's no way the song would have worked sandwiched between, say, 'Electric Funeral' and 'Hand Of Doom' – or anywhere on side one, for that matter: it's simply too laddishly boisterous. However, following the lyrical blank of 'Rat Salad', and as an album closer, the song is gratuitously palate cleansing: almost like slurping down a sorbet after working your way through a toffee pudding.

Chapter Six

Sweet Life / 1971

✝

For most of the world, 1971 proves to be a year of reckoning. As more and more Americans protest their country's involvement in Vietnam – leading to significant US troop withdrawals once again – two eagerly anticipated and much celebrated court cases absorb intense media speculation and coverage: Lt William Calley Jr is found guilty of premeditated murder at My Lai, and Charles Manson and friends are similarly adjudged for the Tate/Labianca slayings.

Excerpts from the first batch of what are to become known as the Pentagon Papers are published by both the *New York Times* and the *Washington Post*. Detailing the extent to which deception was being used (both at home and abroad) in the course of promoting the Vietnam conflict, there is actually little in them to bolster the protestors' case: most of the really incriminating stuff can't positively be traced to Nixon and the White House,* and, besides, most of it is known – or, at least, strongly suspected – prior to the documents being published.

America and Russia sit down together and agree that the exploding of nuclear warheads on the seabed is a bad thing. With the agreement and cooperation of over sixty other nations, the practice is banned unconditionally. Before the year is out, however, America explodes a massive hydrogen bomb under Amchitka Island in the Aleutians, off the coast of Alaska. Environmental pressure groups Greenpeace and Friends of the Earth are both formed: the former in an attempt to prevent the Amchitka incident (it succeeds only in delaying it by two months); the latter to promote recycling and everyday environmental issues (its first action, that May, being to

---

* The Papers revealed that ex-presidents Eisenhower and Kennedy had been warned against involvement and had approved the overthrow of the South Vietnamese president, respectively. Both these figures, however, were now dead.

deliver thousands of empty non-returnable bottles to the doors of Schweppes' UK headquarters).

Following a medical conference in London, doctors and scientists reach consensus on the fact that smoking probably isn't very good for you. America bans tobacco advertising on TV; meanwhile, its cars are pumping a quarter of a million tons of lead into the atmosphere every year. No one thinks to ban car advertising.

As the US lands a car on the moon, the Lunar Rover, three Soviet cosmonauts are found dead in their spaceship after it returns to earth.

There is turmoil in the subcontinent as East Pakistan struggles to gain independence from governing Pakistan. With assistance from sympathetic India, it succeeds, adopts the name Bangladesh and is immediately plunged into famine. In a gesture predating Live Aid by well over a decade, ex-Beatle George Harrison organises a benefit concert for the starving millions of Bangladeshis. Although providing little practical assistance itself,* the concert raises awareness of the plight of the emergent country and helps to further the involvement of contemporary musicians in issues of global or humanitarian concern.

Catholic Republicans and Protestant Loyalists continue to clash violently in Ulster. There are senseless and brutal murders perpetrated on both sides – ending in the year's tally of 173 dead, 43 of whom are British soldiers: the first ever British soldiers to be killed in Northern Ireland and the first in armed conflict on Irish soil since 1921 (i.e. the last time they were there). The authorities' diminishing capability to impose order on the province sees the introduction of 'internment': the right to arrest and detain without trial anyone whom they consider to be a 'man of violence'.

The BBC begins broadcasts of *The Old Grey Whistle Test*, a showcase

---

* It subsequently came to light that there was some jiggery-pokery involved in the handling of the benefit's proceeds; none of this is to be blamed on Harrison, who, oblivious to this, worked tirelessly in organising and promoting the venture. However, it is fair to roundly apportion considerable blame on Allen Klein – one-time Beatles/Stones financial guru and all-round lard-bucket – who served two months in jail for tax evasion over the show's profits, and also funnelled considerable sums from the sale of promotional copies of the commemorative album into his own bank account (Barry Miles, *Paul McCartney: Many Years from Now*, Vintage, 1998, p. 580).

for both established and emerging rock talent, hosted by 'Whispering' Bob Harris, a man of impeccable rock credentials who seemed more at home invigilating at a geography exam.

Maverick director Stanley Kubrick makes his film of Anthony Burgess's *A Clockwork Orange*. Bestowing a balletic grace to acts of random but organised violence and proffering the sweetener that watching a few movies can rid its anti-hero from such sociopathy, the film receives an immediate UK cinema ban from Kubrick himself, after a number of copycat assaults are reported. Jesus, meanwhile, chooses the theatre to make a comeback: *Godspell* and *Jesus Christ Superstar* both premiere on Broadway and in London.

Whilst Dylan is enjoying a lengthy sabbatical away from the task of producing listenable-to records, the rest of the rock world is getting busy with the job of playing catch-up. The Stones reach what many would claim in retrospect to be their peak with *Sticky Fingers*; likewise, Joni Mitchell, Marvin Gaye and The Who hit career high spots with *Blue*, *What's Goin' On* and *Who's Next*, respectively. While Lennon slips out *Imagine*, McCartney releases both *Ram* and *Wild Life* – the latter his first under the name of Wings. Meanwhile, now-established British contemporary rock bands are continuing to consolidate their reputations with well crafted and influential albums: Led Zeppelin with their untitled fourth album, Yes with *The Yes Album* and *Fragile*, Jethro Tull with *Aqualung*, Caravan with *In the Land of Grey and Pink*, Pink Floyd with *Meddle* and, to a lesser degree, Deep Purple with *Fireball*. Jim Morrison, estranged singer of The Doors, draws his last bath and breath: like Joplin and Hendrix the year before, he is twenty-seven years of age.

I leave hospital after Easter. The last thing I remember about it is watching the University Boat Race through the glass walls of the three adjacent isolation rooms that separated me from the television. The television is so small from such distance that if I hold up my hand at arm's length, it completely obscures my view. I am off school for a while, recuperating and reassimilating myself back into an environment where puddings don't come covered in Smarties, and delightfully optimistic

nurses don't wink at me every few minutes.

Every once in a while, I'm taken back as an outpatient. My specialist, a German *Doktor* of an age commensurate with the possibility of his having been involved in the war, is concerned at my recently acquired propensity to faint at only the slightest provocation. He prods my head with interrogative fingers whilst I ponder the odds of his having assisted Josef Mengele in his notable research into paediatrics.

He says, ze vainting vill pass; I say, that's all well and good, but the last time it happened I got covered in beef curry, having been holding my food tray in the dinner queue at school at the time. He shrugs noncommittally; I invite him to sniff my blazer. Dogs follow me around all the time, I explain – one of these days they'll attack.

At least I am alive. I can't remember whether he said that or I did.

On 17 October 1970, *Paranoid* is situated at number one in the album charts, whilst the single is placed at number four. Black Sabbath has become a phenomenon – this despite the constant and unwavering derision heaped on the band by the contemporary music press. Let's just isolate this moment and dwell upon it for a while. They were never to be this big again. This is their high-level watermark. They even appear on *Top of the Pops* and are met with the attendant screaming hysteria of pubescent young girls. A year ago, they were still bashing their brains out in front of apathetic German sailors and prostitutes in Hamburg. The timing is perfect: with Sabbath stocks at an all-time high, the band embarks on its first ever tour of America.* Osbourne:

> When we first played America with Sabbath, and we did Philadelphia,* nobody had ever seen us or heard of us, and,

---

* Chiefly, this was support duty for Leslie West's Mountain, Rod Stewart & The Faces and numerous others: Sabbath headlined only a few of the concerts. Their next US tour, however, they headlined.
* Their first US concert at the Spectrum Theater, Philadelphia, on 30 October 1970.

when I got on stage, two-thirds of the audience were black guys . . . There's this guy at the side of the stage shouting 'Hey, you, Black Sabbath!' – he thought my name was Black Sabbath . . . – 'You guys ain't black.'*

By the time the tour had reached New York's Fillmore East* five performances later, Sabbath were outshining the headliners, Rod Stewart & The Faces. As Iommi was later to recall:

It was just incredible . . . we just went down a storm! An absolute storm! Which I don't think Rod Stewart was too pleased about, because when he went on they started booing and throwing things. It caused a little bit of friction between us for many years.✝

The tour additionally takes in Portland, Columbus, Hollywood, San Francisco and Detroit.⸸ They return to England on 27 November and, two days later, record a session for John Peel's *Top Gear* programme. A whistle-stop tour of Europe follows shortly after, which includes, on 20 December, a much-bootlegged show at the Paris Olympia. Before a tour of Australia and New Zealand kicks off a month later, Sabbath squeeze in a dozen UK performances with the bands Freedom and Curved Air. Although still adhering to a punishing tour schedule, the change in management has at least brought about a rationale to the itinerary: Sabbath are not only playing larger venues, with capacity for two to three thousand seats, they are also benefiting from a more organised route plan which is cutting down the mileage considerably.

Barely having recuperated from their inaugural trip down under,

---

* Stark (p. 11).
* Bill Graham's famous club was to close for good on 27 June that year.
✝ Iommi speaking to Mick Wall of *Classic Rock* magazine, January 1999.
⸸ At Portland, they appeared with Badfinger and Mungo Jerry; with Rod Stewart & The Faces at New York's Fillmore East; Sha Na Na, Arthur Lee & Love, Elvin Bishop, Tower of Power and The James Gang at San Francisco's Fillmore West; and Savoy Brown and Quatermass at Detroit. Siegler.

Sabbath then undergo a second, much larger, tour of North America. Warner Brothers, their American label, primes the market with banners claiming the band is LOUDER THAN LED ZEPPELIN. Starting on 17 February, lasting over a month, and covering, amongst other places, New York, Denver, Winnipeg, Toronto, Detroit, the Midwest and Dallas, the tour further bolsters US sales of both the first album and *Paranoid*, much to the delight of Warner Brothers. At a gig in Memphis on 1 March, an audience member climbs onstage and attempts an attack on Iommi with a knife. Later that night, after retiring to their motel, the band members are met by a group of people dressed in black cloaks; the door to one room had been decorated with an inverted cross daubed in blood.

In early April, it is time for a further two-week tour of Europe, culminating in a triumphant return to London's Albert Hall at the end of the month. In the thirteen months since the release of the first album, Sabbath have played close to 170 concerts, in over a dozen countries, spanning three continents. This, however, is merely a lengthy addendum to the three years spent in almost constant touring that preceded the first album's release. Osbourne again:

> We were on the road all the way through to *Master of Reality*, and then we started to get tired . . . We put in five years on the road. We had *Beatles for Sale* eyes . . . the one-mile stare . . . We were done . . . We were twenty-three years old, and we were veterans.*

With the *Paranoid* album barely eight months old, Vertigo is already encouraging the band to put another album on the market. *Paranoid*'s lofty chart placing, its phenomenal sales* and its shaping of raw musical power into something both influential and, at the same time, inimitable, has generated an explosion of interest from the record company. The

---

* Stark (p. 17).

* *Paranoid* had achieved gold status in both the UK (100,000 units) and the US (500,000 units) by May 1971.

company didn't realise that this stuff could ever sell; but now, with the first two albums having achieved gold status,* it wakes up, and wants more of it out there.

A third tour of America has been booked to start in early July; the band has the months of May and June to record their third album. Led Zeppelin's *III*, released two weeks after *Paranoid* had replaced *Bridge Over Troubled Water* at the top of the charts, and, in turn, deposing *Paranoid* from the top, had disappointed many fans of the growing hard rock genre. Almost entirely acoustic in nature, and introducing a more pastoral approach that was to stay with them in some form or another through their next few albums, the album was received with a little consternation. Dylan, himself no stranger to the idea of putting his fans through trials by ordeal, had similarly dismayed his followers when he released *John Wesley Harding* as the follow-up to the sublime, part amphetamine-driven, part stoned-out *Blonde on Blonde*. With the benefit of thirty years' hindsight, we can see these stylistically incontemporaneous albums as radical masterpieces; in those days, however, when the next Dylan or Zeppelin album was a much-anticipated and talked-over prospect, the perspective was neither so removed nor so perceptive. Although, sales-wise, they didn't bomb altogether, some fans nevertheless felt let down by the lack of electricity, literally and metaphorically, in these albums.* Accordingly, and for the heavy rock brigade in particular, there is considerable anticipation surrounding the release of Sabbath's third album.

The band knows this; they know that, for the first time in their career, they've now got something to lose. Iommi, in particular, is anxious to avoid stretching his hard-won audience's loyalty by straying too far off base. Since *Paranoid*'s release in September of the previous year, it has had no worthy successor in the heavy rock medium. Deep Purple's *In Rock* is still featuring in the charts a year after its release, as is

---

* *Black Sabbath* went gold in June 1971.
* Sales of Dylan's *JWH* were buoyed by the return of the old-school Dylanists to the fold, whereas a mere six months after its release, sales of Zeppelin's *III* had been surpassed by their previous release, *II*.

Zeppelin's *II*; there is clearly a market for the nascent 'metal' scene. Guided primarily by Iommi's steering hand, Sabbath buckle down to release their 'heaviest' record yet. Their confidence boosted by the prodigious sales of *Paranoid*, Vertigo is, for the first time, prepared to lavish some expense on the recording of the third album, *Master of Reality*. Anxious to avoid the unwelcome assessment of Sabbath as only rudimentary, if pioneering, exponents of heavy rock, Iommi and the rest of the band embrace some elements of the studio trickery employed earlier by many of their peers.* As a result, *Master* takes longer to record than both the first album and *Paranoid* put together: two whole weeks.

Although the album includes some very powerful ensemble playing, the record ostensibly belongs to Iommi.* Credited with writing three of the album's eight tracks – the only original numbers in the entire Ozzy-era catalogue not to be credited to the whole group – Iommi is conspicuously present for almost every second of the album's music. His guitar motifs, ever so slightly coloured by the recent upsurge in his consumption of hallucinogens, are graceful without ever becoming slick. Powerful and yet never postural, his guitar work on this album is optimal: it could develop no further without losing its identity in some way. The progression from *Paranoid* to *Master* is slight – but significant. By the time of *Vol. 4*, a year later, there was too much finesse; the rough edges and dark production – felt by many to be almost the quintessence of Sabbath's appeal – were gone, to be replaced by a more layered and textured sound.

Master of Reality was recorded at Olympic Studios in London in June 1971† and released on 1 July. It charted steadily, selling well,‡ and it

---

* Most prosaically, Ward recalls that *Master of Reality* was the first Sabbath album to feature overdubs of any kind. Although this is certainly not true (both the debut album and *Paranoid* featured double-tracked guitar) it is clearly the case that *Master* featured overdubs routinely and as part of its compositional stew.

* Rosen (p. 88) records that Iommi is said to be unhappy with the sound on *Master of Reality*. It is perhaps significant to note that producer Rodger Bain was not asked to work with Sabbath again after *Master of Reality*.

† Like Trident and Regent Sound (where Sabbath had recorded their debut and its follow-up), Olympic Studios had also been used by The Beatles (amongst others) who recorded 'All You Need Is Love' and 'Baby, You're A Rich Man' there in June 1967. Some preliminary work for *Master of Reality* had been done at Island Studios in Notting Hill in January 1971.

‡ By September, a mere three months after its release, *Master of Reality* had been certified gold.

wrestled its way up to a peak placing of number five in the UK, where it battled for status alongside Simon and Garfunkel's enduring *Bridge Over Troubled Water*, The Stones' *Sticky Fingers*, Joni Mitchell's *Blue*, Rod Stewart's *Every Picture Tells a Story*, ELP's *Tarkus*, The Groundhogs' *Split* and McCartney's *Ram*. When you consider that Zeppelin's *II*, Purple's *In Rock* and *Fireball*, Stephen Stills' second solo album, Carole King's *Tapestry*, The Who's *Who's Next* and Neil Young's *After the Goldrush* were also in the chart *at the same time*, you realise several things: how commendable the competition was, how creditably *Master* performed and, ultimately, how lucky we all once were to have so much music of such impeccably high quality from which to choose.

Chapter Seven

Master of Reality

†

This was the first album I bought. True. Were you to ask people born in the late fifties or early sixties to name the first album they bought, they'd probably tell you it was a Beatles album or something by Zeppelin or somesuch. But if it was God asking, and they had to be honest else they'd end up in Hell, they'd probably come clean and say it was something by Ken Dodd, a Disney soundtrack, perhaps, or one of those *Top of the Pops* things that featured scantily-clad young ladies on the front, in poses of, for then, quite precocious suggestiveness. But I can say, with all honesty, that it was *Master of Reality*, and I feel just great about that. It was a toss-up between *Master* and *Paranoid*, and *Master* won out on account of the fact that it came with a free poster – in those days, a fierce and effective marketing ploy:* it did wonders for the long-term sales of *Dark Side of the Moon*.

Long before Richard Branson became the knighted, plutocrat owner of a multifarious, global billion-dollar industry with concerns in banking, aviation and media communications – long before his Virgin trademark became a universally understood byword for mainstream popular culture and was just a risqué and eyebrow-raising imprimatur for all things hairy – he owned a string of small record shops up and down the country, most of which were initially no bigger than garden sheds and were almost exclusively inhabited by young men in greatcoats. It was in his tiny Sheffield shop, situated at the bottom of The Moor, just before Christmas 1974, suitably attired, that I made this historic purchase. If there were more than three people in the place at once, it felt crowded. It always reeked heavily of something resembling patchouli, despite the fact

---

* Warner Brothers included competition forms in five hundred US releases of the albums, posing the question, 'In ten words or less, explain why you love Black Sabbath's music.' Ten words? You can see how bright they figured Sabbath's fans to be.

that it was almost compulsory to smoke whilst you were in there.* The album covers were all there on the racks, protected by plastic sleeves. The plastic sleeves, I remember, came in two types: the ones that smelled of paddling pools and the ones that smelled of dog-shit. It was usually, although not always, the case that the gatefold plastic sleeves fell in the latter category; the single plastic sleeves, the former. This is merely background information; you don't have to remember this: there won't be a test later.

I have the original Vertigo box-like sleeve, although it's now a little squashed, but inside the record is the WWA reissue from 1973. The sleeve misnames 'Sweet Leaf' as 'Sweet Life'. I expect they all did. It's a simple, but nevertheless luxuriant, sleeve: the visual economy of Bloomsbury Group's two colour (black and purple) design being offset grandly by the lavish embossing of the group's name and the album title. On the reverse side, there's the group's name again and the album's lyrics.* There's really very little else I can say about the sleeve; it's the epitome of early seventies, Ford Capri chic.

The freebie poster inside is beautiful and yet a little depressing. Emphatically autumnal in hue and tone, the solarised photo (once again by Marcus Keef, who had shot the gatefold cover for the first album) captures the band in a forest, under the shelter of what appears to be a fir tree. The composition is balanced and well considered, but, on close inspection of the individuals concerned, there is a stupefied exhaustion about their features. Osbourne, in particular, looks all in, and, in adopting a seated position hunched against the bottom of the tree, he is the embodiment of demented – almost lobotomised – withdrawal. Butler, who may or may not be sporting John Lennon-style spectacles – it's very hard to say for sure – claims the honours this time around for most ridiculous costume: the particular item of apparel to which I allude is an ankle-length overcoat, with snakeskin detailing, turn-back collar and

---

* The penny has just belatedly dropped.
* This was the first Sabbath album to do so. The practice was periodically resorted to throughout the Sabbath career – both with and without Osbourne – and became firmly established with the Tony Martin-era albums.

cuffs, and full, body-length zip: Biba on a bad day. He stands in a stern and alert manner; his right arm outstretched and positioned so that his hand establishes contact with the tree. He looks very mannered and posed and not at all at ease. Iommi, caught uncharacteristically in the background, gives Osbourne a run for his money in the I'm-really-out-of-it-man stakes, although I'd pay good money for the jacket he's wearing. Strangely enough, it's Ward who looks the business in this shot: wild flowing hair, penetrative stare, legs crossed like he has to go pee-pee; he looks every inch the moody, broody, charismatic, I'm-like-Jesus-and-in-thirty-years'-time-Billy-Crudup-will-die-for-this-look rock-and-roller – right down to the open-toed sandals. The poster has been reproduced in miniature for the 1996 Castle remaster, but this goes only so far in alleviating my concerns of not being able to retrieve the original from the unruly, adolescent graveyard that is my parents' attic.

For the third and final time, Rodger Bain was hired to produce; again, he achieved tremendous results. The sound is broader – fatter, even – than on *Paranoid*; it whooshes and swirls, and he perfectly captures the periodically strange exoticism of Iommi's guitar phrases and the attendant ensemble playing. More than anything, however, the album is incredibly *heavy*: whereas the numbers on *Paranoid* had been played at concert pitch with standard tuning, three of *Master*'s five heavy tracks* were played with guitars detuned *three* semitones to C sharp.

Having said all this, it seems rather churlish of me to raise the point that the album is a little on the short side. There are only six real songs on the album (two of the tracks are brief, throwaway guitar interludes), and the album clocks in at a rather meagre thirty-four minutes or so. The other five Sabbath albums from this period are all around the forty-minute mark; for me, *Master* would have benefited enormously from another five- or six-minute song. But, as I say, this is probably sullenness on my part: what we have is magnificent; that should be enough. Besides, they did throw in a poster with this album – that kind of makes things a bit fairer.

* 'Children Of The Grave', 'Lord Of This World' and 'Into The Void'.

1) Sweet Leaf

Taking its name from the advertising slogan – 'It's the sweetest leaf' – imprinted on a box of Sweet Afton cigarettes Osbourne had just purchased on a trip to Ireland, 'Sweet Leaf' is Sabbath's elegiac strain to the liberating properties of marijuana. Beginning with an echo-laden cough from Iommi – legend has it that the man had just drawn lengthily from a well-infused bong – this Anacreontic ode is based around a simple, repetitive and intoxicating riff in A. The semitonal descent from the subdominant to the minor third is almost a Sabbath cliché – I shall be writing more on semitonal intervals before this chapter is out, I promise you – but garners an other-worldliness from its replication an octave higher on overdubbed guitar.

Marijuana was still the band's drug du jour in those days – that, LSD and good old alcohol, of course. The period spent between the release of this album and the recording of the next, *Vol. 4,* would see the band transferring their allegiance to cocaine – a not altogether surprising development considering their temporary relocation to Los Angeles. There's much that can be said about the influence of narcotics on Sabbath – how, for instance, they adopt the almost parental stance in 'Hand Of Doom' (LSD and heroin); the wariness of 'Snowblind' (cocaine); the unfettered worship in 'Sweet Leaf' (marijuana) – and it might appear, at first, that Sabbath's stance on these matters, if you consider them to have one, is at best uncertain, if not contradictory.

But, of course, there's all the difference in the world between a crafty toke on a pipe and the more insidious business of ingesting coke or mainlining heroin – just as there's a difference between having a couple of pints down the local with your mates and going to bed with a bottle of vodka every night. There's some who will tell you that coke is a 'social' drug, a 'party' drug – that it's a drug to take with friends to have a good time – but, unless you particularly like hanging around with egomaniacs and self-obsessives, that's a crock of shit. But we'll save further discussion of these issues until we get to the next album.

Osbourne's sheer enthusiasm for the subject matter here – his droll,

street-corner exhortation to indulge at 3:34 – belie the music's trudging momentum. Unusually for Sabbath, the vocal delivery is contrapuntal to the guitar motif: the lyric is delivered amongst breaks in the instrumentation – and this effectively boosts the tempo of what otherwise might have been rather a turgid and painfully slow composition.

After the second verse, the song shifts key and tempo (up in both instances), and, with some exotic cymbal work from Ward and a bubbling bass figure from Butler, we are taken into Iommi's solo, which is enthusiastically delivered over a sustained C sharp. This allegro interlude marks the change from the laborious 'toking' motif to the 'high' of intoxication – the giggling bit. But, after a braking figure at the end of Iommi's solo, it's back to the pipe again for another blast or two and Osbourne's forecast that all of the world will soon be hash-heads.

2) After Forever

Most famous for, and most misunderstood on account of, its reference to swinging pontiffs, Iommi's* 'After Forever' is, in fact, a feisty call-to-arms against disestablishmentarianism.* However, despite its earnest spiritual intentions, it was widely received as yet another 'Satan rules OK; let's go bust up a church' addition to the Sabbath catalogue. Although its evangelical fervour is clearly spelled out in lines such as 'I've seen the Truth, Yes, I've seen the Light' and 'God is the only way to Love', it derived an anti-Christian – specifically, perhaps, anti-*Catholic* – reputation on account of its Pope-on-a-rope✝ and crucifixion❊ references.

It's difficult to maintain a serious argument for this song being heretical or profane; it's somewhat easier, however, to argue that its lyrics are at best naïve – or at worst misguided. The fussy and completely unnecessary internal rhyme scheme✝ gives the lyric – and, by association, the

---

* Together with 'Embryo' and 'Orchid', 'After Forever' is credited to Iommi alone.
* Probably the longest word in this book.
✝ 'Would you like to see the Pope on the end of a rope? / Do you think he's a fool?'
❊ 'It was people like you who crucified Christ.'
✝ 'Is your mind so small that you have to fall . . . Will you still sneer at all you hear . . . I'll be

subject matter – a childish Dr Seuss quality which does nothing to assert the song's intended gravitas. That the lyric assumes the form of Leonine hexameter impresses nobody. Nevertheless, despite its ill-conceived lyric, its unwelcome interpretation as yet another Satanist tract in an ever-increasing portfolio of doom must have proved particularly frustrating – at least for Iommi, its composer.

Whatever criticisms one might to choose to level against its zealous Salvationist lyric, somewhat at odds with the retributive fury of an Old Testament Jehovah, the song's music – especially its clever fusing of the keys of G major and D minor – does much to elevate the song to 'classic' Sabbath status. After a deliberately obscure start, Iommi's guitar rings out a G major phrase that sounds a great deal like the pealing of church bells,* summoning the congregation for the forthcoming sermon. This gives way, in true Sabbath style, to a grinding motif in D minor, over which the verse is sung. The sludging F/E chord change, which punctuates the separate lines of the song's lyric, is both retardant and stimulating: it discourages the listener from being carried away by the sprightly tempo and urges him to focus on the lyric (unfortunate in this case). After the verse, the song seamlessly shifts up to the G major key in which it started, and in which contextually it belongs.

The middle section, modulating from the D minor verse up to the relative major, F, portrays the fervent zeal of the preacher's fist slamming repeatedly against the pulpit, as the lyric ('Could it be you're afraid of what your friends might say . . . ?') encourages the listener to leave one conformity (that of agnosticism or atheism) for another (Christian heterodoxy). In true Iommi style, the drama is intensified by a clever single tone jump up to G major as the lyric – still fastidiously holding on to its internal rhymes – alerts us to the inescapable inevitability of earthly death.

---

prepared when you're lonely and scared . . .' etc. The most outrageous rhyme in the song, however, occurs with the coupling of the words 'Christ' and 'voiced': these words only rhyme if you come from Birmingham.
* The tonic, mediant and dominant are prevalent in the melody – as they would be in a carillon.

Staying in G for a reprise of the carillon theme that begins the song, we are then surprised at 3:26 to come across a four-bar jig-like figure – an interlude which brings to mind Bruegel's* peasants partaking in some vigorous bucolic festivity – which, after a further modulation to A minor, strongly reminiscent of the similar modulation in 'Fairies Wear Boots', gives way to Iommi's solo.

Lyrics aside, 'After Forever' is a very clever song. Its fluid key interchanges and the clever prosodic qualities of its middle section place it in that category of works – best typified by The Beatles, perhaps – which just invites admiration from the music scholar. The predominant (verse) riff is perhaps less colourful than one might be given to expect from Iommi – but this is, no doubt, an unfair analysis: on *Master of Reality*, it abides with truly exceptional company.

3) Embryo

Effectively, little more than an interlude or, alternatively, a prelude to the following 'Children Of The Grave', 'Embryo' is a short, thirty-eight-second etude for unaccompanied electric guitar. Iommi's guitar is detuned by three semitones, taking the chordal key of E minor down to an aural C sharp minor, and the simple melodic phrase is picked out, for the most part, on just the one string. The open B and E strings – detuned to G sharp and C sharp – are left to drone, according the piece a rustic, bygone feel.

---

* I'm thinking of Pieter 'the Elder' (*c.* 1520–69), who never really decided how to spell his surname, and who painted in a richly satirical and well observed style, detached from the Italian Mannerism of his Netherlandish contemporaries. His son, 'the Younger' (*c.* 1564–1638), also called Pieter and also unsure of the spelling of his surname, was called 'Hell' Bruegel because he painted diableries, scenes featuring devils and hags and the like. It took Bruegel 'the Elder' some time to subjugate his initial fantastical influences and develop the pungent 'cartoonery' of his later 'genre' paintings that chronicled everyday peasant life with both fondness and acerbity. Such biographical points have rather delayed me in making the most obvious Sabbath/Bruegel observation: that the cover of the Christmas 1977 compilation, the ridiculously titled *Greatest Hits* (a condensed version of 1975's double-album, *We Sold Our Soul For Rock 'n' Roll*), features the *c.* 1562 'Elder' Bruegel masterpiece *The Triumph of Death*, a grisly panorama heavily influenced by his compatriot predecessor Hieronymus Bosch (*c.* 1450–1516).

The rigid 2/4 time signature does little to lend the piece any elegance, and the elementary runs up and down the fretboard are hardly more sophisticated than those the first-year guitar student would be expected to master for an end-of-term assessment. But we love Iommi because of his invention, his sinister semitonal slurs, his gift for melody, his remarkable generosity with riffs . . . in short, for myriad reasons, but not because he is heavy rock's own Segovia.* There's little point in talking about 'Embryo' as some sort of work of genius – it's a throwaway piece that barely warrants the hundred and eighty odd words I've thus far written about it – but its inclusion on the album is both sympathetic and inconspicuous. This, in itself, is more than can be said for some of Sabbath's later, less judicious experiments.

That it has steadfastly served as an onstage introduction to 'Children Of The Grave' for the last thirty years or so suggests that, for Iommi at least, the piece is not without some charm. That charm derives not from its musical naïvety (or the fact that it requires little in the way of either dextrous skill or mental concentration to execute) but from its almost mechanical, crank-handling pastoralism: some proto-technological device from a primitive industrial age – a corn-chopper of some sort, perhaps, or something you'd affix to the back end of a horse.

4) Children Of The Grave

It's difficult to talk about this song with the sentiments it deserves. Over the years, 'Children Of The Grave' has become, perhaps, *the* classic Sabbath song, and its original manifestation as some sort of pre-apocalyptic caveat has been superseded by its neo-legendary status as a crowd-pleaser. As a latter-day *Anthem for Doomed Youth*, it is certainly meritorious; however, Osbourne's desperate, urgent cries of 'Yeah!' at the end of each verse have since been hijacked and are now offered back to the band in live performances as some sort of yelling triumph.

* Andrés Segovia (1894–1987), a Spanish guitarist who revolutionised the classical technique, enabling his repertoire (and the repertoires of those who followed him) to encompass a much wider range of works. Created a Marquis by royal decree, Segovia was the Steve Vai of his day. His version of 'Red House' is definitive.

Musically, the piece gallops along like the four horsemen of the apocalypse on their way to the end-of-the-world party. The sheer weight of the predominant riff – a repeated, triplet-strewn thunder-strum of the detuned (to C sharp) E string – is probably the heaviest thing that Sabbath (ergo, rock) had thus far produced and was later to provide the blueprint for a host of Iron Maiden songs. This is backed up by Ward's work on overdubbed timbales, which, together with the rhythmic composition of the riff itself, is deliberately evocative of such diabolic equestrianism. The trenchant slashes of C sharp, A and B chords which punctuate this are redolent of mighty swords separating heads from their parent shoulders. It's meant to be frightening – and it is.

And it *has* to be: if the dénouement – this sword of Damocles that is apocalypse – were anything other, then the urgency to keep it in abeyance – or to dismantle it altogether – would not be nearly so pressing. Not that this song is at all descriptive of apocalypse – it's no 'Iron Man' or 'Electric Funeral' – this is a song that tells us to get our acts together, else there'll be an apocalypse. These children are not *from* the grave – they're not infant zombies, for heaven's sake – they're children who will be committed prematurely *to* the grave, unless they can persuade us all to change our ways and provide 'a better place to live in'.

I can barely explain what this song meant to me when first I heard it. In the first two verses, Osbourne sings about these children in the third person: 'Revolution in their minds . . . They're tired of being pushed around . . . Can they win the fight for peace . . . ?' In the third verse, however, he suddenly changes to the second person: 'So you children of the world . . . If you want a better place to live in . . . You must be brave . . . ' In other words, he was singing to me. I was one of these children. I was someone he was entrusting with the responsibility of saving the world: me. It was almost three years before I got my hair cut again. And it would seem that I was not the only one for whom the message in this song struck deep: Marc Bolan took the song's opening lyric, 'Revolution in their minds, the children start to march', as a starting point for his hit with T. Rex the following year: 'Children Of The Revolution'.

For the most part, the song succeeds not on its musical merits *per se* but in its overall effect. As a thundering, animated colossus it has few parallels in rock music. Musically, however, it doesn't get interesting until 2:20. Here, an agitated four-bar phrase, replete with semitone intervals in typical Sabbath style, heralds a sixteen-bar instrumental middle section with warlike tonal intervals and strict regimental tempo. Melodically related both to Gustav Holst's 'Mars' from his *Planets* suite and to Jimmy Page's acoustic work on 'Friends' from Led Zeppelin's *III*, the piece is underscored by Ward's thundering tom-toms, which sound both insistent and menacing, and is given frightening context by the lush peculiarity of the chordal and melodic structure.* Lesser guitarists might have taken a solo over this phrase and, by doing so, would have diminished it; Iommi must have been tempted, but he kept his eye on the bigger picture.

Instead, Iommi takes his solo later – at an altogether more fitting point – where it is used to build further the element of escalating tension and ineluctable catastrophe. The song works to a close through the final notes of Iommi's solo, which, through a prickly staccato, once again evoke the dazzling terrors of impending tragedy. It rather cheesily exits with a synthesised wailing effect (occasionally referred to in Sabbath circles as 'The Haunting')* executed by the controlled use of feedback, over which Osbourne whispers the song's title and we all get the creeps. Rather a shame, this, as it takes the song out of the realms of the motivationally political and plonks it firmly back down into Hammer Horror territory. But maybe that was the point.

---

* Starting on C sharp, the section dives down through B natural to B flat (rather than the anticipated A). On the second iteration, the C sharp hikes up to G natural via an eerie G sharp. The C sharp/G natural interval (a flattened fifth – the same interval as in the track 'Black Sabbath') is something of an Iommi (or Sabbath) trademark: it features in many of their best-loved songs.

* American issues of Sabbath's early output listed introductions or codas of certain compositions under separate names. The bass introduction to 'N.I.B.' was entitled 'Bassically'; the coda of 'War Pigs', 'Luke's Wall'; the introduction to 'Fairies Wear Boots', 'Jack The Stripper' to name but a few. The practice was not adopted in the UK.

5) Orchid

A curious beginning to what, in the old LP-spinning days, was side two of *Master of Reality*, 'Orchid' is another Iommi-only piece, played on a steel-strung acoustic guitar. Iommi's penchant for slinging these slight instrumentals on albums was to continue throughout Sabbath's history.* Sometimes they worked; sometimes they didn't. It's asking a lot of 'Orchid' to open side two of an LP: particularly when it is sandwiched between 'Children Of The Grave' and 'Lord Of This World'. However, with three of the eight tracks on *Master* being, for want of a better term, 'unheavy', you've got to have one of them either opening or closing a side – unless you want to sequence two of them together. And, of the three, 'Orchid' seems the best equipped to take on that kind of responsibility.

Employing a (rather pointless) detuning of a semitone, 'Orchid' is a fairly rapidly paced arpeggio piece, played in the Spanish style, with some surprising melodic highlights and lifts. Again, technically, it's no great achievement, but it is well played and it does not seem either out of place or gratuitous; rather, it establishes a sort of idyll, later to be blasted to Hell by the ensuing 'Lord Of This World'. Not that this has anything to do with juxtaposition, there is no concern with contrast here: what Sabbath are doing is giving you something beautiful and then destroying it. Just as they did with the introduction of the furious guitar break in 'Sleeping Village' on the first album.

6) Lord Of This World

Again using the C sharp tuning found on 'Children Of The Grave' and 'Embryo' (and the later 'Into The Void'), 'Lord Of This World' is, as its lyricist, Geezer Butler, points out, 'our one and only* Satan song . . . it's about Old Nick'. I make mention of this just in case there's any lingering uncertainty. Specifically, however, the song concerns the

---

* See 'F.X.', 'Laguna Sunrise', 'Fluff', 'Spiral Architect' (the intro – sometimes referred to as 'Prelude To A Project') and 'Don't Start (Too Late)'.
* 'One and only' indeed . . .

empowerment of Satan by the greedy and proud amongst us. The message is, we gave Satan our souls – and, therefore, his power – through our materialistic dissatisfaction with the earth God had made for us. It's a sort of cautionary tale, really, based on the notion of Faustian pacts being made on a more or less global basis – and how this will give rise to a demonic superpower with the ability and contractual right to call in our debts.

The initiating riff in C sharp minor, a scalar descent from the tonic to the subdominant, is one of those anthemic, almost fanfare-style, affairs for which Iommi has been so rightly accorded plaudits. The semitonal slurs – from F sharp to F natural and back again (the eighth, ninth and tenth notes of the riff) – chucked in to fatten the motif out and give it a menacing violence, are archetypically Sabbath. If we were to get scholarly about this and set ourselves the task of completing the sentence 'I think Sabbath's riffs are the best because . . . ' in no less than thirty thousand words, we'd have to allow at least a quarter of that treatise for a discussion on Iommi's frequent adoption of semitonal intervals. As often as not, these intervals are not merely musical embroidery – they are not stylistic embellishments thrown in to render the motif more ornate – rather, they are integral to the riff itself. They achieve further substance by frequently being located off-key, and, when used in conjunction with tempo changes or note lengthening (as they are here), they reflect the depth of Iommi's compositional genius. This opening riff, which starts off as a voluntary, is turned into something altogether more sinister and dangerous by the punctuating *duh-duuhh-duh* of the closing notes.

The verse motif is a jerky blues affair, the accent of which falls strongly on the first beat. There is a certain mechanical quality to the riff: like 'Embryo', it seems to recall some prototypical agricultural contraption, cranking and croaking in an eccentric and spasmodic way. It's certainly not demonic, although the semitonal ascent that terminates the phrase is suggestive of some unforeseen menace. This sinister and threatening presence is further bolstered by Osbourne's powerful and vituperative vocal. In fact, this is very much Osbourne's song. The lyric, which

represents an admonishment from Satan himself to the sinners amongst us, is not amongst Butler's best: it seems to come only part of the way in describing the ominous ascent to power of some Dark Destroyer. However, Osbourne deals with the lyrical enjambments well and spits the whole thing out with all the venom he can possibly muster in what is his best performance on the album.

A clever guitar fill at 2:03 momentarily shifts the key *down* a tone before Iommi enjoys a freewheeling, double-tracked solo. This culminates in a further reprise of the introductory theme before the abrupt and brief assertion of a satanic hosanna – 'Lord of this world! / Evil Possessor!' – marking a climax of evil in the lyric. This is the point at which Satan's influence has overcome us – his superiority has been established – and we are bowing down in obsequious worship of the distinguished and doubtlessly smelly beast.

After the final verse, the song briefly departs into more solo territory before a further riff is introduced – probably the most powerful riff of the song and, it has to be said, rather wasted merely as an instrumental coda – taking us to the close.

7) Solitude

If you've been paying attention, you'll recall that, when discussing the *Paranoid* album, I made a big fuss over the minor tonic/subtonic shift evident in many of the songs on that album: 'War Pigs', 'Paranoid', 'Planet Caravan', the initial slur of 'Iron Man' and so on. On *Master of Reality*, we've seen this interval used in the middle section of 'After Forever',* the verse riff for 'Children Of The Grave,'* the middle section of 'Lord Of This World',† and here it is again on 'Solitude': this time in the key of G minor.

There are several striking points to be made about 'Solitude': that the song swings along in a most uncharacteristic 6/8 time is just the least of

---

* 'Could it be you're afraid of what your friends might say . . .'
* The modified version of the main riff played as accompaniment to the verse lyrics.
† 'Lord of this world!/ Evil possessor . . .'

them. Although Sabbath had by this time explored time changes to a limited degree, the introduction to 'Behind The Wall Of Sleep'* aside, they had thus far limited themselves to 4/4 or 8/8 arrangements. The fast waltz of 'Solitude' was thus quite a departure for them – particularly as they were enjoying the accolade of being the heaviest band in the world. Iommi's blues-tinged soloing, which crops up periodically throughout the piece, is clearly a throwback to his pre-Sabbath influences, and it provides the perfect moody accompaniment to Osbourne's plaintive, echo-laden, chorus-inflected vocal.

The piece is further embellished by some uncredited* flute playing, high-register campanology and finger-cymbal work from Ward and a gloopy walking bass from Butler. Overall, the dynamic is strong: musically, this is not, by any stretch of the imagination, some sort of catatonic threnody; rather it bounces along quite merrily – despite the forlorn acrimony expressed in the lyric.

The lyric, which begins with a variation on Dylan's 'With God On Our Side', is pretty much your standard 'she done gone and left me' sort of thing, but it does contain some clever elements. The simple juxtapositions of laughing and crying and leaving and staying are put to good effect in the second verse's final couplet. There's an argument to be made here as to whether the song might have benefited from Sabbath opting for a long instrumental fade-out (as they did on 'Planet Caravan' from the previous year's *Paranoid*) in preference to the self-pitying final verse, in which genuine pathos is allowed to deteriorate into the rather cloying blues clichés of weeping and moaning.

Considering the limitations of his vocal range, however – and the strict pentatonic nature of the melody line – Osbourne handles the singing duties well, and the general effect is undeniably moving, without ever becoming morose in that saccharine and slightly sickly way typical of heavy rock artists tackling a ballad. When Osbourne reaches the third verse, in which he extends the melody beyond its established frame on

---

* Also in 6/8 time.
* Iommi can play flute; however, there is no mention in the credits as to whether he is playing it on this track.

the line, 'The world is a lonely place', it's possible you might, like me, experience a certain shivering down the spine. It's a lovely moment this: the singer's miserable pessimism is compounded by his perception of his surroundings as empty and desolate and being totally unable to shake him from his unhappiness. This cosmic gloom is beautifully comple-mented by Iommi's noodling, the persistent fluttering of the sonorous flute and Ward's continuing endeavours with various tinkling devices. Gradually, we have left the claustrophobic confines of the student bedsit, and we are inhabiting a lifeless suspension in the gravity-free expanses of outer space.

In their first three albums, Sabbath had handled such stylistic departures well: leaving aside the misguided and out of character 'Evil Woman' (which really should have been left aside) 'Planet Caravan' and 'Solitude' possess more than mere novelty value: they actually show a side of Sabbath deserving of further exploration.

8) Into The Void

We're back in altogether more familiar territory with the album's closer, 'Into The Void', a six-minute, environmentally concerned road movie, which features an opening riff of startling originality and fierceness. In fact, it features several.

Once again using the lowered C sharp tuning, 'Into The Void' begins with an octave plunge to the tonic before starting a jerky ascent back up to it in four intermediate steps: the minor third, the fourth, the flattened fifth and the natural fifth. Having done this, the riff then oscillates between the flattened fifth and the fourth (much as it does on the third note of the 'Black Sabbath' riff) and uses the minor third as some sort of grounding base. There then follows a bludgeoning and bellicose interlude,* primarily centred on the minor tonic and subtonic shift, before the initial riff reprises.

---

* Again, this is a tremendous riff, squandered over a mere eight bars and never reprised, that could have formed the basis of another composition. On the one hand, a further testament to Iommi's cre-ative prodigiousness, it might alternatively have been put to better use as the bones of *Master of Reality's* badly needed ninth track.

The verse riff is a supercharged interpolation of the minor tonic/subtonic theme suggestive of enormous mechanical power and ferocity. The slurred semitonal quavering between the fourth and flattened fifth depicts a worrying instability (just as it does on *Paranoid*'s 'Iron Man'): technical fallibility, a screw working loose, the gradual but inevitable process of unforeseen but inescapable catastrophe. When Osbourne's vocal enters, with its observation of how rapidly rockets burn up fuel, we become aware of two things: that the then prevalent preoccupation with space travel is depleting the earth's resources; and that, in doing so, the earth will become a place from which escape is necessary. In other words, these rocket engines are both the iceberg and the lifeboats in Earth's own *Titanic* drama.

And this is where the confusion lies and where the lyrical message of the song is wildly contradictory. There seems little doubt that the song originally began as some sort of environmental protest affair: the idea that man is prepared to squander his and the earth's resources on space travel, whilst ignoring – and contributing to – the manifold human miseries on the planet he meantime occupies. Yet, before the second verse is out, these rocket engines now appear as our means of salvation: as a way of crossing the cosmic void and achieving escape from a final, global suicide.*

The middle section, where Osbourne sings of freedom fighters being sent to the sun, is a rather panicked affair – and how much of this is intentional is hard to say: Ward's drumming is all over the place, and Osbourne has difficulty with his melismas in the untidily sprung rhythm of the lyric. Thankfully, this is but a short passage, and we are soon returned to the main theme. Over the familiarity of this reprise, Osbourne describes an earth now completely given over to Satan, his slaves and nothing to look forward to but death, whilst those lucky enough to have secured a place on a rocket are bound for an unknown land (which we've already been told is the sun – hardly the most hospitable of destinations) where they might enjoy everlasting peace and happiness. It doesn't really seem fair. Incidentally, the 'Sons of Freedom',

* Void and suicide: another Birmingham rhyme.

1. You can see why Madeleine Morgan was so stricken. The urbane, gap-toothed grin conceals the tortured, pre-pubescent artist-genius locked within.

2. A kiss that lasted a lifetime. Madeleine Morgan – as she was and how I will always remember her.

3. Osbourne and Iommi at The Star Club, Hamburg, 1970. Note the village-institute-style pelmet above their heads.

4. The ever amiable Rob Crump *(top left)* and the school where we first met in 1973.

5. Sabbath in the year of the Birmingham barbers' strike. *(Left to right)* Osbourne, Butler, Ward, Iommi.

6. *(Top left)* Edith Sitwell, inspiration behind the poem printed on the inside cover of Sabbath's first album.

7. *(Top right)* Sir Thomas Sydenham, inveterate opium pusher, sex maniac and forefather of rock and roll (see 'St Vitus Dance' entry).

8. – 9. *(Bottom left and right)* Mapledurham Mill in Oxfordshire, as it appeared on the cover of Black Sabbath in 1970 and how it looked when I dropped by a few months ago.

10. Birthplace of a monster: the fifty square yards of studio space that, over five days, spawned the *Paranoid* album.

11. Rock star, legend, icon – Osbourne in 1973. No front-man ever looked this good.

12. Sabbath in 1973 – a Freudian's field-day: while Ward and Osbourne thrust a reassuring hand towards their groins, Iommi and Butler act out the male and female mating ritual.

13. Sabbath after an ill-advised trip down Carnaby Street. *(Left to Right)* Butler, Iommi, Ward, Osbourne.

14. Sabbath on stage in October 1975 promoting *Sabotage*. Note Iommi's occupation of centre stage in preference to Osbourne's.

15. – 16. *La reproduction interdite* (1937), by Belgian surrealist René Magritte, and the cover for *Sabotage* (1975).

17. '10th Anniversary Tour', 1978, mere weeks before Osbourne was fired. The table at the front is groaning under the weight of three commemorative cakes, courtesy of Warner Brothers.

18. Sabbath in 1999 during the Last Supper Tour.

19. The master at work. Iommi on stage, 1997.

who, in the final verse, have bravely relocated to an unknown world, are not to be mistaken for the self-styled Sons of Freedom, exiled Russian Doukhobor Christians, who perpetrated numerous acts of terrorism in western Canada in the fifties and sixties. Sabbath had no connection with this curious sect, and the reference is, as the movie-disclaimer saying goes, purely coincidental.

And although lyrically the song concludes with the successful exodus of these privileged space travellers, the music still has some way to go. After Iommi's obligatory solo and the introduction of what will prove to be the song's closing motif, we arrive (at 5:17) at a most thunderous and surprising passage: sixteen bars of truly monumental riffage. Adopting a call-and-response chordal pattern, Iommi treats us to a particularly ominous interlude: C sharp followed by an F sharp bent up to a G, then an A bent up to an A sharp, a B bent up to a C natural (!) and, finally, a C sharp bent up to an off-the-map D natural. From a compositional perspective, this is really quite astonishing. Indeed, in the entire history of rock music, I'd be hard put to find anything so Out There, so stuck and irretrievable on such a brittle and distant musical limb. After some further soloing, the reverb-drenched closing riff cuts in like an apocalyptic *coup de grâce*: that's it, there's no more to tell; you've had your chips.

Chapter Eight
Going Through Changes / 1972

$\mathfrak{On}$ 9 January 1972, Britain's miners go out on strike. The strike is to last forty-seven days and forces the government to proclaim a national state of emergency. A few days later, it is announced that unemployment in Britain has exceeded a million. Neither of these issues shows Heath's new government in an especially good light as he prepares to sign the Treaty of Accession to the European Economic Community. But worse is to come: in Londonderry, Northern Ireland, on Sunday, 30 January 1972, on a march against internment, thirteen Catholic protestors are shot dead by British troops. The day becomes known as Bloody Sunday. Three days later, the British Embassy in Dublin is burned to the ground. The following month, the Northern Irish parliament is suspended, and Britain assumes direct rule over the province. The year's tally of dead clocks in at 467.

Nixon, with an election scheduled for later in the year, visits China and the Soviet Union – the first US president to do so. The Committee to Re-Elect the President (known by its sinister acronym CREEP) is thrown together by shadowy figures in Washington. In June, five men are arrested for having broken into the Democratic Party's headquarters housed in the Watergate building in Washington DC. The matter is expertly hushed until after the election.

The Olympic Games take place in Munich. The Palestine Liberation Organisation breaks into the compound and takes the entire Israeli team hostage in the Olympic village. Two of the team are slaughtered there and then; the remaining nine are killed later whilst the terrorists are trying to escape the German police. Despite protests from inside Israel, the Games continue. The surviving Arab terrorists are later released by the German police after the PLO takes control of a Lufthansa jet; a hijack that would also entail Germany's handing over of 5 million US dollars for the safe return of the hostages. In Britain, there is a furore over the Tate Gallery's decision to purchase Carl André's *Equivalent 8* – better known as 'the pile of bricks' – and the publication of *The Joy of Sex*.

A few weeks before the presidential elections, Nixon sends Kissinger to South Vietnam to cobble together a peace treaty. It pretty much amounts to a full US withdrawal and to hell with South Vietnam. It's this proposal, together with an earlier pledge not to send any more draftees to the region, which allows Kissinger to proclaim, 'Peace is at hand'. The American public buy it: in the November election, Nixon cruises home. Up against the Democrat George McGovern, who is standing on an anti-war ticket, Nixon polls forty-seven million votes against McGovern's twenty-nine million; he also takes a remarkable 520 out of the 537 electoral votes. It's the second biggest landslide ever, and it gives Nixon the belief that he can do what the hell he wants.

As Coppola's *The Godfather* wins Brando an Oscar on his return to the cinema in a dull year for the medium, a fanatic attacks Michelangelo's *La Pietà* in St Peter's in Vatican City with a hammer. The Coca-Cola corporation recalls three million bottles of Coke contaminated with aluminium: it's the real thing, all right.

The singles charts are swamped by Glam and Teenybop; elsewhere, MOR corners the market in album sales: Bread's *Baby I'm A Want You*, Don McLean's *American Pie* and *Tapestry* albums, and several records by Harry Nilsson and The Carpenters all score well. In something of a contrast, Alice Cooper, making his first tour of the UK, has three albums in the top twenty at the same time.* English proggers Yes release *Close to the Edge*; Purple bring out *Machine Head*; Floyd, *Obscured by Clouds*; and well meaning but not much liked Uriah Heep hit a career peak with *Demons and Wizards* and *The Magician's Birthday*. Santana produce the marvellous *Caravanserai*; Wishbone Ash launch *Argus*; Stephen Stills, *Manassas*; The Stones get back to basics with *Exile on Main Street*; Bowie goes astral with *Ziggy Stardust* and helps struggling Mott The Hoople put together *All the Young Dudes*.

---

* 16 September: *School's Out* (number four), *Killer* (number nineteen) and *Love It to Death* (number twenty-one). Okay, so twenty-one is not top twenty, I know; it's close enough though.

*

I am sitting in my grandfather's vegetable garden, picking peas. I discover that the best way to shell them is to run a thumbnail along the seam of the pod whilst gently applying pressure from above. The pod then springs open, and the peas are there for the taking. My grandfather comes out and joins me. He sits just behind me on a low brick wall and removes a spectacles case from his waistcoat pocket. After turning it over a number of times, he works the hinge and removes his cigarette papers and a pinch of rolling tobacco from within. He can roll a perfect cigarette without even looking, and, on this occasion, he does so – his gaze fixed pointedly at the sky above. He nips the excess tobacco from the end of his cigarette, replaces it in the spectacles case and snaps it shut. He lights the cigarette with a match, extinguishes the match by shaking it and then pushes it head first into the earth. He half smiles at me, the way strangers do when they meet at bus stops, and starts speaking.

'The Germans had gone by the time we entered Belsen. They'd been listening to Allied radio, and they knew we were coming, so they'd got out of there and left the place to the Hungarian SS. We just rolled right in and set up. The stench was . . . It smelled . . .' He shakes his head and starts again. 'It wasn't so much the smell of death, son, it was something else: it was the smell of fear. There were piles of people, dead people; there must have been ten thousand of them. Even the ones who were still alive – well, they were more dead than alive. It was like nothing you could ever imagine. I entered the camp as a soldier and ended up doing the job of an undertaker. I had to move these people . . . Son, they'd fall apart on me; they'd just come to pieces, some of them. There were still people alive there, but we just couldn't stop them dying on us. There was this woman, Polish she was, her arms and legs were covered in gangrene, she had no hair, thin as a rake . . . typhus. I took her to the MO, and he found her a bed. I saw her as often as I could. I wanted to know everything about her: her family, how she ended up miles from home in Belsen. It seemed important to get her story from her. She managed to

tell me her name, and she learned mine – that was as far as we got. She would say my name to me over and over. I think it was the only English she knew, and I would say her name to her, and I showed her pictures of your grandma and your dad – he was only a pup, of course – and she just nodded at me. It was the nearest she got to smiling.'

At this point, he realises his cigarette has gone out, and he lights it again and disposes of the match in the same way. 'I went to see her one morning, and she was dead. No one had noticed – everyone was so busy, you see, and, as I say, there were hundreds dying still day and night. But every day I took a few minutes to remember her, every day for years. Every day, I'd stop what I was up to, say her name and have a little think about her. Every day, son.'

He snaps a pod from its stalk and passes it to me. 'Then it got to be every week; then, every once in a while. And now . . .' He makes a phutt sound, shakes his head and looks at me sadly, 'Now I can't remember her name, son.'

He snuffs out his cigarette, gets up, dusts off the back of his trousers and goes back to the house. He died of a massive brain haemorrhage that night.

The major American tour that Sabbath undertake to launch *Master of Reality* starts on 3 July 1971 in Detroit, bolstering sales of Sabbath's first three albums – all of which remain in the Billboard chart for several months. The tour lasts until November, whereupon the band returns to England. A strategic tour of major British cities has been planned to start at Southampton on 16 November. Owing to the illness of three of the members* – brought on by five years spent in constant touring – the initial dates are cancelled. This gives the four a month away from the road – a window of opportunity Osbourne seizes in order to get married – and sees them through the remainder of 1971 without further incident.

---

* Most significantly, Osbourne was suffering from laryngitis and a septic throat.

By the New Year, *Master of Reality* has been out of the top thirty for two months, and Vertigo are growing anxious for a follow-up. Sabbath's management team,* meanwhile, are keen to keep the band on the road. Up to this point, Sabbath's entire album catalogue has taken less than three weeks to record; as long as the boys are given a fortnight or so's break away from touring, so the management team thinks, they'll be able to assemble another best-seller.

A fresh British tour is put together, including some gigs rescheduled from the ill-fated November roster, and sees the band on the road from January (where they sell out Birmingham's Town Hall two nights running) through to the end of February. Midway through, Osbourne gets sick, and two performances are postponed. The boys are generously allowed three days off before they start their next American tour. Playing some gigs in tandem with Yes (who are promoting the previous year's *Fragile* album – still scoring strongly in the US charts), the tour culminates in what was to have been a headlining appearance at the Mar y Sol Pop Festival, in Vega Baja in the Caribbean, on 3 April. The festival can lay claim to being one of the most impressive ever held: Alice Cooper, The Allman Brothers, B. B. King, Dave Brubeck, Dr John, Emerson Lake & Palmer, The Faces . . . there's more: Fleetwood Mac, Herbie Mann, Osibisa, Roberta Flack, Poco, Savoy Brown . . . there's even more (but the remaining names aren't nearly so luminary). However, although impressive in terms of its line-up, the event was terribly organised: because the festival was taking place in such a remote and poorly infrastructured part of the world, there were all manner of transport difficulties. Sabbath themselves fell victim to these, sitting stranded in gridlocked traffic for several hours and, ultimately, having to withdraw from the festival because they couldn't get to the site!

Before the American tour resumes in July (a tour that will run through until September), the band head for Bel Air for a couple of months to take some sun, get laid, snort box-loads of coke and – in-between

---

* Keith Goodwin, sometime writer for *NME* was appointed as professional publicist in 1972. He performed the same function for a number of artists at various times, including Yes and Dusty Springfield.

times – record their fourth album. Sounds like fun (they even get to trash the pad), and – hey – I'm not going to get all heavy-handed about this, but this is where things start to go wrong. Let's pause: this is a turning point.

Shacked up in the one house,[*] our boys have too much time on their hands[*] and are frolicking in a veritable blizzard of cocaine. Additionally, there is the sense amongst the members that they have already proved everything they had set out to prove; in short, they have made it – and they can now sit back awhile and enjoy the rewards. Ward, Butler and Osbourne are all pretty fried by this time, so it falls to Iommi to exercise some sort of control over both the *esprit de corps* and the preparation of the band's fourth album. Although Iommi is by this time accustomed to this role (remember what we said a while back about Iommi assuming the role of leader), and in many ways is the natural candidate for the job (most of Sabbath's compositions have started life as an Iommi riff, subsequently embroidered by the other members), the arrangement nevertheless cannot be seen as ideal. Although Iommi's guitar playing lies at the very core of Sabbath's music, it is the way his playing interacts with the other instrumentation that truly defines the Sabbath sound and makes their appeal so strong and enduring. Unless the other members are matching him stroke for stroke at the input stage, Iommi's tendencies can drift toward the margins a little. Iommi needs to feed off the full commitment of his fellow band members; when he gets that, he is pushed and he responds.

And this isn't really happening in the Record Plant Studio at the time of the recording of *Vol. 4.* Iommi's benign dictatorship of Sabbath, earnest and well intentioned as it undoubtedly is, is not proving effective – because not everyone is putting the effort in. And this shows in the record now – not so much in terms of the quality of playing, which, it has to be said, is the best so far, but in the overall slickness of the sound.

---

[*] 2023 Stradella Drive. The property was owned by the wealthy Du Pont family, who, appropriately enough, had concerns in the pharmaceutical industry. Tangye and Wright (p. 76).

[*] About two months. Nowadays, of course, two months to record an album (particularly when most of it has yet to be written) doesn't seem at all that long. When looked at in the context of Sabbath's non-stop touring itinerary, however, it's an extensive period.

Ditching Rodger Bain, who had served as producer for the band's first three albums, Sabbath decide to produce the album themselves, with the dubious – and now contested – support of Patrick Meehan, one half of their management duo.

According to Iommi, the band has a happy time recording *Vol. 4*. Tom Allom, who was later to produce much of Judas Priest's more popular work, is drafted in to engineer, and his penchant for cleaner, poppier sounds clearly influences elements of the final mix. And although *Vol. 4* is far from being a bad album, it is, nevertheless, a *different* album from those preceding it. Whereas the progression from the debut to *Paranoid* had been both natural and positive (typical of a band who, having found their niche on a debut, then exploit it fully), and the development from *Paranoid* to *Master of Reality* was slight but significant (the latter being a consolidation of *Paranoid*'s heavy sound but showing tendencies toward more exotic structures), *Vol. 4* is a complete departure. It doesn't carry on where *Master* had left off (as the latter had done in respect to *Paranoid*), it strikes out a new path altogether. Sure, there are elements of 'old' Sabbath still in there, but the patched-in sounds and, for the most part, sharper production makes the record sound more West-Coast American than Midlands British.

Cocaine is at the heart of this transformation. As the seventies' West-Coast scene is emerging through artists such as The Eagles,* Steely Dan,* Jackson Browne,✝ America⚹ and others – and a prototype of disco,✝ too, is beginning to rear its nodding and coiffured head – there is the general belief that cocaine is now the key to mental and musical expansionism. This is in direct contrast to the sixties' West-Coast scene

---

* The Eagles' first album is released in 1972 – bizarrely enough, recorded in England with Glyn Johns.
* Although New Yorkers, Walter Becker and Donald Fagen (the heart of Steely Dan) had relocated to Los Angeles in 1972 and later that year released their first album, *Can't Buy a Thrill*.
✝ His eponymous debut album was released in 1972.
⚹ Formed in England (they were the sons of American servicemen in the UK), America's first album was also released in 1972.
✝ It's difficult to pinpoint precisely the birth of disco, but 1972 was the year when the urban funk of artists such as Sly & The Family Stone and Curtis Mayfield suddenly became mainstream and was no longer seen as being 'black' music exclusively. At the same time, the Motown factory was moving away from its rhythmic soul ground base and edging towards sweeter, more syncopated dance sounds.

– typified by artists such as The Mamas & The Papas, Jefferson Airplane, The Doors, Buffalo Springfield, The Byrds and, later, Crosby, Stills & Nash – who were attuned to pot and acid. Coke is an urban drug – it's a stimulant – but it's also engrossing: it heightens self-regard at the expense of more social or far-reaching perceptions. It's a drug that places your foot on the gas and urges you to get there – rather than pot's tendency to get you to shift down and dig the scenery. And this kind of urgency, this belief that each individual is locked into some sort of awareness race, trespasses into the music of the time. And although it took some time, for example, for The Eagles to get from 'Takin' It Easy' to 'Life In The Fast Lane', they got there nevertheless. And they got there on coke.

And with Sabbath on *Vol. 4*, we get not only 'Snowblind' (an overt coke reference) but 'Supernaut' and 'Tomorrow's Dream', the lush 'Laguna Sunrise' and the frenetic 'St Vitus Dance': all songs dripping with the suffuse self-awareness and sense of exigency that cocaine engenders. And although the musicianship on this album is good, as mentioned before, the overriding impression is that it is good because the band believe it has to *be* good. In other words, with *Vol. 4* Sabbath are choosing to take a step into the unknown, away from their roots. The emphasis here is on construct – rather than atmosphere, as had been the case on their previous albums.

And so the result – the product of cocaine-enmired musical frolics woven together in a touring hiatus – is, on the surface at least, a rather classier affair than that to which we have hitherto been accustomed. Gone (for ever) are the spooky prosaics of Rodger Bain's stark production techniques, and the eerie cavernousness of the group's sound, and we are given instead a slick, glossy, more 'professional' Sabbath. Iommi recalled:

> *Volume 4* was such a complete change we felt we had jumped
> an album, really. It didn't follow suit because we had tried to go
> too far . . . we had reached the limit as far as we wanted to go.*

* Iommi speaking to Mick Houghton of *Circus* magazine in October 1975, printed in *Into The Void: Ozzy Osbourne and Black Sabbath*, ed. Barney Hoskyns, Omnibus Press, 2004 (p. 49).

Vol.4 is a triumphant record, one appropriate to the band's hard-earned success, and it is an excellent record – but it is also a very sad record. In focusing more intently on individual parts* and constructing the pieces, as it were, from partial blueprints, the band are moving away from the organic experimentation of ensemble playing. This is also having an effect on the band's interpersonal relationships. Seldom playing *in toto* in the studio, the individual members of the band are denying themselves the consolidating nuances of being a band; they are now beginning to regard themselves as more separate entities. So much so, in fact, that during Ward's repeated failure to nail the drum part for 'Cornucopia',* together with his increasing estrangement from the group both physically and attitudinally,† there is some consideration as to whether he should play any further part in Black Sabbath. Ward awaits the final decision of the three-man jury whilst camped out in Butler's garden. Happily, for all concerned, he is not fired – but the rot had started, and things were never to be quite the same again.‡

---

* I'm thinking of the multitudinous guitar overdubs throughout the record and Ward's much-assayed drum part in 'Cornucopia' (see subsequent entry).

* As Ward recounts in Rosen (p. 75), he had considerable difficulty in providing a drum track for this song. Tangye and Wright have it that Ward's difficulty was with the track 'Under The Sun' (p. 78); they go as far as saying that the band playfully dubbed the track 'Everywhere Under The Sun' on account of Ward's troubles in laying his part down. Naturally, it's possible that Ward had difficulties with both.

† He wanted to bring Alvin Lee into the group and make *Vol. 4* more of a blues session.

‡ Tangye and Wright have a different take on Ward's isolation from the other three: 'he was so paranoid he convinced himself he was about to be kicked out of the band' (p. 78).

Chapter Nine

Vol. 4

✝

Originally entitled *Snowblind* – but, once again, having its title vetoed by Sabbath's American label, Warner Brothers, this time on account of its obvious pharmaceutical connotations – *Vol. 4* is released on 1 September 1972. It enters the UK Top Thirty on 23 September at number twenty-eight and scraps its way to its highest position of four in the week commencing 21 October. It continues to sell well for two months, achieving gold status in November, before exiting the Top Thirty just before Christmas. You remember Christmas 1972: Little Jimmy Osmond's 'Long Haired Lover From Liverpool' and Chuck Berry's 'My Ding-A-Ling' were at the top of the singles chart. The album also fares well in America – although not *as* well – where it peaks outside the Top Ten at number thirteen.

Again using a gatefold format, the album's cover art is hastily redesigned when Warners reject the originally packaged *Snowblind* album. The band has very little to do with the cover art as we know it now on *Vol. 4*, which once again utilises the stylish design simplicity of Bloomsbury Group.* The decision to elevate Osbourne (only) to front cover status was as bold as it was unprecedented. Can you imagine, for instance, a Led Zeppelin album with a big picture of Robert Plant on the front, with Page et al. relegated to occupying the liner? No, I thought not. And it's a different Osbourne we're seeing here. Whereas formerly he had been portrayed with a sort of tragic fragility – a waif-like persona that both balanced and complemented his manic expressiveness on stage – here he was being represented as a joyous and triumphant figure: his arms-raised-aloft, peace-signs-on-full-view pose indicative of a conquering hero or a messiah. The lithographic monochrome* of Osbourne is strongly reminiscent of the

* Bloomsbury Group had also designed the cover for *Master of Reality*.
* Osbourne is depicted in pumpkin orange against a black background. This particular shade of orange was something of a vogue colour in 1972 (a prototype of the similarly hued Spacehopper was patented in the US in 1971), and it is difficult now to imagine the representation any other way.

ubiquitous representation of Che Guevara: iconic, logotypical and martial. It also invites comparison to Nixon's then predilection for sporting a similar two-fingered gesture (which, in turn, he adapted from Churchill's 'V for Victory' salute): a cynical and ironic summation of his peace-mongering in Vietnam, China and the Soviet Union. The thought of Nixon's aides coming across a copy of the album (it was released two month's before his landslide victory) is perversely intriguing: with Nixon, of course, it was little more than a gimmick, a promotional symbol carefully and affectedly cultivated in order to secure a second term. Upon his electoral victory, it became both socially obscene and mendaciously hypocritical.

The white bubble lettering, depicting the group's name and the album's perfunctory title, is laid out to provide a sort of structural arch over Osbourne's figure: an unstable but still protective umbrella, if you like. The entire front cover design is replicated on the back – only with the text and Osbourne's figure in reversed colouring. So if you spread out the sleeve it looks a little odd: there's a sort of unbalanced symmetry; it looks much better folded up. Inside, you get an additional liner accommodating a number of photographs, taken at Sabbath's sell-out performance at Birmingham's Town Hall that January, by Keith McMillan. The first panel is given over to Butler, dressed simply in an unfastened lumberjack shirt and jeans (a look also embraced by Rory Gallagher and one that the 'construction worker' in The Village People would later bring before a much wider audience). He is hard at work violently punishing a transparent perspex bass. The second panel features Osbourne, with his newly curled hair tumbling about his shoulders, the embodiment of neo-Pre-Raphaelite, early-seventies' hippy chic. After the unimpressive Town Hall shot of the whole band that forms the centre-spread, we then get to Ward's panel: he sits among a quiver of drumsticks, looking a little too meaty for his *Jesus Christ Superstar* outfit, but nevertheless happy enough despite his deteriorating physical state. The final panel, of course, is Iommi's – and he, too, is sporting a new hairstyle: shorter, tidier, more spray and hold – one for the ladies, no doubt. The cover attracted a little notoriety over the

acknowledgement, 'We wish to thank the great COKE-Cola Company of Los Angeles'. Sigh.

And on that subject, it's perhaps appropriate to mention again the pronounced effect that the band's collective coke habit had on the album's music. With a few notable exceptions (the beginnings of 'Wheels Of Confusion' and 'Cornucopia', 'Changes' and the coda of 'Under The Sun'), the album is delivered in a sprightly, cocaine-fuelled tempo. Inveterate boogie-merchants Status Quo also underwent a similar metamorphosis when indulging in amphetamines with their 1976 release, *Blue for You*; and whereas both of these records were fine achievements, they both also signalled turning points in the bands' histories. For Quo, it was a sort of twelve-bar apotheosis, and, having reached this point of elevated dizziness, they were never quite the same again; their next album was the tinny *Rockin' All Over the World* – a truly lamentable affair that marked the start of a brisk career dive. For Sabbath, it represented the end of their 'stoner' period (to adopt more modern nomenclature) and the beginning of a move toward a crisper, punchier sound.

Throughout the remainder of their career, there were still periodic allusions to their lugubrious past; but such instances as there were, the coda of 'Under The Sun', and 'Thrill Of It All' and 'Megalomania' from 1975's *Sabotage* album, now sounded, if not pompous exactly, then at least more grandiose. The decelerated tempi of these tracks came across as an almost regal stateliness – as far removed from the stripped down, groaning simplicity of, say, 'Black Sabbath', 'Hand Of Doom' and 'Sweet Leaf' as it was possible to get without actually leaving the genre. And, although Sabbath could certainly handle faster songs (it was, after all, 'Paranoid' that made their name and 'Children Of The Grave' that exalted them to rock superstardom), their unique and very particular appeal had always been based around the slower ones: you could rock out to Purple or Zeppelin or – if you were less choosy, perhaps – Heep, but only Sabbath could conjure that very special sludginess that seemed to embody those dark, broody feelings associated with having a bad day.

But although this emphatic downer style won them many fans, it brought them nothing but derision from the music press. Basing their asinine observations on the dubious conclusion that, if they played slowly, they *thought* slowly (i.e. they were just a bunch of morons)* – or that they played slowly because they couldn't handle faster arrangements – the British music press took perverse pleasure in dismissing the band as comic-book *Unterkultur* for teenagers.* And, to a gifted musician like Iommi, this must have been particularly distressing. No real surprise then that, by 1972 and the time of *Vol. 4*, efforts were being directed at the press to convince them that Sabbath were a vital and relevant musical force – rather than just an inexplicable phenomenon. As a result, *Vol. 4* met with guarded praise from British music critics, who welcomed the attempt the band were making to 'progress'.

But music critics don't buy albums: they don't have to. And in following a course that intended pleasing – or, at least, keeping at bay – the British press, Sabbath were moving away from the ponderous, mantric rock that their fan base had grown to love. And although a certain degree of latitude was tolerated – even welcomed – a complete departure was not: *Vol. 4* marked the start of a decline in album sales that was to continue through to *Technical Ecstasy*, *Never Say Die* and the eventual break-up of the original Black Sabbath.

1) Wheels Of Confusion

Starting with a bent guitar note of disgustingly lardy fatness played against a sombre waltz, 'Wheels Of Confusion' soon dissolves into a turgid and repetitive 4/4 riff on a B power chord. Over Ward's splattering, Zeppelinesque drum pattern, Osbourne sings a Mixolydian, folk-infused vocal melody of surprising depth and colour – especially when given the fact that it is based on a literally monotonous riff. The lyric,

---

* A logical non sequitur that would make Napalm Death geniuses.
* Although efforts were made to redress this as early as 1976, it was only after the Nirvana-led legitimisation of Sabbath that the British press started to re-evaluate the Sabbath catalogue in a more considered and perceptive way.

which is uncharacteristically rhyme-free for the most part, concerns itself with introspective mental self-analysis, a coming-of-age sort of thing, hinging on lost innocence and the gaping doors of adulthood and, in some senses, can be read as their first statement of disillusionment with their increasingly demanding surroundings.

We get two verses of this sort of trudging navel-gazing before a simple Iommi fill takes us into a more threatening and dramatic middle section. It is here that we are introduced to the eponymous wheels of confusion, which seem to stand as a metaphor for the sad, mechanical inevitability of our own progression through this unhappy vale of tears. Only the music here, which is both frenzied and demonstrative, hints at a more sinister and conspiratorial presence at work behind the façade of poetic melancholia. The siren motif played on Iommi's guitar at 2:58 suggests the mournful lacrimae of some familiar Madonna-like* figure as she bears witness to the sad passage of life and the endless parade of human suffering.

We then arrive, at 3:32, at a big dirty riff that, although indicating a degree of chaos, is strongly suggestive of arrant malice. We're cutting away from the dismal panorama of assembly-line deprivation and looking behind the scenes at the architect responsible for it. The music handles the metaphysics: its Miltonic dénouement expounded in Iommi's savage bravura.

After a final reprise of the verse pattern, the song then changes tack completely. Fixing on yet another minor tonic/subtonic chordal motif of hoary wickedness, Iommi delivers a counterpoint of uplifting sweetness. We've never heard Iommi doing this before – delivering honeyed phrases devoid of sadness on his guitar. For the next couple of minutes, which takes us through to the end of the song, a battle is being fought music-ally between the grunting malevolence of the riffing guitar (which gives way to a pained solo at 5:46) and the mellifluous tones of the over-riding octaved staccato which accompanies it. As this duality is allowed to develop, a certain agreement is reached. It's not total harmony (there

---

* As in the Mother of Jesus, the Catholic 'Our Lady of Sorrows' – not the trumped-up disco Jezebel.

is still an element of contradiction in the discourse), but there is an over-arching sense of serenity and all being well with the world: an Eden, perhaps, albeit an Eden with a serpent. As T. S. Eliot put it, 'The world turns and the world changes, / But one thing does not change . . . The perpetual struggle of Good and Evil'.*

But as the coda draws to a close, the sweetness of Iommi's chiming tones, which maintain a melodious and persistent supremacy over the turgid undertow, suggest that good is, for the moment at least, triumphing over evil – an optimism rarely found in either Milton or Eliot.

2) Tomorrow's Dream

Once again using the dropped C sharp tuning that proved so effective on *Master of Reality*, 'Tomorrow's Dream' was intended as the follow-up hit to 'Paranoid'. It was released as a single in September 1972, along with its parent album, but failed to make any impact. Although this is in some respects not remarkable – the single and its B-side, 'Laguna Sunrise', both featured on the album, thus rendering it obsolete for all but the most ardent of Sabbath completists – it is in other respects surprising, nevertheless. 'Tomorrow's Dream' certainly bears comparison with 'Paranoid' as a song; more to the point, it shares certain similarities in its construction that make its absence from the charts all the more notable, especially considering the unexpected yet emphatic success of the 'Paranoid' single.

The riff is based around the now familiar minor tonic/subtonic shift we've come across in a number of earlier Sabbath songs ('Paranoid' included). The tempo of the song, its Aeolian modularity and its habit of terminating a free-flowing and rapidly paced riff with a chordal braking pattern* are all properties it shares with 'Paranoid'. So too its lyric: 'Tomorrow's Dream's third verse (2:29), in which the singer archly bemoans the dissolution of his relationship on the grounds of safeguard-

---

* From *The Rock* (1934).
* In this case, the minor subtonic and the subdominant; in 'Paranoid', the minor mediant and minor subtonic.

ing his mental health, paraphrases 'Paranoid's remarkably similar opening lyrical gambit, and a general sense of dissatisfaction and dissociation is common to both songs.

But there are sufficient differences between 'Paranoid' and 'Tomorrow's Dream' to render the latter song something more than just a rewrite of the former or a variation on its successful formula. Most noticeably, 'Dream''s Roy Orbison-like bridge at 1:28, a simple alternation of B and D chords* played in a chiming style similar to Pete Townshend's work with The Who, is quite unlike anything on 'Paranoid' and brings the song a much-needed relief from its locomotive tempo. Iommi's simple fill at 0:39, co-opted from *Master of Reality*'s 'Into The Void', can be seen in the context of *Vol. 4* generally as a brief over-the-shoulder glance at a style they were in the process of leaving behind – and, without wishing to get too overemotional about it, engenders a very real sense of poignancy in the song.

Where it fails – and I say 'fails' only because it has never achieved the status envisaged for it – is in its mixing. The sound is subterranean, the pitch is too low to support the incisiveness of its attack, and the overall effect is deadened by a slapdash rendition, the players losing sight of one another in the soup of the track's dismal crepuscularity.

3) Changes

'Changes' is a peculiar departure for Black Sabbath. There's really no way that it should work – let alone work as well as it does. One can only imagine its genesis:* after having come up with a rudimentary piano figure in the player-friendly key of C (yet, perversely, in the curious, proggy, limping-waltz tempo of 6/4), a lyric is hastily construed detailing the dissolution of a romantic affair and, finally, a mellotron is plastered all over it like you would add syrup to a pudding. When you consider the fact that, additionally, there's no guitar in the piece (nor bass,

---

* This is the actual pitch. Because of the detuning, the chords Iommi plays are D and F.
* As Rosen did (see Foreword); however, it is extremely unlikely – in view of the finished recording – that the number was ever an ensemble piece.

nor drums) it becomes a difficult package to sell. On paper, the whole thing looks like a massive cop-out into the sticky world of sub-genre rock balladry that – let's face it, *rightly* – deserves all the scorn one can energetically and two-fistedly throw at it.

But 'Changes' is not at all like that. The hypnotic repetitiveness of the piano figure and its awkward 4/4+2/4 time signature, the peculiar whining pathos of Osbourne's delivery and the, thankfully, under-scored mellotron combine to produce a work of some considerable stature and lasting grandeur. Quite whether I'd agree with Joseph Adair's assessment on the sleeve notes to Castle's triple-CD compilation, *Black Sabbath: The Ozzy Osbourne Years*, is another question. Here's what he had to say:

> 'Changes' had more than a ring of the epic to it. Shades of 'Stairway To Heaven', anyone? . . . a prime candidate for Ozzy Osbourne's best ever vocal performance.

I do have to say that amuses me greatly. Quite where the similarity between 'Stairway To Heaven' and 'Changes' lies, I'm not at all sure: 'Stairway' doesn't even have a piano in it; in fact, aside from a suggestion of mellotron in 'Stairway', the two songs have no instrumental elements in common. However, Adair does have a point regarding Osbourne's vocal. It is nothing like his career best, but he does manage to generate some feeling out of a lyric that sounds like it was lifted from the Peter & Jane books: 'I feel unhappy / I feel so sad / I've lost the best friend / That I ever had'.

Sadly, the lyric gets no better than that. In blaming the break-up of the relationship on 'the world and its evil way[s]', Osbourne refuses to scrutinise either his own shortcomings or those of his lost lover. All of which, in a manner of speaking, makes him come across as either grossly insensitive or seriously deluded. Unlikely as it may seem, 'Changes' is the solemn partner piece to 'Paranoid''s vaunted hubris: this is where Osbourne got to after he finished with his woman for not helping him with his mind.

All he wants is to 'go back and change [the] years' – the one thing no man can do; all he is capable of is 'tears' – understanding is quite beyond him, jettisoned some time ago in the monomaniacal fug of 'Paranoid''s rampant hysteria. His complete failure to get to grips with his situation – all played out against a lachrymose backdrop of painfully elongated string sounds and mournfully hobbling piano – is genuinely provoking. It's like watching a blind cripple trying to walk on ice. His inarticulacy in no sense diminishes the listener's perception of his pain; rather, it intensifies it. Our hearts go out to the lumbering misfortunate – even though he is now squirming in the bed he has himself made – because he simply seems unable to cope with what he's done.

All of which will be of little consequence to those of you determined not to like this song.

4) F. X.

I'll admit, the prospect of writing a couple of hundred words on this pointless whimsy is not one that fills me with any kind of confidence. What the 'song' is about, I have no idea. Why it found a place on the album, likewise. Had it featured on *Never Say Die*, it would perhaps have been one of the stand-out tracks (okay, I'm joking), but here . . . I'm lost for words. It's been recounted that the piece was executed by Iommi tapping his crucifix against the guitar strings;[*] I'm not even going to attempt to say anything meaningful about this inconsequential fart of a noise.

5) Supernaut

Starting with one of Iommi's most irresistible and engaging riffs, 'Supernaut' is 'new' Sabbath at their best; or, rather, it's transitional Sabbath – Sabbath experimenting with doom-free, upbeat riffery whilst still not forgoing their established and identifiable trademarks. These trademarks – and we've discussed these before – include detuning; the

[*] Tangye and Wright (p. 71).

minor tonic/subtonic shift (which, I guess, you're bored with hearing about now); semitonal slurs (ditto); and the unexpected exoticism of certain tonal intervals, most notably, the flattened fifth (which has been with us since the first track we discussed, 'Black Sabbath').

'Supernaut' employs all but the last of these trademarks or signatures; so, on the one hand, it can be said to be typical of earlier Sabbath – whereas the assertive melodic optimism of its initial riff and the calypso-like frivolity of its drum break and ensuing middle section at 2:38 accord it a new identity more closely associated with the two following albums. Much the same case can be made for 'Sabbath Bloody Sabbath' (which we'll get to in due course), and this goes to prove that there were new grounds (or new sounds) that Sabbath were capable of exploring with successful results. The problem was that having explored them they then occupied them more or less exclusively – and this merely shifted their box further down the line; it did not free them from it. More to the point, it meant that they could not easily revert to their earlier tried-and-tested downer style without looking like they'd regressed.

Compositionally, the piece makes much of its rather meagre raw materials. The main riff is a reiteration of the tonic/minor subtonic interchange employed exhaustively throughout the Sabbath – and, it must be said, *rock – oeuvre*. It is garnished with a semitone slide between the minor subtonic and the submediant in order to give the motif a sense of uneasiness, counterbalancing the uncharacteristically upbeat tempo. The alternate section – Sabbath's own take on the jukebox evergreen 'La Bamba' – provides a welcome break for those heads being repeatedly bashed against the wall.

The vocal is triumphant – it's almost as if Osbourne *knows* this song is something special – and Butler's hungry, galloping bass pattern, interplaying with Iommi's restrained verse riff and Ward's fevered and insistent drumming, gives 'Supernaut' a sense of charging rapacity: a great, sleek shark-like thing, elegant and deadly, voraciously consuming all in its path.

6) Snowblind

Despite the efforts put into, and the intentions behind, 'Tomorrow's Dream', it has been 'Snowblind' that has emerged from *Vol. 4* as the 'hit' track and which has, from the perspective of fans at least, weathered the years better. Originally intended as the album's title track, 'Snowblind' is a song that lyrically propounds an anti-coke message, but, in doing so in such an I'm-a-naughty-boy manner, completely divests itself of any sincerity. But, let's not forget (as if we could), cocaine was pretty much what they were in Bel Air to do: the music on *Vol. 4* was just a very welcome bonus for the rest of us.

Iommi recalls that he first tried coke before a gig in Madison Square Garden in 1971;[*] after that, he says, it was around all the time. Butler can be more specific:

> America was where we really discovered drugs. We had this house in LA we lived in while we were doing *Volume 4* and the place was just full of drug dealers.[*]

And Osbourne recalls it with equal vividness:

> We'd have coke dealers over every day. We'd have stuff on the drip, you know: coke, dope, morphine, acid . . . [†]

You get the picture. And, unlike 'Hand Of Doom', which was written in the second person and was clearly admonitory, 'Snowblind', written in the first person, is more flirtatious with the subject matter. As a consequence, there is a certain ambivalence to the song: the icicles in Osbourne's brain contrast with the happiness running through his veins;

---

[*] Iommi speaking to Mick Wall of *Classic Rock* magazine, January 1999. Tangye and Wright has it that the band first experienced the drug at The Whiskey A Go Go in Los Angeles.
[*] Butler speaking to Mick Wall of *Classic Rock* magazine, January 1999.
[†] Osbourne, ibid.

he craves both happiness *and* cold.* And although the ambivalence is explicit, as it is in Lou Reed's 'Heroin', J. J. Cale's 'Cocaine' and a host of other pharmaceutically flirty songs, the overriding impression is one of embracement. It's the same sort of dangerous thrill you might procure when paying for a dominatrix to whip you: it's not genuine enslavement (or so the song goes); it's some sort of kinky fix. Osbourne's audible whisper 'Cocaine!' at the end of the song's first verse is both schoolboy naughty and wise-guy dumb.

The song starts with an 'unusual' riff – unusual in that it mixes power chord motifs with arpeggios in a style that was, then at least, not all that common, Paul Kossoff aside – configured for the now familiar C sharp tuning. The verse riff, again based around the minor tonic/subtonic shift, is similar in effect to the verse riff found on the earlier 'Wheels Of Confusion' and provides Osbourne with a blank enough canvas on which to splash his vocal. The guitar fill at 0:41 leads us into a reprise of the arpeggio A major/B major chords and, from there, back into the verse pattern.

The song's major highlight occurs at 1:40 with a splendid arpeggio descent from C sharp down to G sharp, stopping at the usual places on the way, over which Osbourne delights in snowflakes glistening on trees, perceptible yet through the dazzling effulgence of freezing light. So insistent, in fact, is the hibernal imagery that you almost expect him to segue lounge-style into 'Winter Wonderland', but he somehow manages to control himself. Iommi's following solo is simply gorgeous, and then we find ourselves back in the verse riff. Iommi's almost obligatory 'bonus' riff occurs at 3:28, over which a rather belligerent – almost adolescent – Osbourne proudly proclaims his belief in what he's doing, that it's what he *wants* to be doing and that we are the losers, the ones who don't get it. This has much the same effect as the final 'Yeah!' in 'Fairies Wear Boots' and encompasses precisely the ethos of the song: reprehensible complicity. From here we are taken back to the 0:41 guitar fill and then

---

* There are similarities here with Charles Baudelaire's 'Chant d'automne' ('Autumn Song') in which may be found, 'All winter will return in my soul: / Hate, anger, horror, toil, and sudden chill, / And, like the sun in its Antarctic hell, / My heart, a red and frozen block, is still'.

– and this is a big mistake as far as I'm concerned – back into yet another reprise of the verse riff. Someone* must have realised it was sagging a bit here because, out of nowhere, we've suddenly got Mantovani and his merry men pitching up in the background. The thing is, the string-embellished verse actually works – it really does – but it should have come earlier: this is verse *four*, for heaven's sake, *terra incognita*. We've never had a verse four in a Sabbath composition before – and this is not the song in which to introduce one.

7) Cornucopia

Sticking to the C sharp tuning to emphasise the bottom-heavy nature of this song's turgid opening riff, 'Cornucopia' is a real horn of plenty – at least in terms of its generous allocation of musical ideas. The opening motif's first seven notes, which climb unsteadily, but with great purpose nevertheless, from the C sharp root note, through some wobbly G sharps and naturals to a most unstable D natural, sound like some awful slime-covered beast emerging from the pit of Hell with an enormous headache and an overdue bill to pay. Truly, it's monstrous. We then get the semi-tonal slur down to the tonic before the quavering C sharp – D and G – G sharp (for which a debt must be acknowledged to Hawkwind's 'Paranoia' from their 1970 debut album)* before the catatonic tempo is usurped by the sforzando prestissimo (I'll have nuts on mine) that forms the verse riff.

The lyric concerns itself with consumerism gone wild. Butler's initial inspiration came from a news report that stated there were 'only twenty-five' deaths in Vietnam the previous week. Coupling this seeming disregard for human life – making it merely a numbers game – with the issue of pollution and the earth's ever-depleting resources, the lyric sets out to lambaste the senseless and prodigal attitudes toward the environ-

---

* Probably Bill Ward – Stark (p. 21).
* The riffs differ slightly in that Hawkwind's goes C sharp – D, A – A sharp, E – F, but the mood is similar particularly from 0:25–0:30 in 'Cornucopia' when the quavering is repeated.

ment and man's future on the planet. It only succeeds, however, to a point: the lyric is barely discernible at best, and Butler's implied criticism of men seeking to shield themselves from the terrors and stupidities of contemporary life through 'illusion' and the comforts of a large income is one that could be levelled at the band members themselves.

Whatever the song's dubious arguments, its merits stem almost exclusively from its abundance of riffs: at 0:56, there's a curious little four-bar phrase redolent of a Celtic dance; the powerful chorus motif with its B natural – B flat descent shored up by a resounding F sharp – G sharp answering phrase; then, later, there's some ethereal cymbal work accompanying an arpeggio descent from F sharp through E to B – and we're less than two minutes into the song.

For me, the song reaches *excelsis* at 2:26, with Iommi and Butler locked into a surging and pumping F sharp motif and Osbourne singing that he doesn't know what's going on, that he's cracked up. This is precisely the kind of lyric for which Osbourne has no equal in delivering. If Robert Plant, for instance, were given that lyric, he'd translate it to the relational: he wouldn't know whether his baby (pretty bay-be) would be leaving or staying; *his* head would be torn from emotional uncertainty. With Osbourne, however, you just feel the guy's a total mess and he hasn't the first idea how it came about or what he can possibly do about it. This is genuine pathos: a quick 'I'm sorry, baby' and bridge-building shag is going to do nothing to help him out.

8) Laguna Sunrise

An instrumental interlude of little complexity, 'Laguna Sunrise' has, nevertheless, some charm on account of its striking melody line, plucked out by Iommi on steel-strung acoustic guitar, and the almost 'Wild West' nature of the accompanying string sound. The trouble is that there are not enough musical ideas to sustain interest in a piece that, at 2:53, is twice as long as it needs be.

With 'Embryo' and 'Orchid' from *Master of Reality*, and, to a lesser degree, 'Rat Salad' on *Paranoid* and 'Warning' on *Black Sabbath*, Iommi

had established a pattern of including instrumental passages on albums. This is not a bad idea, and, given that Iommi was the only member of Sabbath who could lay claim to being a musician in the traditional sense of the term, it was really to be expected – in the same way that Jon Lord was indulged on Deep Purple's early albums. It has to be said, however, that these inclusions did not always work. 'F. X.' was an execrable waste of time, and it comes close to spoiling the whole mood of the record; 'Embryo' and 'Orchid' I would have gladly forsaken for the inclusion of one more half-decent vocal track on *Master of Reality*. That aside, 'Laguna Sunrise', written in Laguna Beach earlier in the year, is pleasant enough. Despite its drawn-out length, it certainly fits better on the record than the ephemeral nonsense of 'F. X.' – and it also provides welcome respite from the sludge-and-thrash of 'Cornucopia' and the peculiar rock jig that is 'St Vitus Dance'.

Perhaps the most significant thing to note about 'Laguna Sunrise' is that, like many tracks on *Vol. 4*, it marked a transition of sorts. Hitherto, Iommi's makeweight instrumentals had been largely solo, single-guitar affairs; here, the guitar was double-tracked, and the arrangement was further embellished by the panoramic sweep of the luscious string sounds. This newly found confidence in more complex, quasi-orchestral arrangements was to lay the foundation for the glorious 'Fluff' on 1973's *Sabbath Bloody Sabbath*.

Sitting somewhere between Stanley Myers' 'Cavatina'* and John Barry's *Midnight Cowboy* theme, 'Laguna Sunrise' is a laid-back, Spanish-inflected shuffle, suggestive of long and unfeasibly coloured cocktails sipped from the recumbent comfort of a sturdy recliner.

9) St Vitus Dance

This really is a curious little affair. Beginning with a repeated, frantic two-bar jig figure, the song then descends to the familiar minor tonic/subtonic shift pattern found on so many of the songs already

---

* The theme for the 1978 Michael Cimino movie, *The Deer Hunter*.

discussed. This pattern is substantiated by a quavering between the minor mediant and the supertonic, the semitone differential — once again, a Sabbath signature — this time suggestive of drunken incapacity, perhaps, or some kind of gurning dementia.

And really, that's about all this song does. There's a bizarre modulation at 1:17 — in which the key is shifted *down* from its initial B to A flat, indicating the slamming of a cell door (whether it be in the local nick or the county sanatorium, we don't yet know) — and this gives the song a much needed shot in the arm (sanatorium then) from the incessant recapitulation of its two-bar hopping frenzy.

Reportedly, much of *Vol. 4* was written and recorded in the (not particularly) drawn-out gaps between cocaine deliveries. *When's the next batch due? Half an hour. Right, let's do a track then* sort of thing. Given that this was most probably the case, this must have been one of those knocked-off affairs, accomplished whilst Osbourne was hastily scribbling his signature on the delivery note. It's underwritten in the extreme: there's no solo, little musical content or texture and the lyric sounds like it was cribbed from the agony pages of a teen magazine. Its saving graces are two: its gonzoid fury is actually quite amusing for a while, and the track's brevity assures that its dubious novelty value does not pall.

St Vitus' dance is the parochial term for Sydenham's* chorea — a nervous disease that affects children. The symptoms include uncontrollable and sudden spasms. It derived the name St Vitus' dance on account of the fact that, traditionally, its sufferers would pray to St Vitus for relief. Vitus himself, by way of completing your education on this matter, was born toward the end of the third century AD and, whilst still a child, was denounced by his father for being a Christian. After being soundly thrashed and scourged by his intemperate old man, he fled to Rome.

---

* Thomas Sydenham (1624–89) an English physician and fighter (as Captain of Horse for the Parliamentarians) in the English Civil War. Interestingly, he backed the use of liquid opium (a substance he dubbed 'Sydenham's laudanum') in the treatment of severe nervous disorders. He also believed that senile decrepitude could be remedied by sending the patient to bed with a nubile young woman. There's certainly a lot to be said for such forward-thinking treatment — talk about holistic — and, given that he clearly dug sex and drugs and only missed out on the rock and roll, there's every indication that he would probably have got on famously with our boys.

Whilst there, he saved the emperor Diocletian's son from demonic possession but then refused to give thanks to the Roman gods. He was consequently treated with the utmost suspicion – before being thrown to the lions as punishment. The lions, however, refused to touch him, so poor little Vitus was then boiled in oil: nasty and probably bad for his cholesterol level. At this moment, so the story goes, an impressive storm blew up and with well deserved, karmic promptitude destroyed one or two of the nearby Roman temples. By the sixteenth century, his veneration had attained such heightened frenzy in Germany that people would dance and cavort wildly in front of his image – believing, if they did so, that it would give them a clean bill of health for a year. Amongst other things, Vitus has been the patron saint of actors, dog bites, oversleeping (yes, this really has a patron saint), epilepsy and the former Czechoslovakia.

10) Under The Sun

Beginning with a sludgy riff straight out of the Iommi textbook – a riff that utilises the now familiar C sharp detuning, semitonal intervals and that hellish flattened fifth, in short, three of Iommi's trademark devices – 'Under The Sun', the last song on the album, bids a loud and final farewell to the old Sabbath sound and provides a fitting and powerful close to the band's transitional fourth album.

The opening riff is, in some respects, a hybrid of the riff in 'Black Sabbath' and the verse riff in 'Electric Funeral'. Starting from the tonic for the first three notes, the riff then arrives at the flattened fifth by way of the natural fifth,* before lurching awkwardly to the augmented sixth via the minor seventh, and from there diving in semitones back to the natural fifth.* This is *exactly* the kind of scalar exoticism that makes Iommi's riffs so conspicuously unmistakable.

---

* In 'Black Sabbath', the tonic is reproduced an octave higher (the second note of the riff) before arriving at the flattened fifth and, whilst there, suggesting the natural fifth by a finger-induced vibrato effect.
* This arrangement of notes is completely different from the semitonal descent in 'Electric Funeral', but the feeling of trudging despondency suggested is similar.

The verse riff, by contrast, is a far less complex affair, little more than a slowed-down boogie really, which allows Osbourne's searing vocal to come to the foreground. The lyric, bearing something of a resemblance to the coda of John Lennon's 'God',* is a fierce assertion of individuality and self-belief intended as a warning against all those who would tell you what to do and attempt to indoctrinate you. Its irony is that, in denouncing preachers and their ilk as unsound and not worth listening to, Osbourne unwittingly places himself in that same unwelcome category when he dogmatically urges credulous listeners to believe what he tells them.

At 1:56 the song ups tempo again as the band hammers out a simple figure based on F sharp, while Osbourne bemoans the quotidian and all-consuming nature of his drug habit. A few seconds later, at 2:21, the same riff is taken up a tone to G sharp, then at 2:46 – the start of Iommi's solo – it ascends another full tone to A sharp. We're back to Bach again here – or, at least, the intro to 'Fairies Wear Boots'. But whereas 'Fairies' started its modular climb from the tonic, here the ascent has begun from the more difficult subdominant. No matter: from A sharp the key is raised a further semitone to B at 2:54, which further heightens the sense of tension and panic which has been developing in the song since this section began. From there, it jolts back into the verse riff (in effect, a full tone modulation – only it drops down five full tones rather than pushes up a whole tone) at 3:11. This section, just over a minute long and effectively using five different keys, is a work of truly inspired craftsmanship. Although a modulation can often be a rather hackneyed way of injecting a sense of excitement into a song,* with Sabbath, modulations have always been used temporarily and sequentially to portray an escalating mood of uneasiness, instability or tension.

But all that has happened so far in 'Under The Sun' is of little

---

* From the 1970 release, *Plastic Ono Band*. Lennon sings of his disbelief in, among other things, gurus, mantra, Jesus and Beatles and that he only believes in himself; Sabbath's lyrics cover similar ground in an identically declamatory manner, registering the singer's disavowal of violence, peace, preachers and God, whilst concluding – like Lennon – with an assertion of his belief in himself as the only true thing. A rare occasion where Sabbath grappled with the Ancient Greek Skeptics.
* Think Eurovision and the final choruses of most of the songs.

consequence when compared to its mighty coda, the first notes of which kick in, after a reversed cymbal splash,* at 3:57. The descent in question (the first three notes of the theme) is worth looking at in some detail. It actually consists of dominant-mediant-supertonic – instead of the more typically rock-friendly dominant-subdominant-mediant. The difference may appear slight, but it is significant. By omitting the subdominant, the descent is leaping further with its first interval (from G sharp to E, instead of G sharp to F sharp), and this infuses the motif with a sense of droning grace normally associated with traditional folk melodies. The next step down (to the supertonic) suggests tension or suspense, and the whole effect is like a hypnotic carillon, given a sinister injection of downward-spiralling doom by the chordal descent from C sharp, through B, A and G sharp, to F sharp. The effect is further abetted by a slowing down of the figure coupled with the increasing weight of guitar sound. The crisis reaches completion when both guitars conjoin in a ponderous sludging unity at the end. This is a truly glorious coda, saved from triteness and bombast by the clever construction of the carillon, which brings a very fitting close to a brave – but, possibly, over-optimistic – album.

Vol. 4 saw Sabbath moving on: not very far, perhaps – but onwards, nevertheless. The stylistic 'leap' many critics perceived between *Vol. 4* and the following year's *Sabbath Bloody Sabbath* was not so pronounced as it struck them. The clues were to be found splattered all over *Vol. 4*: from the innocuous string sounds in 'Laguna Sunrise', providing knowing indications for both 'Fluff' and 'Spiral Architect'; the piano on 'Changes' (their first recorded use of this instrument, it was to feature again on *Sabbath Bloody Sabbath*); the up-swinging riffs in 'Supernaut', 'Tomorrow's Dream' and the coda of 'Wheels Of Confusion', which prefigured *Sabbath Bloody Sabbath*'s 'Looking For Today' and 'Killing Yourself To Live', amongst others; and the triumphant farewell paid to their stoner style in the unholy coda of 'Under The Sun'.

---

* How very Beatles.

Chapter Ten
Looking for Today / 1973

†

January

1973, and the peace treaty which brings to an end the Vietnam War is signed in Paris. The first American prisoners of war are released and sent home by plane. Well over a million people have been killed in the conflict, ninety per cent of them North Vietnamese. America has lost 55,000 servicemen and must nurse a further 150,000 wounded. In contrast, the number of road deaths in America during the period of the war has exceeded 400,000. In other words, almost eight times as many Americans have died in domestic vehicular accidents as have in combat during the Vietnam War.

The Watergate trial begins in earnest. Nixon admits overall responsibility for the bugging but denies any personal involvement. He forbids his staff from giving evidence at the hearings, but after the heat is intensified – due in no small part to *Washington Post* reporters Carl Bernstein and Bob Woodward – he has to relent. Tapes subpoenaed by the grand jury, and believed to contain vital evidence in linking Nixon directly to the break-in, mysteriously go missing, are wiped or are otherwise tampered with. Presidential aides G. Gordon Liddy and James W. McCord Jr. are convicted of spying on the Democratic Party's headquarters; four other aides quit. Suspicion builds, Nixon declares he isn't a crook and talk of impeachment begins in the House of Representatives. Vice-President Spiro Agnew, a man whose name is an anagram of 'grow a penis', pleads guilty to a charge of tax evasion after taking backhanders from government contractors and is replaced in office by bumbling gawk and future president Gerald Ford.

On 11 September, a date later to gather a searing significance for all Americans, the CIA, in a move aimed at safeguarding American business interests in the country, sponsors a *coup d'état* in Chile: General Augusto Pinochet, at the head of a fascist military junta, wrests power from a democratically elected Salvador Allende. Allende is found dead, reportedly a suicide but almost certainly not, and Pinochet sets about the American-backed killing of three thousand 'undesirables', including many parliamentarians, university professors and students, trade union leaders and activists, a foreign diplomat and members of the clergy.

In the Middle East, OPEC doubles the price of crude oil and reduces its supply to Western countries it perceives as having Israeli sympathies. This includes not only America but Britain also, who, before the year is out, will see the introduction of, first, another national state of emergency and, then, the three-day week: the latter a measure imposed by Prime Minister Heath in an attempt to conserve energy reserves in production industries. The Ecology Party – later to become known as the Green Party – is formed in Britain in the wake of the oil crisis and, amongst other things, attempts to steer the conscience of the British populace toward more environmentally friendly alternatives to non-renewable energy sources.

As Soviet leader Leonid Brezhnev cries 'Uncle!' on the Cold War, Irish Republicans begin a murderous Christmas bombing spree on mainland Britain. This is taken as Republican condemnation of the Sunningdale Agreement: a treaty ratified by the British government which protects the province's status as a sovereign dependency and assures there will be no Irish unity while there is a Protestant majority in Northern Ireland.

Technological advances give us the 'Skylab' project – an American incentive which allows manned space exploration over prolonged periods of time – and the effective exploitation of cryogenics: a calf is born from a frozen embryo.

William Friedkin's *The Exorcist* (a film Osbourne is to sit through a reported six times and one which Iommi lists as a personal favourite) and Robin Hardy's *The Wicker Man* portray an ailing Christian religion in futile combat against satanic and pagan forces. Bernardo Bertolucci's *Last Tango in Paris*, Nicholas Roeg's *Don't Look Now* and Terrence Mallick's *Badlands*, meanwhile, provide an ugly/beautiful look at, respectively, sex and dependency, sorrow and longing, and anger and dissociation. *Deep*

Throat alternately shocks and titillates an American public whose mouths are caught open in either appalled disbelief or salacious expectation, and Martin Scorsese announces his arrival with *Mean Streets*, springing both Robert de Niro and Harvey Keitel on a movie audience barely ready for them.

The singles charts continue to be dominated by MOR, teenybop and glam: The Carpenters, The Osmonds and an oven-ready Gary Glitter compete with The Sweet, Wizzard and Slade for the seven-inch market. Album-wise, it's more of the same from British stalwarts The Rolling Stones, The Who, Led Zeppelin, Free and Deep Purple, as they all produce new works of continued stylishness.* Status Quo, having found their niche the previous year with *Piledriver*, release *Hello!*, and Alice Cooper capitalises on his newly found British popularity by issuing his rite-of-passage suite *Billion Dollar Babies*. Prog sees the launch of five concept-related albums: Yes's criminally maligned *Tales from Topographic Oceans*, ELP's *Brain Salad Surgery*, Genesis' *Selling England by the Pound*, Mike Oldfield's debut, *Tubular Bells*, and Pink Floyd's evergreen *Dark Side of the Moon*. Elsewhere, many bands are taking the opportunity to release their concert recordings – a format that, other than The Stones' *Get Yer Ya-Ya's Out* and The Who's *Live at Leeds* (both 1970) has been little exploited: Hawkwind, Uriah Heep, Yes, Ten Years After, Genesis, Lindisfarne and Clapton* all release live records.

Do you want to touch me?

The voice belongs not to Gary Glitter but to my fifteen-year-old babysitter. My parents are out for the evening, and my sister, at eight years of age and three crucial years younger than I, has been consigned to bed an hour ago. It is eight o'clock, and I've only thirty minutes left of being up before I, too, will be headed the same way. She lifts up her top, a horizontally striped, sleeveless nylon affair; she is not wearing a bra.

---

* *Goats Head Soup, Quadrophenia, Houses of the Holy, Heartbreaker* and *Who Do We Think We Are* respectively.
* *Space Ritual Alive, Uriah Heep Live, Yessongs, Ten Years After Recorded Live, Genesis Live, Lindisfarne Live* and *Eric Clapton's Rainbow Concert* respectively.

You can touch me here if you like.

She takes my hand and places it on her stomach so that it completely covers the bullet-hole of her navel. I offer her a brief smile, as I don't want her to hit me or tell me off. I'm too young to feel inhibited over what I'm doing, so when she takes my hand and pulls it onto her right breast I offer no resistance. A group of sand-brown freckles on her sternum resembles the constellation Orion. She shows me how I am to stimulate her nipple by gently squeezing it between my thumb and forefinger – the same action my grandfather used when rolling cigarettes. I am amazed how the nipple grows under my touch, but my interest is more scientific than sexual. The silence in the room is occasionally punctured by her short, high-pitched gasps and the curmudgeonly grunting of the family dog, collapsed in front of the fire. Her top teeth bite down on her bottom lip, and her small pink face fixes me with the same type of stare my mother would employ when trying to get to the bottom of something.

She edges forward on the couch (for that is where we are), reaches forward and pops the button on her jeans. A second later, she has undone her zip and, after pushing herself even further forward, peeled the jeans down as far as her knees. Her pants are white – or once they were – and seem several sizes too small for her buttery hips, into which they sink slightly like the tape round the immersion jacket. They fit so snugly that the contours of her body beneath them are fully evident. I know enough to know that she has no penis; I just don't know what the thing she has instead of one is going to look like.

And I never get to find out, for, as suddenly as it had begun, the show has ended. Five minutes later I am in bed thinking of Orion: mistakenly killed with an arrow by Artemis, his betrothed, whilst swimming in the Aegean Sea.

Sabbath return to Britain to finish off the record, and, a few weeks after all has been done, *Vol. 4* is released in September 1972. By this time, the band is in the middle of a sizeable US tour with British proggers Gentle Giant. There is cause for concern when Iommi collapses after the gig at the Hollywood Bowl on what was to have been the penultimate date of the tour; consequently, the Hollywood Bowl gig, on 15 September, ends up being their last on American soil until February 1974. With *Vol. 4* nestled comfortably in the upper reaches of the album charts, Sabbath begin a four-month touring hiatus in mid-September before embarking on their second Australian tour in January 1973.

Although Sabbath are pleased at the reception *Vol. 4* is getting, and have every reason to be happy with the record themselves, there are worrying signs, nevertheless. Ward's periodic lack of commitment to the making of the album, his coke-induced incapacity to nail the drum part in 'Cornucopia' and his careless persistence over getting Alvin Lee in to jam on the album* leads to the band's first real falling out in the four years or so they have been together. It is not to be their last. Equally worryingly, Iommi's onstage collapse has taught the band that even the oldest, most responsible amongst them is not impervious to the rigours of a hectic professional life combined with a prodigious drug intake.

Osbourne, who had married in 1971, has his first child, Jessica Starshine Osbourne. Together with his wife and a son from her previous marriage, he now feels part of a family – a family for which he feels at least some modicum of responsibility – and, largely at his insistence, the touring schedule for 1973 is a more relaxed affair. Ward, on the other hand, who had split from his first wife prior to the recording of *Vol. 4*, doesn't so much care what the schedule is like – just as long as he can fit in his pharmaceutical pursuits *en route*. After a two-month tour of Europe and Britain concludes with a show at Newcastle's City Hall on 18 March, the band – now with Gerald Woodruffe featuring on keyboards for their live appearances – takes a break from the road until December, its only touring commitment during this period being an

---

* This occurred after the band had returned to Britain to mix down *Vol. 4* and re-record some of the tracks. Alvin Lee, late of the British power trio Ten Years After, was a close friend of the band – they had often performed together – and was about to embark on his first solo project.

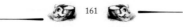

appearance at Alexandra Palace for the London Music Festival in August.

Happy with the way that *Vol. 4* had been written and recorded – Iommi, in particular, had been relieved to find the compositional ideas flowing freely – and enjoying the tableaux of experiences available to them in Los Angeles, come summer, the band decide to begin work on their fifth album in the same environment as its predecessor. Studio time is once again booked in the Record Plant in LA, and the band gathers in Bel Air to set about recreating the *Vol. 4* vibe. On arrival at Record Plant, the band are alarmed to discover the studio has been revamped and modernised: owing to Stevie Wonder's presence, there is an abundance of synthesisers – not really their bag – and the band find themselves ill at ease in an environment which, although familiar to them, proves oddly alienating.

Worse, Iommi appears to have dried up, riff-wise. Having long shouldered the burden of initiating and polishing compositions – he has often recounted that the other band members would repair to the nearest pub and leave him with the task of writing and finishing songs – Iommi is struggling to weld together riffs in a constructive and viable manner. Despite strenuous efforts to recreate the free-flowing energy of *Vol. 4*, the music is proving stubbornly elusive. After several weeks, the band reluctantly decides to quit Bel Air and return to Britain. After a couple of weeks' rest, time is booked at Rockfield Studios, a rehearsal and recording facility located in the Monmouthshire country-side in Wales.

Deciding to bed-and-breakfast at nearby Clearwell Castle on the Welsh borders and make the commute to Rockfield on a more or less daily basis, the members of Sabbath are relieved to discover that the old magic is still there. However, lodging in such atmospheric surroundings, their stay is not without incident. Osbourne falls asleep in front of a roaring log fire one night, is ignited by a flying ember, and almost burns to death. He is saved by Dave Tangye and some of the road crew, who, whilst still awake and catching the unmistakeable miasma of Osbourne flambé, promptly drag the singer from the fire and douse him in cider.

There is a further scare for Osbourne when he and Iommi are walking the castle's corridors on another evening. After spotting a mysterious figure, dressed entirely in black, enter a room ahead, they follow the individual only to find that he has vanished completely.

In the middle of this, Sabbath come up with the track 'Sabbath Bloody Sabbath', the title of the song, which Ward claims to have coined,[*] simultaneously a nodding reference to the events in Londonderry the previous year, John Schlesinger's 1971 film *Sunday, Bloody Sunday* and a riposte to the Melody Maker headline BLOODY HELL, BLOODY SABBATH! This track effectively busts Iommi out of his creative block, and the rest of the album's numbers are written shortly thereafter. In compiling his own profile for a Black Sabbath Appreciation Society newsletter in 1989, Iommi recalled 1973 as being his most memorable year – 'because of the general vibes at the time, and it saw us at a good peak'. Hell, he feels so good he even shaves off his moustache. Butler, also, has fond memories of the year *Sabbath Bloody Sabbath* was put together:

> [It was] a whole new era for us . . . before then, we were in a terrible slump. We were all exhausted from touring. We weren't getting on very well. Then Tony came up with the riff for 'Sabbath Bloody Sabbath', and everybody sparked to life . . . That was a really good year, personally. I'll always remember that album and look back on it with a good feeling.[*]

Ward concurs with the general feeling of happiness and unity:

> Went to Wales. Felt really good about that . . . We were in this beautiful castle . . . I can remember doing that. It was just, ah, I loved that album.[†]

Osbourne, too, is happy with 1973. Being reunited with his wife and

---

[*] Ward in Stark (p .24).
[*] Butler speaking to John Stix for *Guitar for the Practicing Musician* magazine, May 1994.
[†] Ward in Stark (pp. 23–4).

baby daughter comes as welcome relief from the months spent away from home on the road – particularly for a man who is, let's face it, as suited to fatherhood as a hammer is to dentistry. It's significant to note, too, that Osbourne – whilst pottering about his kitchen one day – comes up with the basis of the track 'Who Are You'; although this is certainly not the most impressive number on *Sabbath Bloody Sabbath*, it does demonstrate how committed Osbourne is to adding to the creative stew of the forthcoming record.

But it's not all seriousness and hard work. Despite spending much of their time rehearsing in the castle dungeons – by all accounts, a particularly spooky environment which informs a lot of the music on what is to become *Sabbath Bloody Sabbath* – the band are prone to the boyish high jinks typically associated with young lads spending too much time together. Amusing each other by scaring themselves half to death, this light-hearted japery goes to such protracted limits that the band become so scared they collect their sleeping bags and head for safer suburban accommodation.

In an attempt to secure Sabbath a better recording deal, manager Patrick Meehan, whose interference during the making of *Vol. 4* had been stoically tolerated by the band, wrests Sabbath away from their Vertigo contract and signs them exclusively with Warner Brothers; the Warner subsidiary World Wide Artists (WWA), operated by Meehan's father, Patrick Snr, has exclusive rights to the issue of the forthcoming album. Happy with Meehan's promise that this new contract will ensure them a higher income, Sabbath are nevertheless reluctant to consent to his appearing in the studio. Accordingly, they decide to produce the record themselves and, it has to be said, make a fine job of it, too.

Sabbath Bloody Sabbath is released in December 1973, just in time for the Christmas market. It strikes its way rapidly to its peak placing of number four before slipping promptly out of the Top Thirty by the end of February 1974.

Chapter Eleven

Sabbath Bloody Sabbath

✝

Hailed by many to be Sabbath's finest achievement, the album *Sabbath Bloody Sabbath* is a dedicated and upbeat assertion of the band's growing confidence and resolve: from the title track itself – a defiant two-fingered gesture to the British music journalists who constantly scorned the band's efforts – to the increasingly experimental instrumentation found throughout the album and crafted into shape by Sabbath's own hands-on production. There is no doubt that all four members rate the album highly, and this proud satisfaction helps strengthen the band's unity. Bill Ward:

> We're never going to split. We couldn't be more together now, because we love each other and because we dig each other's music, both individually and as a group.*

And it is as well that the band has discovered this renewed sense of togetherness. 1972 was a fun-filled, successful but difficult year for Sabbath: *Vol. 4* had been a remarkable achievement, but the seeds for later discord had been sown in the band's growing substance abuse and their occasionally jarring musical aspirations. Furthermore, 1974 was to be another difficult year: with lawsuits flying in all directions and management changes to come, it was to be the first year in which they wouldn't release an album since they started. *Sabbath Bloody Sabbath* helps cement the band together – musically and, as it were, socially – and its successful reception is to keep the band pulling in the same direction, despite the onset of difficulties, for another couple of years. In short, had there been no *Sabbath Bloody Sabbath*, the troubles of 1974 might have proved too onerous for the band to withstand, and it all could well have ended there.

* Ward in 1973, quoted in Alexander Rack's Black Sabbath FAQ on www.black-sabbath.de

In the spring of 1972, whilst they had been touring the US with Yes, Sabbath had met and struck up a friendship with Yes's keyboard player, Rick Wakeman. Wakeman, a committed drinker, hellraiser and meat-eater, was finding Yes's almost Buddhist restraint amidst the trials of touring somewhat less than fulfilling. Accordingly, whilst the bands were on the same bill, he shacked up with Sabbath and found Ward and Osbourne's refreshingly liberal attitude to life on the road rather more to his taste. The friendship was to last for the remainder of the tour, and, when pulling together *Sabbath Bloody Sabbath* the following year and realising that help might be required in working out the keyboard arrangements, Sabbath remembered their old drinking buddy and gave Wakeman a call.

There is some confusion over what, precisely, Wakeman contributed to *Sabbath Bloody Sabbath*. On the album notes, he is only credited with piano and synthesiser on the one track, 'Sabbra Cadabra'. However, Iommi has since mentioned that Wakeman appeared on 'Who Are You',* and there have been vague allusions to the effect that he is present more or less throughout the album. Although Iommi is himself no stranger to the piano – Bill Ward has said that Iommi is a 'beautiful piano player'* – it seems likely that the gorgeous, if slightly kitsch, right-hand arpeggios in the middle section of 'Who Are You' are Wakeman's and not Iommi's.

The album is richly presented in a gatefold sleeve dominated by Drew Struzan's✝ dramatic front cover, apparently entitled *The Rape of Christ*. According to Osbourne:

> The front of the cover represents a man dying . . . There are all these distorted figures bending over him and gloating as he lies there. These figures are actually him at different stages of his life. He's a man of greed – a man who's wanted everything

---

* This may be found in Joe Siegler's website, black-sabbath.com, in an interview with Iommi from March 1996 entitled 'The Iron Man Speaks'. Unfortunately, the magazine in which the article first appeared is not mentioned.
* Stark (p. 30).
✝ Struzan was later to design the poster art for the 1977 film *Star Wars*.

all his life and done all this evil stuff. The back [cover] represents the good side of life. The person dying on the bed has been really good to people. He's got all these beautiful people crying over him as he's dying . . . All in all, this represents the good and bad of everything.*

Should Osbourne ever tire of his current role as self-proclaimed 'Prince of Fucking Darkness', a future as an art critic assuredly awaits him. But, regardless of what the cover art pertains to be about – and I'm certainly not about to venture my opinion – it is positively striking. Rather like the reptile house in a zoo or close-up pictures of medical trauma, you are repulsed but, at the same time, fascinated. The artwork is complemented by the album's title, appearing in an angular geometric font – a variation of which was to be used for Spinal Tap's logo – above the grisly tableau. The design of the capital 'S's, evocative of the SS regalia in Nazi Germany, and the prominent inclusion of 666* on the front cover made it unlikely that Sabbath would win over the Mothers' Union with this release. Inside, you get a rather bizarre shot of the band stripped to the waist and striking some curious postures. By the manner in which they are, for the most part, shielding their noses with their arms, it could be that one of them has just parped; be this the case, I would suggest Osbourne as the culprit, as he is the only one brave (or accustomed) enough to lift his face away from his arm and thereby expose his nose to the miasma. This rather unsettling photograph, credited to Shepard Sherbell – about whom I know absolutely nothing, I'm afraid – is superimposed upon an interior shot of a Jacobean-style boudoir, replete with timber four-poster, laminated chipboard shelving and a mains-voltage power socket. It's just a shame they couldn't squeeze in a waste-paper basket and a radiator. The rear panel, with 'the person dying on the bed [with] all these beautiful people crying over him', as

---

* Osbourne in the magazine *Circus Raves* in 1974.

* The number of the beast, of course. Oddly, it wasn't until the 1976 release of Richard Donner's film *The Omen* that this particular excerpt from St John's Book of Revelations (13:18) became absorbed into the currency of the non-theological mainstream.

Osbourne put it, was revisited by Bowie on his 1999 release *Hours* . . . right down to the gothic lettering, the pose of the recumbent and the cool blue colour palette. As with *Master of Reality*, we are given the lyrics (with a line from 'Spiral Architect' mysteriously missing);* only this time they appear printed on the inner sleeve, not on the cover itself.

Although Sabbath credit themselves as producers, it seems likely that Mike Butcher (who is listed as engineer on the album) also had a valuable contribution to make in regard to the overall sound of the record. Unlike *Vol. 4*, on which the sound quality varied from hard and crystalline to loose and sludgy, there is a constancy and uniformity about this record which allows the – at times – disparate pieces to hang together well as a whole. The instrumentation is closely knit, and the musical departures – upon which the majority of the songs embark – work well in according the songs a composite unity. Iommi's guitar, which is fed through a Rotosound effects box,* is defining without it ever monopolising the mix, and it sounds at times like an organ. With two exceptions, the title track and 'Sabbra Cadabra', the guitar sound is light and punchy – reminiscent of a featherweight at the height of fitness – and explores more fully the melodic inroads made on the previous album, *Vol. 4*.

1) Sabbath Bloody Sabbath

> I'd rather not talk about 'Sabbath Bloody Sabbath'. It was a very personal thing, and I wouldn't like to embarrass the person it was written about.✝

Beginning with a multilayered guitar riff of almost soupy viscosity, the title track of Sabbath's fifth and most ambitious album to date starts off as a mean, bitter affair, picks up wistful sweetness along the way, gets

---

* At least on the original pressing of the album – although I note that the same line is also missing from the 1996 Castle remaster. What *is* that line anyway? I always assumed it to be 'Even martyrs cry', but I have since come across alternative suggestions: 'Even fathers cry' and 'He was father's pride' being but two.

* Iommi disclosed this in the October 1974 issue of *Guitar Player* magazine.

✝ Osbourne in Stark (p.23), speaking to Paul Long of KNAC Radio.

downright furious and then ends in a cacophonous mix of brutal, architectural sonic structure and aeroplane noise. It's a mighty, strident piece, breathtaking in its alternating ugliness and beauty, which manages to capture the band's rediscovered unity and channel it into an angry *pièce de résistance*, whilst simultaneously providing the band with a truly classic track – their first of such stature, perhaps, since 'War Pigs' – alongside which the future output of heavy rock would come to be measured.

There's such an energy to the opening motif, a C sharp detuned sequence alternating between the tonic and minor subtonic, brought full circle by an ascending chord sequence of A – B – C sharp – E, upon which Butler's spectacularly vituperative lyric has been nailed. The interpolated acoustic quatrain which immediately follows the first verse at 0:43, an ornamented alternation of the supertonic and tonic along the lines of The Beatles' 'Don't Let Me Down', and which is both melancholic and resentful, provides but a momentary respite from the acrid\astringency of the preceding figure, before the heat is intensified by the infuriated rancour of the second verse. 'The people who have crippled you, you want to see them burn', Osbourne sings, speaking for the whole group and providing the sort of catharsis necessary to release years of frustration, accumulated from the snide derision and derogatory criticism of Britain's myopic music press.

There's so much pent-up anger and dissatisfaction in Osbourne's vocal that he can't help but allow it to overspill in the second iteration of the acoustic section. In the line '[they] fill your head all full of lies', the acrimony is patent, it is too strong and pronounced to be subsumed, and it reaches climax with the extraneous shout of 'You bastards!' that prefaces Iommi's pungent solo.

Following the power chord concretion of a bonus middle section at 3:02, we arrive at a lugubrious and wallowing semitonal blues riff at 3:19 over which Osbourne's searing vocal, pitching in at a top C sharp, effectively blends that potent mix of frustration, bitterness and anger which embodies the song's very nature. After the desperation of 'Where can you run to? / What more can you do?' in the first of these two closing verses, we get to the simultaneous denunciation and self-assertion of 'Bog

blast all of you! / Sabbath Bloody Sabbath!' and the gruelling sarcasm of 'Living just for dying / Dying just for you' in the second.

There is then an almost triumphal chord sequence, as if to underline the vehement vindication of the band's ethos, at 4:42 which leads us into a brooding, simmering coda evocative of a smoking battlefield: the conflict has been fought, won, and it is now time to pick up the casualties and regroup for the next onslaught. There is no lasting peace here – the war is still raging, as evidenced by the chaotic assemblage of sonic concretion and aeroplane noise – but there is at least time to bury the dead.

2) A National Acrobat

Famously dismissed by its lyricist as a song 'about having a wank',[*] 'A National Acrobat', with its references to conception, embryonic life and the post-partum hereafter, is something of a philosophical and ethical springboard. Butler was later to say about it:

> That was just me thinking about who selects what sperm gets through the egg.[*]

And although the song falls short of providing a full and frank philosophical analysis of prenatal politics – preferring instead to offer an encrypted message from an unborn child, paradoxically at some existential point of death – it does, at the very least, predispose one to afford some consideration to these matters. I'll get on to reviewing the song's musical merits in a moment, but, before I do, I should just like to open up the discussion a little. It's a bit of a gamble this, but you might find it interesting.

There are people who consider abortion unethical. As far as I can determine, their reasoning – and by 'reasoning' I mean the rational part

---

[*] Butler speaking to Mick Wall for *Classic Rock* magazine, January 1999.
[*] Butler in Carol Clerk, *Ozzy Osbourne: The Stories Behind the Classic Songs*, Carlton Books, 2002 (p. 49).

of their argument as opposed to the emotional – goes something like this. (a) It is wrong to harm an innocent human being. (b) A foetus is an innocent human being. (c) Therefore, it is wrong to harm a foetus. If you accept the first two statements, you are bound to accept the third: such is the infallibility of syllogistic logic. You just can't argue with it. There are others, however, who take issue with the second statement: they argue that a foetus is *not* a human being – that human being-ness does not begin until birth. Finally, there is a sort of middle ground – and it is this grey area of compromise which current legislation inhabits: a woman has the legal right to terminate a foetus less than twenty-four weeks old.*

Now, I'm fairly confident I could provide a coherent argument against all of these standpoints. I'm not going to because I don't want this digression to drag on, and I want to throw some other issues at you whilst we're on the topic: IVF,* 'saviour siblings' and foetal harvesting. Most IVF treatments are straightforward; however, UK law✝ still provides that *both* parents must consent to all stages of the treatment. This means that an estranged partner who has withdrawn consent after donating sperm can deny a woman her child – all of which raises the questions of who owns the right to make that decision, and what rights, if any, the foetus itself possesses. UK law is in even more of a tatter over 'saviour siblings' – embryos which are developed with the express intention of providing 'spare parts' for existing children: Britain's fertility watchdog, the Human Fertilisation and Embryology Authority (HFEA), effectively banned the procedure, only to have its ruling rejected by the European Society of Human Reproduction and Embryology, who maintained the practice was morally acceptable. Foetal harvesting provides for perhaps the muddiest quagmire of the lot. The technology now exists to manufacture children from mothers who have never been born. It is now possible to harvest ovarian tissue from an aborted foetus that, bathed in female

---

* The current UK legal limit.
* In vitro fertilisation (literally, fertilisation in glass): where an egg is removed from a woman unable to conceive, fertilised in a laboratory and then reinstated into the uterus.
✝ Human Fertilisation and Embryology Act, 1990.

hormones, will eventually develop into a human egg. Once fertilised and implanted in the uterus, this egg will develop into an embryo and, thence, a child. The ethical considerations may well be complex, but the philosophical ramifications are startling. The science fiction of the seventies has now provided a very real moral dilemma in the early twenty-first century. Butler's omniscient unborn child, never conceived, then a paradox, has now come to exemplify an ethical battleground upon which the conflicting arguments of science and progress, religion and tradition, wage a messy and ultimately unwinnable war against one another.

At eight years of age, Butler converted to vegetarianism, and the Buddhist essence of this credo mildly flavours the song's lyrical conundrums throughout. Another vegetarian, the poet Shelley,* published an early essay entitled 'The Necessity of Atheism',* a work that essentially argues that had God not existed then we would have had to create Him, and which asks the question, 'Have we existed before birth?' It answers this by stating, 'As far as thought and life is concerned, the same will take place with regard to us, individually considered, after death, as had taken place before our birth.' I make this point not in any inflated, show-offy way but to invite comparison between Shelley's take on extraneous reincarnation and Butler's, in the second half of the song's final verse (4:24-4:35), in which he speaks of the cycle of reincarnation, the transmigration of the soul and the anticipation of future life. All topped off with a wickedly hammy laugh from Osbourne. Before we put him back on that dusty top shelf upon which many of you might consider him to belong, I'd just like to conclude with a further observation about Shelley. He was, as the vernacular has it, a bit of a lad. For several years, he had a *ménage à trois* with his future wife⁺ and her half-sister, he established a commune, generally lived the rock and roll lifestyle (such as it was in the early nineteenth century) and, like Butler, he dressed in an outlandish and flamboyant manner.

---

* Percy Bysshe Shelley (1792–1822), nicknamed 'Mad Shelley' at Eton.
* Published in 1811 and revised in 1813.
⁺ Mary Wollstonecraft Shelley (1797–1851) who gave us *Frankenstein*.

Now, as promised, we will talk about the music. Once again featuring the C sharp tuning, the song's opening riff is a jerky baroque figure strongly suggestive of the proto-technological agricultural husbandry briefly alluded to in 'Embryo' from 1971's *Master of Reality*. The har-monic thirds in the opening few bars are a splash of autumnal evening sunlight: low on the horizon, orange-hued and gently warming. The verse riff which follows – a progression comprising tonic, minor mediant, minor subtonic and subdominant – sounds at once familiar and yet original: the musical equivalent of Butler's lyrical paradox. As Osbourne's ascending vocal peaks at a B on the second syllable of 'secret' – giving the word a heightened sense of furtive conspiracy – the Dorian arrangement hangs suspended on the subdominant like the vascular placental sac anchored to the motherboard of the song's mysterious and mechanical momentum.

At 2:15, the song gets angry. Osbourne's frenzied and desperate *cri de cœur* at 2:20 for people to sit up and listen introduces the subject of precognition foreshadowed in earlier works such as 'Electric Funeral', 'Planet Caravan', 'Into The Void' and 'Wheels Of Confusion'. These Cassandrian* visions are made all the more significant and viable given the song's context of placing the seer in a position of having endured a thousand lives. Whilst Osbourne is making these exhortations, the remaining band members lock into a savage and blistering riff, exotically punctuated by a consecutive C sharp major/minor seventh,* the discordant nature of which assails us like a fetid cloud of poisonous smog – a blast of Satan's breath. The song finds an uneasy home in this figure

---

* Greek mythology: Cassandra was the most beautiful of King Priam's and Queen Hecuba's daughters. In an attempt to seduce her, Apollo gave her the gift of prophecy. When Cassandra still refused his advances, Apollo turned on her and corrupted his earlier gift – he made it that however she might prophesy, she was never to be believed. She foresaw the sack of Troy, but the Trojans ignored her. As Troy fell, she was raped by Locrian and then given as a spoil of war to the mighty warrior-king Agamemnon. When Agamemnon took her back to Greece, Cassandra tried to warn him of the dangers that would await him there. Once again, she was ignored, and both she and Agamemnon were murdered by Clytemnestra. Contemplation of Cassandra's fate reminds us of how onerous and yet how futile it is to have such a gift. Although Butler's adaptation of the Cassandra story is somewhat muddied by the contradictory lyrics 'I've found out what it means to be believed' and the later 'You've got to believe me', the apparent contradiction nevertheless reflects some of the frustration and desperation felt by the subject.
* Occasionally used by Hendrix, this construction contains both the major and the minor third as well as the seventh.

for some time before Osbourne's sardonic and embittered laugh, followed by a descending guitar figure underpinned by a sympathetic bass, takes us to a surprisingly upbeat and melodic instrumental section at 4:50.

Whatever gloss with which this interlude might first appear to sheen the song is soon tarnished by the dirty, explosive coda at 5:33 and the crazed accelerando that brings 'A National Acrobat' to a close. Reminiscent of the final few seconds of 'War Pigs', the structure of the finale suggests a violent ripping of flesh: a hastily executed birth into a world of chaos and terror.

3) Fluff

Enough of your brazen cynicism: this is a lovely piece of work, and, what's more, it fits perfectly on the album. If you're not prepared to accept this, skip this entry and go straight on to 'Sabbra Cadabra' – but believe me, you'll be missing out.

We'll start with the title. 'Fluff' can mean four things: any light downy substance, an object or matter of little importance, a mistake and a young woman (as in 'a bit of fluff'). The insensitive amongst you will no doubt proffer the argument that the title here refers to the second meaning; the more hard-nosed, the third. There are some who maintain that the title honours the veteran BBC Radio disc jockey Alan Freeman; there are others who argue with similar conviction that Freeman actually gave himself the nickname as a consequence of hearing the piece. Not true: it was Freeman's mother who was actually responsible for his nickname. If you really want to know why, read this footnote.*

---

* Condensed version: his mother buys him a sweater – rather like the ones worn by submariners (it says here, in the Alan Freeman section of the uproar.fortunecity.com website) – which he would invariably wear for his Saturday night radio shows. After he'd finished a show, there was usually a party to go to, and the sweater would accompany him there. It never got washed. I can barely believe you're reading this. Anyway, after three years the sweater was starting to look a little soiled, and Freeman decided it was time to cart it off to a dry cleaner's. On its return from the cleaner's, it had developed a curious fluffy bobbliness – akin to a sheep's fleece. Undeterred, and presumably unabashed, Freeman resumed wearing it. One night, at one of these obligatory showbiz get-togethers, he was spotted by an acquaintance who blurted out, 'It's Fluffy Freeman!' and, ever since, the name has stuck to him more fiercely than the damned sweater ever did. You see, if you'd skipped straight past this entry and on to 'Sabbra Cadabra', you'd have missed out on this.

But whatever the word refers to exactly – and I should like to say it's a mixture of the first and fourth definitions above – it is nevertheless a fitting title for a near-perfect instrumental interlude: it is mildly disparaging without it belittling unduly the song's undoubted merits.

Which are many. Taken at a leisurely waltz dictated by a simple guitar arpeggio in D, the song has an undemanding and engaging melody picked out by a second guitar. This three-note tune is answered by a third guitar – couched in numerous special effects making it sound a little like a horn, similar to Peter Green's guitar in Fleetwood Mac's 'Albatross' – and all this is wrapped up in extraneous piano and harpsichord arpeggios and underscored by Butler's sure-footed bass. The 'chorus' to the tune – a simple alternation between the subdominant and the dominant – is a particularly sad but hopeful phrase, suggestive of heartbreak and longing.

At 1:41, just as its charms are starting to wear a little thin, we arrive at a middle section of inspiring, uplifting beauty. Somehow, with little more than a few chords from Bert Weedon's *Play in a Day* book, Iommi manages to conjure a progression which surprises at almost every turn and is transfixing with each and every note it contains. No exotic chords, nothing at all flash on the guitar and only a couple of off-key C naturals: with just these raw materials, a whole new perspective is opened up. Escaping the confinement of the predominant chamber accompaniment, the piece suddenly reveals expansive vistas of tear-jerking loveliness. When we are presented with a recapitulation of the original theme at 2:31, the effect is one of greeting an old friend. Go back and listen to this track again: it's more than worthy of your attention.

4) Sabbra Cadabra

Sabbath go Zeppelin – only in a way that Zeppelin could never have managed. Set against a ballsy, rootsy riff (one which Metallica's Lars Ulrich was to term 'the fucking riff from hell'), this is a lusty, my-woman-she's-the-bee's-knees affair that was as out of character for Sabbath as it was first nature for Zeppelin. Similarities between the two bands are few:

other than their shared West Midlands ancestry,* their occasionally abstruse dabblings in dungeons-and-dragons-type lyrics and their respective commitments to pioneering a style of music later to be categorised and emasculated under the term 'heavy metal', the bands had little in common. Whereas Sabbath had more or less shed their blues heritage by the time of *Master of Reality*, Zeppelin clung onto theirs, taking it with them throughout their career, right through to *In Through the Out Door*'s 'I'm Gonna Crawl'. Although they were never just a blues band, the blues remained at the very heart of Zeppelin's music and provided both a lyrical focus and a musical template upon which many of their more exotic compositions were based: even on such eclectic material as 'Stairway To Heaven' and 'Kashmir', Plant's vocal strains 'There walks a lady we all know . . . When all are one and one is all' and 'I am a traveller of both time and space' are as firmly rooted in the blues idiom as his tom-caterwauling on 'I Can't Quit You, Baby' and 'Whole Lotta Love'. But Plant and Page were bluesmen; Iommi and company were not, and upon that point their styles and careers diverged.

So it is interesting to come across something like 'Sabbra Cadabra', with its references to a woman who gives good loving and who lacks the sinister attributes typical of her sex found in the band's earlier 'love' songs. Indeed, such is the libidinous nature of the lyric, it almost borders on Zeppelin parody. And it is interesting because it proves that if Sabbath had been content to make it as just a good-time, wine, women and rock and roll band – a prototype Whitesnake, if you will – they very probably could have done so. The track is splendidly played: it is tight when it needs to be tight, and fat-arsed and sloppy when the occasion warrants it. Osbourne's vocal is almost rabidly enthusiastic, and the band's ensemble playing intoxicatingly heady.

Nowhere more so than on the slow-burning middle section starting at 1:58: here, the C sharp minor* arpeggios of Iommi, and Ward and Butler's pulsating accompaniment, evoke the candles-burned-out, cigarettes-lit, fusty aroma of the post-coital bedroom. And, despite

* Only Bonham and Plant of Zeppelin were from the West Midlands; Page and Jones were 'Southerners'.
* Once again, the guitars are tuned down to C sharp.

Osbourne's promise-cum-boast to keep going all night long, you feel he's got to rest up sometime – or, at least, the recipient of all this good lovin' must – and that this is the point at which he – or she – is doing so.

At 2:52 we get the first disintegration of the song. After Osbourne has declared his intentions of never leaving this lucky lady, the song, as it were, removes its accentuated, rhythmic corset and all the fleshy treasures of the gluteal curvature spill out onto the bed. The ad-libbed piano, unquestionably Wakeman's, is crucial to the song's momentum; no more so than at this point, where its flighty, bar-room adroitness complements the song's gratuitous carnality perfectly. The song picks up again for one last go at it – a reprise of the smoky figure replete with double negatives and promises of undying fidelity – before two minutes of slap and tickle [3:51–5:51] dissemble into a loss of consciousness and exhausted sleep – the final note like a flat-lining bleep on an ECG.

5) Killing Yourself To Live

Yet again using the C sharp tuning, 'Killing Yourself To Live' begins with a riff in F sharp minor not unlike 'Sabbath Bloody Sabbath's – only a fourth higher. Both riffs feature tonic-based motifs shored up by bolstering chord progressions comprising the minor submediant and subtonic. However, the similarity ends there. 'Sabbath Bloody Sabbath' is a terrifying riff embodying anger and loathing in equal measure; 'Killing Yourself To Live''s opening progression, by comparison, is not nearly so emotionally charged. Although it indicates menace with the insistent bass underscoring the hard-working guitar, it does so in a manner that is, if not exactly subliminal, at least more temperate. In a song so full of unbelievably imaginative and stimulating riffs, the preliminary figure is restricted to just opening the song and is never reprised. At 0:31, it gives way to the B minor verse riff (from which Nirvana drew heavily for *Nevermind*'s 'Come As You Are') while Osbourne addresses lyrically the futile exhaustion of workaday lives suggested by the song's title.* When

---

* Butler wrote the lyric in reference to Sabbath's punishing 1972 tour schedule. Tangye and Wright (p. 81).

we arrive at the chorus, the words of the song's title are sung over a dirty, descending guitar figure running from B minor through A and then in semitones down to F sharp. The low-register guitar in this section contrasts effectively with the high-pitched, moaning vocal, leaving you with the impression of a great and vacuous chasm — into which we endlessly piss away all of our energy and hope — lying between the one extreme and the other.

The verse pattern is then repeated whilst Osbourne continues lyric-ally in the same vein, and, after a variation on the chorus, we arrive (at 1:45) at Iommi's solo. The solo possesses a sort of metronomic quality — suggestive, perhaps, of work on a factory production line — and, although elementary enough, it provides the perfect instrumental interruption at this point in the song. We don't require some climactic release here (remember this is only 1:45 — it's a little premature for an orgasm); what is required is something to build tension, elevate the mood and add detail to the picture. That's precisely what Iommi's solo achieves. The solo gives way to a bridge at 2:30 — a staggered, decelerating recapitulation of the chorus's chordal structure — before we get Osbourne in 'Sweet Leaf' mode exhorting us to roll a fat one at 2:51 over an incendiary middle section. This brief interlude, which burns moodily for a few bars and is, for me, the riff of the song — if not the whole album — then explodes in an accusatory frenzy at 3:16, with the singer addressing either his baby, the listener or even the whole world on the volatile nature of the human condition. This is followed by a short solo and then yet another riff (3:38) that marks a turning point of sorts in the song: the song is now not about the common drudgery of routine lives; it is hereon in about escape and taking a reckless plunge into the unknown.

Iommi's second, brief solo, richly coloured in autumnal browns and oranges and suffused with the sweet and intoxicating stench of hashish, curls and wisps its way towards the ceiling before the tempo is picked up dramatically by the closing section at 4:07. Osbourne lays bare his discomposure at 4:12, his confusion shot through with blind rage, while guitar and bass jerk out a groovy and infectious riff, deliberately dis-orientating, before another solo and a thunderous, machine-gun riff

(5:26) bring the song to an exhausted close.

There's a whole album's worth of music in this one song. Looked at in terms of its constituent parts, it really oughtn't to work as well as it does: there seems to be too *much* going on – there's too much light and too much shade – but it has been so expertly wrought* that it hangs together in a, quite literally, breathtaking manner. Not just an album highlight, this song is one of Sabbath's most estimable achievements.

6) Who Are You

Much derided at the time, and proving stoically resistant to attitudinal revision throughout the intervening years, 'Who Are You' (mysteriously and eccentrically robbed of its question mark) is perhaps the least fancied of the tracks on *Sabbath Bloody Sabbath* – 'Fluff' aside, of course. And, before the great shout of 'Unfair!' goes up, there's very good reason: it's really quite boring. It has merits, but only two of them: its glacial sound and its amends-making middle section – a passage of admirable restraint and delicate frailty.

Osbourne came up with the three-note motif by himself, reportedly whilst watching his wife cook breakfast, and, with its incorporation of the Iommi favourite the flattened fifth, it is, compositionally at least, very Sabbath. The decision not to augment the simple phrase harmonically – it appears desperate to grasp the dominant but is restrained from doing so – and then to repeat the riff in a dropped-tone reiteration makes the song's initial chill quickly pall. The relentless icy tundra engendered by the first few bars of the song's introduction, which first strikes the listener as overawing and eternally desolate, quickly melts into a colourless sludge that must be waded through in order to get to a dull roundelay of a chorus which can't justify the arduousness of the journey. That chorus, such as it is and if we can call it a chorus, despite its suggestion of 6/8 timing and The Beatles' 'Norwegian Wood', is simply not sufficiently robust; neither can its flimsy structure support the plangent

---

* You can hear a work-in-progress version of this song on the 1980 release *Live at Last*.

dreariness of the preceding verse structure with which it is so onerously encumbered.

This dismal panorama is burdened with further monotony by Osbourne's anodyne vocal that achieves little in the way of lifting the song out of its ponderous, pedestrian momentum. The lyric, which, at two verses, is rather under-written (so much so that the second verse has to be repeated in order for the song to break three minutes), is engaging enough – dealing, as it does, with the kind of paranoid insecurity with which much of Sabbath's material has been associated.

However, at 2:02 we are treated to the sixteen-bar phrase to which I alluded in the first paragraph of this otherwise entirely negative review of the song. Sadly, it cannot save the song from tedium altogether (and there is further disappointment when we realise that the insistent and nauseating synthesiser drone persists throughout), but it does, at least, provide welcome and overdue respite from the tiresome drudgery of the glumly insistent three-note phrase that, by this point, has severely outstayed its welcome. It's possible that you may not immediately recall the phrase I'm talking about – at only sixteen bars, it is rather swamped by the enveloping mass of the rest of the song – and this is a great shame, because, really, it deserves more of a platform in order to speak for itself. The chordal structure is unpredictable – after a repeated D minor/Am7 interchange, it quite surprisingly lands on an E major* – and lavishly embellished by some cheesy cocktail-lounge piano for which we may have to thank Rick Wakeman.*

Sadly, and rather pointlessly, after this all too brief interlude, we are plunged back into the merciless gloop of the main structure for a patience-stretching reprise of the second verse. As if we hadn't had enough already.

* This is not the only surprise: from E major, it progresses through F, A minor and A major (a lovely touch) before returning to its base, D major.
* Although Iommi is credited with piano on this track, and although Wakeman is only listed on the album notes as playing on 'Sabbra Cadabra', it seems likely, as we mentioned before, that this work is Wakeman's and not Iommi's – particularly in light of Iommi's revelation that Wakeman helped out on this track, too.

7) Looking For Today

It's hard to equate the almost evangelical fervour of this song's music (it even features 'praise be' handclaps) with the Sabbath of 'War Pigs', 'Hand Of Doom' and 'Children Of The Grave'. In fact, had Sabbath squeezed it onto 1971's *Master of Reality*, they might have ended up losing half their fan base. However, prefigured the previous year by *Vol. 4*'s 'Supernaut', 'Looking For Today' finds a sympathetic and contextual home on *Sabbath Bloody Sabbath* it could not have found anywhere else, least of all on the following album, *Sabotage*. Centred around a swinging guitar motif that wouldn't have been out of place on The Beatles' *Revolver* album, the song melds the sneering fury of an attack on consumer faddism and critical vogues with an emphatic and infectious accompaniment that almost defies sober analysis.

Pitched in the awkward key of F sharp (most probably as a result of the band's detuning to C sharp and playing in what would have been the key of A – there are very few Sabbath songs from this period that aren't in the 'played' key of E, G or A), the enthusiasm of the various band members, from Ward's splendid drum track right through to Osbourne's exuberant vocal, is hard to avoid; the passion is as prominent as it is on *Paranoid*'s 'Fairies Wear Boots'.

The lyric features an internal rhyme scheme which, unlike 'After Forever''s, is wholly appropriate to the song's contextual attack on marketing and consumerism: it becomes a sardonic parody of the advertising jingle. Its Dorian hook is blasted out over the swinging tonic/subdominant instrumental backing, and is a bitter and scathing attack on the transitory nature of fame, fashion and popularity. It is both cynical and off-hand – as is its target: the ephemeral and fleeting obsessions with which marketing gurus and consumer apostles are so temporarily preoccupied. Written before the notion of a single global market had been fully embraced by industrial conglomerates and then-nascent multinationals, the song provides a caustic tirade against both the corporate avarice of artificial obsolescence and the apparent willingness with which we, the buying public, play ball.

The sixteen-bar phrase which slides in just after the first and second verses – a chorus masquerading as a bridge – comes as something of a surprise. Delicate and sympathetic, augmented with a flighty and inconstant flute accompaniment and not dissimilar to the title track's 'Nobody will ever let you know . . .' section,* this plaintive quatrain seems to offer some balm amid the vitriol of the verse's outpourings. The final line of this section, an honest, heartfelt plea for your tears, is a wake-up call: the suggestion being that, in complying with the greedy manipulation of the mass-marketeers, we are cutting ourselves off from all that is – sorry to sound so damned psychotherapeutic about this – spiritual and emotional.

After the second iteration of this quiet section, we arrive, at 2:36, at a simple chorus iterating the song's title, a simple chord pattern – much used by The Beatles ('Dear Prudence', 'Lucy In The Sky With Diamonds', 'I'll Follow The Sun', 'Magical Mystery Tour', the same four-chord sequence* appearing also in their cover of 'Devil In Her Heart') – in the modulated key of B. Although repetitive, the chorus is effective, largely on account of Osbourne's piercing delivery (encompassing a whole octave!) of the do-re-mi-fa-so-do melody and Ward's splattering drum pattern. After a final interpolation of the verse, we arrive back at this musical figure, which this time is extended into an escalating coda, featuring a low-key Iommi solo and, again, some firecracker drumming from Ward. The song rather disappointingly fades out at this point; I say 'disappointingly', as, for me at least, it still has somewhere to go.

Inexplicably sidelined as the album's single (a rather cut-and-paste version⊕ of the title track was put out, backed with *Vol. 4*'s 'Changes' instead), 'Looking For Today' was the closest Sabbath had come, at that point, to recording a 'pop' song. It is saved from pop vacuity only by

---

* Structurally, they are miles apart: 'Sabbath Bloody Sabbath's 'quiet' section alternates between the supertonic and the tonic, whilst 'Looking For Today''s modulates a fourth up to the key of B and then alternates between the supertonic and the minor inversion of the dominant. There is more than a passing similarity, however, in the finished product.
* Tonic, tonic 7, major subdominant, minor subdominant.
⊕ In a crude attempt to reduce 'Sabbath Bloody Sabbath' to something approximating single-length, the first verse is followed by the quiet section, which then cuts straight to the final (alternative) verse of the song. Outright butchery.

Ward's inventive and infectious drumming throughout and Osbourne's unsuitable-for-radio vocal style. Their next venture into this territory, *Sabotage*'s curious 'Am I Going Insane', was neither so effective nor so pardonable.

8) Spiral Architect

This is a beautifully constructed song, a real departure for Sabbath (even when looked at in the context of this album as a whole) and the perfect blend of melancholy and resignation required to bring *Sabbath Bloody Sabbath* to a close. Initial hearings of the song might at first lead the listener to conclude that there is a sort of 'prog' complexity to the number, but this is not in fact the case. The song is straightforward enough; it is just that it has been so lovingly and expertly crafted that it seems to suggest much more than is really there.

Starting with Iommi's acoustic prelude, a brief arpeggio along the lines of *Master of Reality*'s 'Orchid', we can see that much is made from the rather basic raw materials at hand. The progression from an eerie and hollow-sounding Bm9 to a dangerously unstable Bm9sus4 and then to a precipitous Bm9/add7 is rudimentary enough – particularly as Iommi has tuned down three semitones to his customary C sharp – but it conjures an enticing air of mystery in the proceedings; a benign mystery, that is, suggested by the F sharp9 – E/F sharp sequence which follows. The trepidation and drama invoked by the recurring ninths belong to the smoke-filled worlds of Arthurian myth or Tolkien, and the bolstering confection of the F sharp9 – E/F sharp answering sequence ensures the prelude steers clear of the more typical sinister colourings associated with minor chord suspensions.

The unusually high-registered motif at 0:46, which is brought to an end by Iommi's downward-spiralling fill at 1:05 (the nearest he gets to a solo in this song), is a heady mix of acoustic and electric guitar, providing the perfect blend of levitated exoticism necessary to complement the surreal futurism of the lyric. With its baffling allusions to sorcerers, undertakers and oceans of plasma – together with the curious neologism

'synchronated' – chanted mantra-like over a rising Mixolydian scale, the lyric is nothing if not a progger's paradise of beguiling assonant and rhythmic wordplay and arrant nonsensicality.

It is saved from the stuffy and over-perfumed realms of the sci-fi boudoir, however, by its chorus; this benefits enormously from steering clear of the Asimovian mumbo-jumbo of the verses with its plaintive and poignant reflection of the narrator's past. Bill Ward reportedly penned the chorus lyric, a genuinely mature piece of writing contrasting markedly with Butler's chaotic symbolism. This is offset against a descending chordal pattern, embroidered up to the point of decency yet not beyond by Will Malone's like-minded string arrangement. The overall effect some might find cloying – there's a certain element of toffee-like sweetness to it, for sure – but it is sensitive and sympathetic, not overly sentimental, and it further colours the album with the burning, golden shades of autumn, death and decay.

In lieu of an Iommi solo, the strings strike out an agreeable passage of their own at 3:19. This pleasant interlude – the strings passage is just long enough to remind the listener of their presence – together with the vocal harmonies* in the chorus are the only intentional concessions made to the orangey-brown loveliness of the song; its wistful melancholy is as graceful and captivating as a leaf falling from a tree.

And were that not enough, Sabbath manages to invent drum 'n' bass with the mock outro.

---

* Vocal harmonies, eh? Who'd have thought . . . ?

Chapter Twelve

Killing Yourself to Live / 1974–75

✝

As 1974 begins, OPEC's continuing stranglehold on oil reserves intensifies the major fuel crises in both America and the UK.* Pump prices hit the roof, and suburban garages turn into secret petroleum hoards as car-drivers prepare for the worst by building up lethal stockpiles at home. On 28 February, the British electorate returns a hung parliament; five days later, Harold Wilson forms a minority Labour government and brings an end to the three-day week almost immediately.

India becomes the world's sixth atomic power after it explodes a bomb in May, and the summer is dominated by the coverage of the Watergate case and its aftermath. Following an order for him to surrender all subpoenaed tapes, the US House Judiciary Committee formally recommends Nixon for impeachment. On 5 August, Nixon finally admits complicity in the cover-up, and, four days later, he cheats the hangman by resigning from office. He is succeeded by Gerald Ford who, unable to exonerate his predecessor and despite widespread protests, pardons Nixon for his part in the scandal. In a sweet twist of irony, the predominance of the media's massive coverage of Watergate during the summer is threatened only by their near-equal fixation with the newly prevalent practice of streaking. In both instances, the cover-ups are as ham-fisted and intriguing as what is known to lie beneath them.

As Britain prepares for its second general election in eight months, the IRA launches another major bombing offensive on the mainland: bombs in two Guildford pubs kill five and injure a further sixty-five, and there are more explosions at the Tower of London

---

* The price of oil was pushed up ten-fold as a result of Israel's besting of Egypt and Syria in the Arab–Israeli War. In an organised gesture of pan-Arab, anti-American protest, leading Arab nations colluded to push the price of crude beyond the reach of many of the world's poorer countries.

and the Houses of Parliament. After scraping home in the October election with a parliamentary majority of just three seats, Harold Wilson navigates the successful passing of the Prevention of Terrorism Act: a law that allows the police to arrest suspects and detain them without charge and which also restricts movement between Ireland and mainland Britain.

Skylab 3, part of America's ongoing space exploration programme, spends eighty-four consecutive days in space, the longest period so far, while a Mariner 10 satellite transmits pictures of Mars and Venus to an increasingly curious Earth. Patty Hearst, daughter of media mogul William Randolph and millionairess-in-waiting, disgraced British MP John Stonehouse and aristocrat friend-of-babysitters Lord Lucan all disappear in suspicious circumstances. Hearst resurfaces on CCTV, seemingly in cahoots with her abductors, as a soldier of the Symbionese* Liberation Army; Stonehouse is collared with a false passport and considerable funds in Australia; Lucan stays disappeared.

John Guillermin and Irwin Allen's *Towering Inferno* and Mark Robson's *Earthquake* usher in a spate of disaster movies; John Carpenter's *Dark Star* and Tobe Hooper's *The Texas Chainsaw Massacre*, meanwhile, provide Americans with a burst of much needed, post-Cold War paranoia that will be intensified further with the publication of Peter Benchley's *Jaws*. *Washington Post* journalists Bob Woodward and Carl Bernstein publish *All the President's Men*, and Solzhenitsyn unveils his epic and disturbing *The Gulag Archipelago: 1918–1956*.

Ably assisted by The Band, and following his first New York appearance in eight years at Madison Square Garden, Dylan releases *Planet Waves*, but it is a poor year generally for music. Aside from Bad Company's wholesome, eponymous debut, Blue Oyster Cult's endearing *Secret Treaties*, Paul McCartney's *Band on the Run* and the overlooked and underrated Budgie's *In for the Kill*, 1974 proves to be a year of retreads and last gasps: David Bowie's *Diamond Dogs*, Status Quo's *Quo*,

---

* And the whole world reached for atlases in an attempt to find out where Symbion or Symbiona or Symbionia was – only to discover that it didn't exist. One is now left to ponder exactly what it was this ambitious pressure group were trying to liberate – and from what.

Alice Cooper's *Muscle of Love* and the Coverdale/Hughes incarnation of Deep Purple's *Burn* and *Stormbringer* are all sad facsimiles, poor relations or unwelcome departures from rock's stagnating musical gene pool. The situation is so bad in fact that when Mike Oldfield releases his second album, *Hergest Ridge*, it drags the year-old *Tubular Bells* with it to the top of the UK album charts: for a whole month those two dismal albums share the top two positions.

As 1974 turns into 1975, the Leader of the Opposition, Edward Heath, is fighting a losing battle holding onto the Conservative Party leadership. After a party vote, Margaret Thatcher takes over and strikes a blow for womankind twenty years of postmodern feminism couldn't even begin to heal. As inflation in Britain hits an all-time peak of almost twenty-seven per cent, the electorate decide they'd like to join the European Economic Community with a yes vote comprising much less than half the total number of those eligible to vote.

There is trouble in the Far East as the communist forces of the Khmer Rouge overrun Cambodia's capital, Phnom Penh. The bloodshed and butchery inspire Vietnam's communists to do likewise as they run riot through Saigon and force the surrender of South Vietnamese President Minh. America gathers its diplomats, withdraws the last of its troops from both countries and scurries home.

Iceland further extends its fishing limits from fifty to two-hundred miles and sends gunboats to confront German trawlers. Spain quickly gets over the death of its leader, proto-Fascist and head of the military junta Generalissimo Franco, and returns a king as head of state, whilst neighbouring Portugal sees all executive powers transferred to the military. King Faisal of Saudi Arabia is assassinated by his nephew, who, in turn, is beheaded.

American President Ford survives two assassination attempts and looks on as friends and ex-colleagues are convicted of criminal conspiracy in the Watergate cover-ups: John N. Mitchell, John D. Erlichman, H. R. Haldeman and Robert C. Mardian join E. Howard Hunt, G. Gordon Liddy and numerous other luxuriantly initialled party bigwigs in jail. The Supreme Court rules that the beating of unruly students is

acceptable under certain circumstances. A federal jury, meanwhile, clears Governor of Ohio James Rhodes and the National Guardsmen from any wrongdoing during the 1970 Kent State student massacre; so it would seem that killing them is okay, too.

Jim Sharman's *The Rocky Horror Picture Show*, Ken Russell's *Tommy* and Michael Apted's *Stardust* demonstrate the uneasy marriage of film and rock music: the first is meant to be funny and isn't; the second, intended to be serious, is periodically hilarious; the third, plainly abominable. Steven Spielberg edges a step closer to superstardom with the film *Jaws*, but the movie honours go to Jack Nicholson, if not the whole cast, in Milos Forman's *One Flew over the Cuckoo's Nest*.

The year 1975 proves a much better one for music than its predecessor: Zeppelin unveil the sprawling and majestic *Physical Graffiti*; Dylan, the aching magnificence of *Blood on the Tracks*; and Pink Floyd, the sublime-but-queer-in-parts *Wish You Were Here*. The Who struggle to follow *Who's Next*, fail and release the lukewarm *Who by Numbers*, a return to the four-minute songs from which they claimed to have been liberated on their previous album;* Queen's apotheosis of high-camp prog, *A Night at the Opera*, bolstered by the phenomenal sales of their Christmas hit 'Bohemian Rhapsody', elevates Englishness from the quaint to the downright ludicrous in much the same way *Sgt. Pepper* had done eight years earlier. Bruce Springsteen successfully fuses Spector, Orbison and Duane Eddy into his urban masterpiece *Born to Run* – an album as long in the making and as troubled in its gestation as Sabbath's *Sabotage* – and provides the blueprint for Bob Seger and Tom Petty's careers, Meatloaf's *Bat out of Hell* and Thin Lizzy's *Jailbreak* and *Johnny the Fox* albums, amongst many others. The Eagles and Bowie embrace the blossoming disco movement in their own ways with *One of These Nights* and *Young Americans* respectively, while Bad Company, Jethro Tull and Alex Harvey plough their own individual furrows with *Straight Shooter*, *Minstrel in the Gallery* and *Next*. As Deep Purple, minus guitarist Ritchie Blackmore, hit a new nadir with the bottom-of-the-barrel-

---

* *Who's Next*'s 'Won't Get Fooled Again'.

scraping *Come Taste the Band*, the errant guitarist strikes out with the underwritten but promising-in-parts *Ritchie Blackmore's Rainbow*, featuring pint-sized, guttural Elf and future Ozzy replacement, Ronald James Padavona (or Dio, as he likes to be known).

For Sabbath, 1974 starts with a brief mini-tour of several major European cities, followed by a month-long tour of the States in February. The latter proves valuable in promoting *Sabbath Bloody Sabbath*, which, like all of Sabbath's early albums, is released in America some time after it is available in Britain.* After wrapping up the American tour in Nassau, where they perform with Bedlam (featuring future Sabbath member Cozy Powell) and Lynyrd Skynyrd, the band decamps to Britain and the members enjoy a month off. They return briefly to America the following month, where, on 6 April, they perform at the Ontario Raceway in California in what becomes known as the California Jam.

The California Jam is a massive festival at which Sabbath had been booked to appear some time earlier. Whether through poor management communication or just sheer apathy, as the time approaches, Sabbath show no inclination to perform in it; after having given their assent, they simply forget all about it. A few days before the festival is to take place, manager Patrick Meehan receives a reminder, and the news is filtered through to the band members. Still reluctant to accommodate the performance in the break of their schedule, the band despatch their road manager on a reconnaissance mission to check that the festival is still taking place and that tickets have been sold.

After receiving the news that the festival is, indeed, a legitimate affair and not just another disorganised free-for-all, Sabbath pack their bags and set off for California. Were further enticement necessary, it comes in the form of a letter threatening legal action should the band pull out. Sabbath are the pre-penultimate band on the bill (Emerson, Lake & Palmer and Deep Purple follow them)* which also includes Earth, Wind

* This is in sharp contrast to Led Zeppelin's early albums, which were released in the US before the UK.
* Sabbath gracefully withdrew from the inter-band arguments about who, exactly, should top the bill. In the end, it was ELP who won out.

& Fire, Black Oak Arkansas and several others. Over 250,000 visitors attend the one-day event, which is broadcast to an estimated twenty million TV viewers stateside. Although bettered by Coverdale and Hughes' energetic performance in Deep Purple, Sabbath throw together a creditable show* – a remarkable achievement considering the band has but half an hour's rehearsal before going on and have not played together for a month or so.

Another British tour begins in May, and this is followed by a week of commitments in Australia, before a subpoena, served to Osbourne on the instruction of former manager Jim Simpson, effectively prohibits Sabbath from performing live until the matter of Simpson's firing as manager – an event which took place four years earlier, in 1970 – is settled in court. As a result, Sabbath are grounded for the eight months through to July 1975. During the court proceedings, it comes to light that millions of pounds of royalties held by Simpson have never been paid to Sabbath. Sabbath had been having suspicions over Simpson's integrity – which was one of the reasons they fired him in the first place – but it is nevertheless sobering to discover that his mendacity had run so deep.

It's about here in the story that Osbourne's slide into the murk of drugs and alcohol really begins. It's always difficult for a singer to maintain his sense of focus in a group when that group is in the process of recording and re-recording, mixing and remixing, editing and re-editing tracks for hours on end. *Sabbath Bloody Sabbath* had taken months longer to record than their previous albums; *Sabotage* was to take over a year.* Once Osbourne had recorded his vocals, his job was done and his commitment

---

* Their performance of 'Children Of The Grave' can be seen on the DVD/video *The Black Sabbath Story: Volume One*, Sanctuary Records, 1991, together with a brief interview with Osbourne about the festival. While we're in this footnote, it is worth pointing out that Iommi and Butler, speaking in the same DVD/video, recall Sabbath's not having played together prior to the Cal Jam for several months. Rosen, too, quotes Osbourne as saying that the band hadn't *been on the road for three or four months*. In actual fact, although they played only one gig between April and December 1973, they had performed thirty shows in January and February of 1974.

* After having recorded the album, the tapes were inadvertently wiped – reportedly by a careless studio hand (most probably tape operator David Harris, who is credited as 'saboteur' on the liner notes). The whole album, therefore, had to be recorded again.

exhausted. So it's all too easy to see that whilst Iommi, Butler and Ward were twiddling knobs and tinkering with the mixes for Sabbath's later albums Osbourne must have been at his wits' end.

To make matters worse, Osbourne and Iommi have been butting heads over who is to occupy centre stage during performances. Osbourne, a born showman, would seem to be the obvious choice, but it is Iommi who, borne out of his status as the band's leader, is more frequently taking precedence. This struggle – as pointless as it is to prove ultimately destructive – is merely symptomatic of a much more fundamental crisis: Iommi wants to move on musically and take the band with him; Osbourne wants Sabbath to stick to what they do best – and what their fans most expect and desire from them – the no-holds-barred heavy stuff upon which they have built their reputation. This is an issue that has been covered in Rosen and much alluded to in other biographical essays on Black Sabbath. However, the point that has escaped these writers is that, on *Sabbath Bloody Sabbath*, it was Iommi who came up with the title track, the most traditional-sounding of the album's eight pieces; Osbourne, on the other hand, brought the least typical vocal number, 'Who Are You', to the table. The matter then is not one that merely confines itself to the issue of whether to experiment; rather, it appears that Osbourne was happy to venture out stylistically – as long as the undertaking met with his approval, and that, in doing so, Sabbath did not forsake their blood-and-thunder roots. Iommi, on the other hand, has always maintained a pronounced liking for Sabbath's earthier, more prosaic compositions – you only have to hear him speak about 'Paranoid' on the DVD/video *The Black Sabbath Story: Volume One** to realise that. Additionally, as the band's leader and the only true musician out of the lot of them, he probably felt the most pressure to advance the group's musical identity.

In short, the matter should not have been insoluble; certainly, it shouldn't have proved fatal – as it was to do in the years that followed. And if success is to be measured in the quality of the finished product,

* Sanctuary Records, 1991.

we must conclude that their decision to compromise — from whichever laudable direction it came — only ended in disappointment. *Sabotage*, which was to be the following release, was to be a great album, but the wayward, and in retrospect rather desperate, inclusion of 'Am I Going Insane (Radio)' and the overblown 'Supertzar', respectively seen as Osbourne's unhappy marriage of experimentalism and basic four-to-the-bar rock and Iommi's ersatz sophistication, did not build that greatness; rather they threatened to diminish it — particularly as the two tracks were sequenced together on the album. *Sabotage* succeeded where its blending of straight-no-chaser rock and proggish finger-dipping was less forced: the extended acoustic sections of 'Symptom Of The Universe' and 'The Writ', for example. And although *Sabotage* deserves to be called a great album, or even a classic album, it could have been all the greater had the band not suffered so many distractions during its lengthy compilation.

The Simpson court case — perhaps the single most significant of these distractions — occupied the rest of 1974 (indeed, it consumed a fair part of 1975, too), and Sabbath were not to return to the road until the following summer. Amidst Osbourne's increasing unhappiness and his subsequent decline into alcohol abuse, Iommi's whimsical philandering with ever-diversifying musical forms, Ward's continuing ill health (he was drinking heavily, addicted to cocaine, riddled with hepatitis and was to suffer a mild heart attack in 1975) and the general sense of frustration and anger resulting from the protracted legal wrangling with Simpson, 1974 proves to be Sabbath's most difficult year yet.

As *Black Sabbath v. Simpson* drags on into 1975, it is discovered that Patrick Meehan, Simpson's replacement as Sabbath's manager, has been siphoning much of the band's earnings into his own bank account. There is a strong suggestion that Meehan's interests in both Sabbath and WWA (Sabbath's UK label at the time) are conflicting: that in his having financial interests in the record company as well as the group, the band are not getting the best deal. However, it is information concerning the California Jam that proves to be the most emphatic. It comes to light that the band was paid in the region of $250,000 for the appearance; the

individual band members, however, only received $1,000 each. Setting aside a generous allocation for travelling expenses, insurance and taxes, around $150,000 remained unaccounted for. Contractual niceties mean that the band is not at liberty to sack Meehan outright; instead they bring in an overseer, Mark Forster,* and simply discontinue negotiations with Meehan. Eventually, Meehan and Sabbath part company on mutual terms, and, for the first time since 1968, Sabbath are without a manager.*

Meanwhile, the final settlement in the Simpson case – which comes as another bitter blow for our boys – ensures that Simpson receives a further pay-off ✝ on the grounds of his 'wrongful termination'. Yeah, you read that right. The good news is that the matter is now behind them, and they are free to begin working in earnest on their new album. *Sabbath Bloody Sabbath* is proving a hard act to follow: although the record has met with a favourable response from both fans and critics, it is going to be difficult transforming that response into a blueprint for the sixth album. Should they, musically speaking, repeat the experimental formula of *Sabbath Bloody Sabbath*? Should they move further on – or should they go back?

It proves a difficult quandary to settle. As far as the band is concerned, *Sabbath Bloody Sabbath* had represented a new pinnacle, and this is what is presenting them with such difficulty. If they merely repeat it, they will encounter a creative stasis – their first ever; if they are to move further afield and occupy more experimental and proggy ground, they may jeopardise their identity, or it simply might not work; if they move back, on the other hand, they risk the chance of losing all the ground and respect they have gained with *Sabbath Bloody Sabbath*.

But this is rather simplifying the matter: it is not, after all, a case of the band collectively scratching its head and trying to figure out the next move. It is more a case of the individual band members – Iommi and

---

* Mentioned by Ward in Stark (p. 27); Stark misspells Forster's name as 'Forrester'.
* Don Arden, father of Osbourne's second wife, Sharon, was appointed as Sabbath's next manager in 1976.
✝ Simpson was awarded £35,000 by way of compensation; most of this, however, was payable by Meehan and not Black Sabbath.

Osbourne in particular – pulling in different directions* and how it might be possible to proceed without the group falling apart. Osbourne is at the beginning of a steep slide into alcohol and drug abuse, and his commitment to the group is to receive a further test later in the year when his wife gives birth to his first son, Louis.

With management troubles, at least temporarily, behind him, a critically acclaimed album still selling well almost two years after its release, and an infant son in tow, Osbourne has little obvious reason to be at odds with the world. However, the constant struggle with Iommi over the band's musical direction is intensifying and driving a wedge between Osbourne and Sabbath. It has to be said that this is barely discernible on *Sabotage*: indeed, Osbourne's disenchantment and frustration are put to good purpose, externally, in his embittered renditions of 'Hole In The Sky', 'Symptom Of The Universe' and 'The Writ' in particular.

The lengthy interval between the release of *Sabbath Bloody Sabbath* and the recording of *Sabotage* should have seen the band eager to capitalise on the success of the latter. However, with Ward's continuing ill health and the general uncertainty over how to pitch the album, much of the laid-back spontaneity and dynamism of their earlier releases is missing from the record. The album is not so much overwrought, as some critics have, in retrospect, determined, as over-*thought*: had Sabbath been in a position after *Sabbath Bloody Sabbath* just to go ahead and make *Sabotage*, there probably wouldn't have been a problem. With the enforced hiatus of the Simpson court case, however, and the various other managerial issues plaguing them at the time, this was never a possibility.

Coming so long after *Sabbath Bloody Sabbath*, *Sabotage* is something of a last gasp for the original Black Sabbath. Torpedoed by bad management and legal wrangling, the band had spent the eighteen months since

---

* There were rumours at this time suggesting that each of the four members of Black Sabbath was working on material for a solo album. Rosen, too, suggests that Osbourne's 'Am I Going Insane' was originally intended as a solo project (pp. 85–6). However, these plans, if such they were, came to nothing.

the release of their last album flailing in and under the water. *Sabotage* was the last breath of air the original Black Sabbath was to take before sinking: for the two following albums – *Technical Ecstasy* in 1976 and *Never Say Die* in 1978 – they were inhaling water.

Sabotage is slipped out in September and enters the UK album chart at number twenty-one. Rod Stewart's enduring *Atlantic Crossing* sits at number one – it was to spend seven consecutive weeks there – and Pink Floyd's *Wish You Were Here* is also vying for the top position. *Sabotage* enters the Top Twenty the following week, and, the week after, it reaches its peak placing of number eight. It remains in the Top Ten for the following two weeks and bobs in and out of the Top Thirty for another month before making its exit.

Sabbath convene a further tour of America to promote *Sabotage*. This begins on 14 July in Toledo and is split into three legs in order to save the band from exhaustion. The first leg sees them appear with Slade in Chicago and Peter Frampton in Savannah. Additionally, there are performances at Lincoln, Minneapolis, Lakeland, West Palm Beach, Baltimore and Providence (with Kiss), Asbury Park (where the show was recorded for the *King Biscuit Flower Hour*) and Philadelphia. After a two-week rest, the band then go on to play Chicago (again), Houston, El Paso, Tucson and Albuquerque, Sacramento (with Frank Marino's Mahogany Rush) and various other venues in California, before a filmed appearance at Long Beach* and appearances at Las Vegas, Spokane, Seattle and Portland.

The band returns to Britain in mid-September, before embarking on a national and European tour in October. There are ten performances in Britain in thirteen days, before the band honours commitments in Germany and Scandinavia. Before the year is out, Sabbath returns to the States for one-off appearances in New York, Boston and Syracuse.

It's probably safe to say that the release of *Sabotage*, and the fact that it broke the Top Ten, ensured the continuation of the original Black Sabbath through to 1978 and the disappointments of both *Technical*

---

* *Don Kirshner's Rock Concert*, broadcast on US television on 25 October that year: Siegler.

Ecstasy and *Never Say Die*. Had Sabbath not managed to get anything out of 1975, it seems certain they would have splintered there and then. As it was, and for better or worse, at least Sabbath were still breathing by the time punk came, did its thing and left a year or so later.

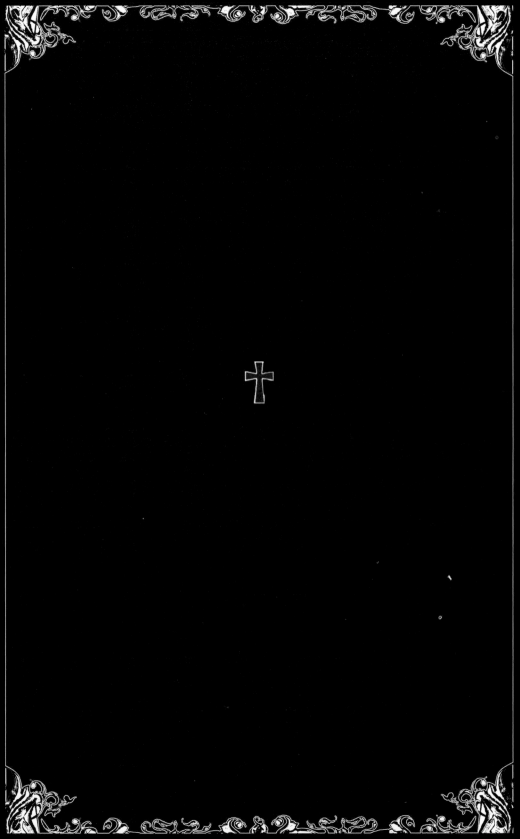

Chapter Thirteen

Sabotage

†

This was Sabbath's first release on the NEMS* label. Although NEMS was to reissue all of the Sabbath back catalogue, as well as bringing out the compilation double album *We Sold Our Soul For Rock 'n' Roll*, Sabbath were to revert to Vertigo for their following release, *Technical Ecstasy*. *Sabotage* was also the first Sabbath album to display the group on its front cover. My guess is they regret that now. Originally conceived by Bill Ward and his drum roadie, Graham Wright,* and executed and overseen by the art company Cream, the cover is so spectacularly awful it's difficult to know where to start with it.

It's not the concept, such as it is, that's so bad – and it's not the execution of the concept that stinks either – it's just that the band look like complete idiots. Remember, this is the first (and, indeed, only) time that any manifestation of Black Sabbath has decided to put itself up front pictorially on an album cover.† It would have been very easy to commission some dark nebulous artwork for the piece or something more symbolic, perhaps, along the lines of *Master of Reality* and *Vol. 4*; instead, they made the deliberate move of foisting themselves up there, and – it has to be said – none of them looks all that happy about it. And that was then. Heaven knows how they feel about it now. In defence of the project, Wright, co-author with David Tangye of the book *How Black Was Our Sabbath*, states therein that the shoot was only intended to be preliminary and that more fitting images of the band members were later to be superimposed. To everyone's eternal embarrassment, this

---

* The label started life as an offshoot from Brian Epstein's family's business. Epstein's father owned a chain of music stores in northern England, North East Lane Music Stores. Brian Epstein started the label, which grew with signings such as Billy J. Kramer & The Dakotas, Gerry & The Pacemakers and others, during the sixties.
* Ward in Stark (p. 28). The liner notes credit only Wright.
† The nearest Sabbath came to repeating this was Iommi's 1986 release, *Seventh Star*, which featured the guitarist only.

never happened, and what we are left with is a cover that manages to be simultaneously excruciating and perversely endearing.

The front shows our boys lined up, facing forty-five degrees away from the camera, in front of a large mirror emblazoned with the album's title, SABOTAGE. The mirror is displaying not the backs of the foursome, as would be normal under the laws of reflection, but their fronts. So it's like each member has a ghostly double of himself standing behind him – or, in Iommi's case, sitting behind him. When you turn the cover over, you see the same image but from behind: the boys are similarly posed, facing the mirror, backs to camera, and their backs are likewise reflected in the mirror in front of them. The cover is typical of the absurdist-influenced styles most notably embraced by contemporary cover artist Storm Thorgerson* and may be traced back to the Belgian Surrealist Magritte.*

Starting from the left, Butler is kitted out in some prescient incarnation of Sonny Crockett from the eighties' TV series *Miami Vice*. His lapis lazuli jacket, boasting slightly padded shoulders, foreshortened sleeves and a tailored waist, sits over a skin-tight camisole-type top, horizontally striped, with a plunging 'V' motif drawing the eye to what, under normal circumstances, would be the cleavage. His left hand sits uncomfortably in his jacket pocket, crooking his elbow at a rigid ninety-degree angle. In what is either a continuity gaffe or a subliminal message to his fans, Butler's left hand is positioned by the side of his body on the back of the album. His trousers are tight-crotched, loose-fitting cream Oxford flares, neatly pressed and snugly showcasing what is either a priapic hernia or a very large cigar. He supports himself by means of a neatly folded umbrella, which suggests an infirmity at odds with the otherwise healthy, neo-Restoration grandeur of his dress.

Iommi, seated in Zen-like contemplation, his fingers knotted in the here's-the-church-here's-the-steeple manner, looks like he has just

---

* Pink Floyd's *Wish You Were Here* (1975) and Led Zeppelin's *Presence* (1976) amongst others.
* René Magritte (1898–1967), a former wallpaper designer and commercial artist, and later at the forefront of the Belgian Surrealist Group. His 1937 painting *La reproduction interdite* (*Not to be reproduced*) uses the same contravention of the laws of reflection as *Sabotage*.

returned from an unsuccessful audition for the Travolta part in *Saturday Night Fever*: light blue, brushed denim flares, white satin shirt with a collar so pronounced it looks capable of propelling him into orbit, a deep tan and one of those prototypical digital watches that required two hands for operation (one upon which it was worn, the other to push the button to display the time). But at least he doesn't look like he's just rifled his wife's closet to cobble together his outfit. Which is more than may be said for . . .

Bill: forgot his trousers, forgot his shoes, forgot his shirt. Ward is resplendent in his wife's scarlet tights and leather bomber jacket, his thumbs hooked into his pocket as if in the early stages of dancing to Status Quo's 'Down Down' or 'The Birdie Song'. Turn the album over and you get to see his underpants. Featuring a brown and white check design, these can only be described as 'bachelor pants': no self-respecting woman would allow her man to wear such a thing, and one can only wonder what kind of a man would want to.*

And finally there is Osbourne – 'a homo in a kimono',* as he would describe his appearance later. It's a *quality* kimono – mainly black with some nice print-work, a suggestion of a brocade around the throat, fine ornamental detailing and colourful *japonaiserie* throughout – but, for heaven's sake, *it's a kimono*.

In terms of the album's music, the sound is both crisp and biting. Mike Butcher, who had served as engineer on *Sabbath Bloody Sabbath*, was retained, and the mix keeps hold of that album's impressive latitude. At times, the drums sound a little too removed from the mix, but Butler's bass and Osbourne's embittered vocals sit perfectly alongside Iommi's emphatic guitar work. The album's various songs demonstrate a sophistication – first assayed on 'Sabbath Bloody Sabbath' and 'Killing Yourself

---

* Osbourne, apparently – for it was he who loaned Ward the particular item for the shoot (Osbourne, quoted in Clerk [p. 55]). This makes me concerned over two issues: is Osbourne himself not wearing pants, and did Ward just slip the pants on after Osbourne had divested himself of them (I mean, without washing them or anything – whilst they were still warm)? And in case you were wondering what happened to Ward's original pants (the ones he was wearing prior to the shoot), he's stuffed them down the pants he *is* wearing.

* Clerk (p. 57).

To Live' – that shows a band happy to embrace contrasting musical styles within the one composition. Osbourne's searing vocals – a clear refutation to all those who contended that he was never much of a singer – Butler's acid lyrics and the seething fury of much of the album's music all testified to the pronounced state of resentment and hostility the band felt toward the music business generally and their own mismanagement within it specifically.

1) Hole In The Sky

It was a conscious move to start *Sabotage* with a no-holds-barred, guitar-bass-and-drums rocker in order to re-establish Sabbath's credentials as the world's heaviest rock and roll band. The field was being deserted at the time: Deep Purple and Led Zeppelin had moved towards lighter, funkier, poppier sounds, and 'heavy rock' (for want of a more specific term) was about to be hijacked, broken down, reassembled, and churned out as eighties 'heavy metal' – a process that started as early as 1977 with the release of Jim Steinman and Meatloaf's high-octane pap-balladry, *Bat out of Hell*, and which was to continue throughout that decade and beyond, first by acts falling under the New Wave of British Heavy Metal umbrella and, later, by myriad American floozies in spandex, make-up and tattoos.

'Hole In The Sky' sees Sabbath inhabiting the new musical ground they had successfully annexed with tracks like 'Sabbath Bloody Sabbath' and 'Killing Yourself To Live' from the previous album. The execution is tight and precise, and the band are caught in spirits at least as high as those put to work on the joyous 'Fairies Wear Boots' and the lubricious and lavishly sprawling 'Sabbra Cadabra'.

The main riff, essentially nothing more than a detuned* and accelerated pentatonic blues lick in F sharp, shored up by alternating A – B and B – A interchanges, is a simple affair; the second motif at 0:26, a

---

* C sharp again – although the riff is based on the fifth string, and, accordingly, the song is keyed in F sharp.

swinging, descending pattern with broad intervals, likewise. The chorus – the persistent hammering of a single chord – is more prosaic still. Yet despite the lack of any technical invention in the song, and despite the uncharacteristically short register of musical ideas, the song succeeds triumphantly.

Butler's lyrics, developing from the modestly outré on the previous album to the downright absurd on this track (1:23–1:32 is a quite spectacular example), revisit the theme of ecological meltdown he so emphatically exploited in songs like 'Into The Void' and 'Looking For Today'. Like 'Into the Void', an escape is offered from this encroaching and inevitable catastrophe, and, just as it does in the earlier song, that escape takes the form of speeding full-tilt through the ether to some unspoilt cosmic utopia.

With four identical verses, two identical choruses and no extra-curricular extraneousness to fatten it out, four minutes seems a long time to fill with such little material. However, the band's sheer exuberance, their energetic enthusiasm for the piece, not only carries the song, it makes it one of *Sabotage*'s most compelling and infectious pieces. The spirited abandon of the ensemble playing – this is, by far, the most live-sounding track on *Sabotage* - more than compensates for Butler's occasionally questionable liberty-taking with the lyric. His reckless and bathetic rhyming of Mars and cars – the almost cantankerous perversity of it – qualifies as either jejune fatuousness or borderline genius.

2) Don't Start (Too Late)

A brief but rapidly paced acoustic guitar interlude along the lines of 'Orchid' and 'Laguna Sunrise', 'Don't Start (Too Late)' serves as a clever introduction to the following 'Symptom Of The Universe'. It may not be immediately evident on first listen that the two pieces share the same chord structure: an alternation between E and B flat. The interval between these two chords is the by now familiar flattened fifth or tritone found throughout the early Sabbath catalogue from the track 'Black Sabbath' onwards.

Although superficially resembling the Spanish style of 'Orchid', 'Don't Start' in fact bears a closer relationship with the other instrumental from *Master of Reality*, 'Embryo': the furiously quick melody actually shares the same sequence of notes as its more lugubrious predecessor. The piece reaches an abrupt conclusion at 0:49 after an alternation between B flat and A major, just short of resolving on the adapted home chord of A major. This is an efficient device: the unexpected halt on the lip of resolution further dramatises the start of the following 'Symptom Of The Universe', making the latter's initial motif sound like a fall into the very pit of despond.

The title of the piece, together with its parenthetic appendage, is a reference to the oft-repeated (and frequently ignored) exhortations of sound engineer Robin Black for the band not to start playing until he had the tapes ready.

3) Symptom Of The Universe

Essentially the riff from the track 'Black Sabbath' – only with the gaps filled in – 'Symptom Of The Universe' has proved the most enduring of the eight tracks on *Sabotage*. Whether it necessarily deserves such an accolade is questionable. However, it is sometimes the case that a song, without ever being particularly interesting compositionally, can nevertheless have something about it – something that makes it special and ensures its future through the years. There's very little going on musically with some of The Beatles' most famous songs, from 'I Saw Her Standing There' through to 'Let It Be'; however, they do have *something*, nevertheless. In terms of Sabbath's output, 'Paranoid' has proved the most popular song from the *Paranoid* album; similarly, 'Children Of The Grave' has endured from *Master of Reality* and 'Snowblind' from *Vol. 4*.[*] These songs don't bear comparison compositionally to their album mates, 'War Pigs', 'Into The Void' and 'Under The Sun', yet they

[*] Siegler, in polls conducted on the fan site black-sabbath.com between September 2002 and May 2003.

nevertheless have something that endears them to the Sabbath fan base. It's probably something as patent as the fact that these songs have steadfastly remained in both Sabbath's and Osbourne's repertoires over the intervening years; it may also be something to do with lowest common denominators.

'Symptom' is a good song – there's no doubt about that – it's just not a particularly interesting one. It rips through three highly paced verses, each replete with Butler's lyrical preoccupation with matters mythological and paranormal, and the chorus – if such it may be called – consists of the single word 'Yeah!' staggered out over a pulsating, descending figure of three chords. At 4:24, it disintegrates into a two-chord jazz figure – not without interest but, at a further two minutes, somewhat needlessly protracted.

However, it does have its merits. The energetic delivery of the vocal is most compelling (regardless of the fanciful and fantastical lyric), and the sublime, Joe Cocker-style vocal coda beginning at 4:34, laid out in Tennysonian trochaic octameter and employing the Dorian mode of 'A National Acrobat' and 'Looking For Today', is rather affecting. Iommi's spiralling riff at 3:14 and his piercing solo at 3:49 are also well considered. Butler's bass and Ward's pinpoint drumming do much to underscore what is undeniably an infectious verse motif.

My grumble is that however well the song has been executed, and it *has* been executed well, it just doesn't add up to a full measure. It comes over as two half-songs crudely nailed together by means of a startling hinge figure and solo. The clattering images conjured throughout the lyric – all this Mother Goose stuff, for instance – I find a little distracting. The urgent, oft-repeated, never-dying love, I can handle, but the final salvo promising conjugal happiness under the loving skies of summer belongs to 1967 and an ideology Sabbath never bought into and, moreover, set out to subvert.

4) Megalomania

At 9:41, 'Megalomania' is Sabbath's longest ever, self-penned studio cut

and, at times, shows every inclination of trespassing into the proggy territory suggested by the track's longevity. Compositionally, at least, there's a lot going on here — certainly enough for it to warrant consideration as 'progressive' — but the credit in this song derives not so much from the content itself but in how the various and diverse musical themes fit together within it. Lyrically, the song is a bitter concoction of mental psychoses: paranoia, obsession, schizophrenia, delusion and denial, fantasism and phobia all loom large in the singer's long list of psychosocial problems. The term 'megalomania' — a clinical diagnosis exemplified by a lust for control and delusions of grandeur — barely does justice to the pathological diversity of symptoms evinced in the song's lyrics. It's almost as if all the characters featuring in earlier Sabbath compositions — the haunted quarry from 'Black Sabbath', the junkie war vet from 'Hand Of Doom', the manic fantasist from 'Fairies Wear Boots', the evangelical pot-head from 'Sweet Leaf' and so on — have fused into the one, poor, unfortunate individual in 'Megalomania'.

The melancholy arpeggio that starts the piece — a sinister and brooding alternation comprising the minor tonic augmented with the submediant* — artfully conjures the same sense of pervasive introspection and withdrawal as, say, the opening figure in 'Hand Of Doom'; the treated vocal repetitions which preface the delivery of the lyric* make plain the singer's paranoia. The limping slide into the subdominant at 1:03, accompanied by Osbourne's hostile vocal, and the progression to the dominant eight bars later are archetypal Iommi⚕ and serve to increase tension in the song at a point where it is already building irresistibly.

The musical sequence is then repeated for a second verse, in which the singer's psychoses are further expounded and which concludes with the smouldering reiteration of a Garboesque call for solitude at 2:52. There then follows a short bridge at 3:07 which, other than marking the

---

* Again the C sharp tuning is employed. The played chord is an A minor later augmented with an F; the detuning produces an F sharp minor augmented with a D.
* ('I find . . . I find . . . I find . . .')
⚕ The same progression may be found in many of Sabbath's earlier material: 'Fairies Wear Boots' and 'Lord Of This World' are but two.

end of the beginning of the song, brings the song back to its home key of F sharp from the transitional C sharp in which it was lately rooted. The following section at 3:23, where Osbourne sings of his being taken he knows not where – the dirtiest riff on the album by some measure and possibly the dirtiest in their entire recording catalogue – gathers a somewhat frightening momentum and evokes, as it does so, equal measures of fear and mania in the listener as surely as it represents those feelings in the singer.

The fear transmutes to loathing in the following section at 3:07 – a familiar-sounding barrelhouse figure – in which the mania is no less evident, although it is now fuelled entirely by self-recrimination. At this point in the song all the musical ideas have been aired, played out and exhausted; musically, the song has nowhere else to go – and goes there. Lyrically, however, the listener is subjected to more poisonous outpourings from this most troubled of human spirits. As the tower of corrupt emotions builds unsteadily ever higher – and the remote possibility of resolution sinks lower beneath the increasingly ponderous weight of the singer's encyclopaedic pathology (this song could well have been titled 'Universal Symptoms') – we arrive eventually at what can only be described as a happy ending.

From the initial paranoid introspection, we went to outright fear; from fear, to self-recrimination; thence, via abject hatred, to a final sense of liberation. The singer has found happiness from the depths of his sorrow; this gives him the strength to despise the way in which he worshipped and was led by his anonymous nemesis. This has been a whirlwind whip round the emotions, but it has ended up on a high note. I guess he just found the right pills at last.

5) Thrill Of It All

The major shame with CDs is that you don't get a side two. Okay, you also miss out on all that expansive, large-scale cover art, too, but their fliplessness is, for me, the greater crime. There are some songs in the rock canon, if you'll forgive the slightly grandiose term, which can only *be*

side-two-track-one songs: Zeppelin's 'Heartbreaker', for one, then there's Pink Floyd's 'Money', Steely Dan's 'Show Biz Kids' and Springsteen's 'Born To Run' to name a few more – you just couldn't place them anywhere else on their respective albums. In the old vinyl days, you always got the impression that the sequencing of tracks was quite deliberately structured: you needed something specific to start off side one, something of a drama to close it, something renascent to open side two and something really exceptional to finish it off. There were some recording artists who considered that was *all* you had to do. And the significant thing was that there was a break between the end of side one and the start of side two. And it was a natural break, too – it wasn't like hitting the pause button on a CD player. You could go off and make a cup of tea, empty your ashtray or hit your parents for some going-out money. And then, when you were ready, you could put on side two, and something different and wonderful would happen.

And here's another thing: because albums came in two twenty-minute chunks, you could really listen to them properly. Listening to music used to be an intense affair: you gave it everything you had. Now what happens is you put on a CD (in itself a less fulfilling task than the protracted ritual of committing a stylus to vinyl), sit down and, after about twenty minutes, you get up and wander about or pick up a paper or start thinking about fixing the exhaust, and you're not really giving the music – which is still playing – your all.

'Thrill Of It All' is a side-two-track-one song. You've just got through 'Megalomania', and you want more – you just don't want it *yet*. But when you do put it on, it does the business. There's something both arresting and familiar about the opening figure. Whether it's the temporal similarity to the main motif in the first movement of Beethoven's Fifth Symphony* or its anagrammatic rearrangement of the main riff from 'Hole In The Sky', there's something that tells us it's going to be a bumpy, if halfway familiar, ride. At 0:33, Iommi lets fly a lick right out of

---

* You know the one . . . da-da-da *daaaah*. Apparently, Beethoven used this as a musical interpretation of the phrase 'Thus Fate knocks at the door . . .'. Very dramatic.

the *Rock God Handbook*, vintage Clapton meets stoned-out Santana, which not only takes us into the verse riff but cleverly modulates the song to a fresh key.*

The verse riff itself – a big, squeaky affair accompanied by echo-laden drums* – possesses the sort of awkward purpose and creeping portentousness exemplified by the earlier songs 'Iron Man' and 'Electric Funeral'. The semitonal interchanges at the end of the riff again hark back to earlier Sabbath compositions. Unusually, the first verse leads straight into the second, and Butler's lyrics, which in the first verse amounted to little more than a barrage of polysyllabic gobbledygook, become less verbose and take on more meaning in the second. Addressing the question to Mr Jesus, Osbourne asks whether, given the trouble in the world, Christ still believes in man. This is quite a deft reversal of the ontologically more insoluble 'How can there be God when evil is so prevalent in the world?' and resurrects the assertion of man and God being on speaking terms with each other.

There's then a delicious, six-bar instrumental interlude at 2:39 before the song changes completely into a sprightlier tempo, driven by a well moderated Moog at 2:59. Lyrically, the two halves of the song don't fit – there's little in common with the existential sci-fi of the first half and the cynically motivational exhortations of the second – but, musically at least, the two contrasting elements are effectively conjoined into a pleasing whole by this six-bar instrumental bridge.

The second half of the song – a real smoke and spotlights affair – does much to further the argument that, when they wanted to, Sabbath could occupy successfully the traditional centre ground of mainstream seventies' rock. The rampant tempo, the sinuous intervention of the synthesiser and the propulsive accompaniment are suggestive of *Who's Next*-era Who, and the sound could have provided the blueprint for further musical development for Sabbath had they not dampened it down into the bloodless and disheartening turgidity of the following

---

* The song starts with a riff in F sharp minor (played in A minor, the guitar is detuned down three semitones); the verse is in the key of B minor (D major).
* The rather brutal rhythmic construction is reinforced by handclaps (as it is in 'Looking For Today' from *Sabbath Bloody Sabbath*).

album's 'Back Street Kids' and 'All Moving Parts (Stand Still)'.

The title, incidentally, alludes to Aleister Crowley's *Duty*, in which he states (with his customary good humour), 'Thrill with the joy of life & death . . . thy death shall be lovely: whoso seeth it shall be glad' and has nothing to do with the 1963 Doris Day movie of the same name.*

6) Supertzar

Although some favourable words have been spoken about this song (mainly, it has to be said, by those who recorded it), I can only assess this particular offering in terms of its failure. Whether it was a failure waiting to happen – a bad idea from the start, if you will – or merely a failure in its execution is uncertain; that it *is* a failure there can be no doubt. The practice of blending rock with 'classical'* music was piloted through acts like Electric Light Orchestra, Captain Beefheart, Frank Zappa, ELP and others throughout the seventies and was about to come to its awful, full-blown apotheosis with the release of the London Symphony Orchestra's *Classic Rock* in the post-punk, power-pop summer of 1978.

The song's connection with the gothic is tenuous: despite the lush and wordless exertions of the English Chamber Choir, the song repeatedly fails to tie itself up to the atmospherically disconcerting nature of its more sepulchral predecessors, 'O Fortuna!' (from Carl Orff's *Carmina*

---

* Actually, the movie's called *The Thrill of it All* (note the definite article), and, although you probably remember Rock Hudson being in it (he usually had the responsibility of partnering Ms Day), it was actually James Garner who in this movie took on that task. Osbourne's 'Mr Crowley' (which featured on his first solo album, *Blizzard of Ozz*, in 1980 and which clearly had nothing to do with the Doris Day film) featured the lines 'Your lifestyle to me seemed so tragic / With the thrill of it all / You fooled all the people with magic / You waited on Satan's call'.

* The habit of dubbing any music played by musicians in formal evening wear as 'classical' is as infuriating as it is inaccurate. The Classical period – which really only lasted from the late eighteenth to the early nineteenth century, and was perhaps best typified by composers such as Mozart and Haydn – was but one genre in the history of orchestral or instrumental music. The middle of the nineteenth century saw the beginning of the Romantic movement – presaged by Beethoven and more closely associated with the great Germanic composers Wagner, Bruckner, Richard Strauss and Mahler – which, and the irony here is lost on most people, was diametrically opposed to the almost architectural strictures of Classicism. Similarly, the early eighteenth century composers – Johann Sebastian Bach, for instance – were more tail-end baroque than they were Classical. Elgar's *Enigma Variations* are no more Classical than the outpourings of the Wu-Tang Clan are rock and roll.

214

Burana), Verdi's 'Dies Irae' (from his *Requiem*) and others, upon which it is imprudently predicated. There is the very distinct possibility that the song's title is serving some sort of diabolic alternative to the then prevalent biblical rock opera – most obviously, *Jesus Christ Superstar*. However, as a barb, it is less effective than the Christian musical soaps it sets out to deride. (The title 'Supertzar', intended as a *nom de guerre* for our illustrious nemesis down under, is a neologism marrying super and tzar.) Despite Ward's impressively martial percussion and the inclusion of some portentous campanology, there is little that saves this choric ode from an overall sense of ugly pointlessness; it sits on *Sabotage* like a Sunday painter's worst watercolour in a room full of Vermeers.

The initial E minor motif, sharing its melodic structure with both the main riff of *Paranoid*'s 'Electric Funeral' and the opening vocal line to Irving Berlin's 'Let's Face The Music And Dance',* falls short of its maleficent intentions by dint of it being played too quickly and in too high a register. The trademark Iommi semitone intervals are there, but they lose their menacing nature from being played staccato rather than glissando. The lumbering 9/4 time signature (which is thankfully dropped at the bridge), intended to give the piece a sinister ghoulishness, merely renders it more awkward and unwieldy. At 1:17, the song has the opportunity to redeem itself – an 'Iron Man'-style semitonal guitar break offers to take the song in another direction – but the door closes too soon, and what promise there might have been comes to nothing.

Written at home by Iommi on guitar whilst accompanied by his wife on harp, and clocking in at 3:44, the piece is not only too long but thoroughly exhausts the meagre allocation of musical ideas it bases itself upon. In a way, this is its most substantial failing: had 'Supertzar' merely arrived, waved its fearsome satanic claw in front of our faces and left us within a couple of minutes, it might have proved more successful; at 3:44, it is asserting itself as a bona fide song rather than a brief musical interlude, and the compositional paucity of its construction cannot support the sheer weight of its posturing grandiloquence.

---

* Iommi is a lifelong Sinatra fan.

7) Am I Going Insane (Radio)

And this one's no better really, which is a shame, as, structurally speaking, it is, again, not without moments of promise. The problem is, however, that such promise as there is fails to deliver, and the overall impression is one of either indolent experimentation or misguided intention.

The entirely major chord sequences in the song are archetypically Spanish – so too the interval between the E major home chord and the F major which follows as the first change in the verse pattern – and they could have been made to sound a great deal more interesting than they do. Broadly speaking, the song is badly let down by the monotonous melody of the chorus. However, such a blithe criticism suggests that the song has merely the one, however major, flaw; in fact, it boasts several.

That the song is under-written is to be expected: it was an Osbourne composition and, as Rosen has intimated, was to form part of an Osbourne solo album – a plan that, for better or worse, came to nothing. With an eight-bar, two-chord introduction, a repeated eight-bar, two-chord verse and a repeated eight-bar, three-chord chorus and a comically blundering lyric written in dismal quatrains, the song severely outstays its welcome at 4:16. At its worst – specifically, the moribund and perfunctory execution of its choruses – it sounds like a post-watershed Status Quo leading a group of tone-deaf drunks in a gymnasium singalong.

Ward's drumming in the verses is of some interest: it slaps and tickles its way through a momentum entirely independent of the song, in much the same manner that Keith Moon's did in his best work with The Who. Iommi's trenchant guitar, which is completely at odds with the laboured vocalisations of Osbourne, is also significant. It was this trebly and whooshy sound that he was to adopt on subsequent Sabbath albums and which led to the final disintegration of the Sabbath sound formulated through the band's first few records: it is this guitar sound that you hear throughout *Technical Ecstasy* and *Never Say Die*.

The instrumental middle section is merely a recapitulation of the verse and chorus structure over which Iommi takes a completely out-of-

character solo. From here, we inevitably end up with verse three (as we did in Osbourne's other composition, 'Who Are You', from *Sabbath Bloody Sabbath* – something which rarely happens with Iommi/Butler compositions) which ends in a farcically grotesque melic couplet in which Osbourne takes pains to elucidate that the reason he may not be sounding too cheerful is because he's a 'schizo-brain'. The anodyne chorus is then repeated a further three times in an attempt, presumably, to drive the listener insane too.

The speeded-up laughter, followed by the harrowing and stridulous sound of vomiting which closes the song, comes as some sort of relief. I remember feeling quite shocked and frightened when I first heard these noises; now I find them merely embarrassing, like bad situation-comedy, *The Jerry Springer Show* or splitting an infinitive in public. As with Osbourne's previous composition, 'Who Are You', the title inexplicably omits its punctuational requirement, the question mark. Psycholinguists amongst you are at liberty to consider whether Osbourne's then predilection for interrogative song titles was indicative of his insecurity or, alternatively, his hunger for control. The effort was pushed out as a single* on both sides of the Atlantic in February 1976 but failed to stimulate any interest – the parenthesised 'Radio' in the song's title indicative of the band's deprecatory opinion of its commercial success.

8) The Writ

'The Writ' is one of Sabbath's biggest songs and arguably their most adventurous. Starting with a rumbling bass figure in B, reminiscent of *Paranoid*'s 'Hand Of Doom', the song explodes in a furiously delivered vocal at 0:39. As its title suggests, the song embodies Sabbath's seething resentment toward a catalogue of managerial misdemeanours and legal fusillades that had beset the band throughout its short professional history. Most of this rage is, no doubt, directed at Jim Simpson, whose serving of a writ to an onstage Osbourne the previous year had effect-

---

* b/w 'Hole In The Sky'.

ively stymied the band for the most part since the release of *Sabbath Bloody Sabbath*. Osbourne's singing is fevered and possessed, while the lyric – a latter-day Archilochian* epode – additionally displays both vulnerability and hurt.

The livid opening salvo, blasting in at 0:39 and stridently setting out the high dudgeon of the lyric, mixed with the brooding and explosive fury of the music, firmly establishes this credo of wounded pride and resentment. The next lines, detailing the depths of emotion the singer has endured and the hopelessness he now feels at continuing this bitter conflict, betray the helplessness and desperation which help steer this song away from mere truculence and lend it a genuine poignancy.

The song then abandons the brooding two-chord structure established thus far for a scathing assault at 1:32. An additional dynamic is forced on the song by this passage, based around a very Who-like A major – E major – B major sequence. Butler's bass then cuts in for a reiteration of the opening motif (although it starts on the dominant F sharp before it returns to B) and the entire sequence is repeated.

The second time around, however, the lyrics – and Osbourne's delivery of them – intensify in both their bitter fury and their wounded dignity. The singer – long-suffering and clearly now at breaking point – has stomached so many broken promises and lies that he is now driven by his indignation to the point of exacting violent revenge.

The second phase of the song begins at 3:37. Over a fractured and troubled riff, played almost mechanically by Iommi, Osbourne sings Butler's lyrics that, again, show no sign of relinquishing their acrimony. This marks a turning point: hereafter, the mood changes to first-person narrative. At 4:23, there is the introduction of a thumping riff on C sharp (featuring the eerily discordant flattened fifth, a G natural) which takes the song through to its first note of sneering triumph: a suggestion that the band, despite the suffering and setbacks, will overcome these problems and will then set about grinding the faces of their tormentors

---

* Archilochus (seventh century BC): a Greek poet who specialised in composing verse based entirely on his own experiences.

into the dirt by way of acknowledgement. The optimistic tacit major-chord progression E – F sharp – A – G sharp, over which Osbourne sings that a smiling face means the world to him, marks the dramatic turning point of the song: if you've seen the 1954 film *On The Waterfront*, it's the bit near the end where Marlon Brando's just been beaten up by Lee J. Cobb and gets to his feet again. It is big, angry, ornery power, unvanquished by the organised brutality of oppression.

The ensemble build-up on the final syllable of Osbourne's 'misery' from 4:58–5:06 (probably his boldest ever melisma – it climbs robustly and without hesitation through three-quarters of a diminished major – C – D sharp – F sharp – to the dominant G sharp) leads us into the third and final phase of the song at 5:06. With bass, multi-tracked guitars, xylophone and a suggestion of harpsichord playing an abstruse sequence of chords,* Osbourne slips back into world-weary self-reflection, as he did in the choruses of 'Spiral Architect' from the previous album, whilst retaining just a suggestion of the bitterness for the tribulations that have brought him to such a state. The pitifully defeatist lines starting at 5:39, where the singer rues his prior, unfounded confidence, transmute to the sardonic and ironically triumphal statement that everything will turn out fine; however, any overtones of optimism suggested by the lyrics are entirely quashed by Osbourne's sneering delivery of them. The singer's performance here is both trenchant and morbidly playful – like a mental patient half-heartedly slashing at his wrists with a scalpel he purloined from the attending physician.

The recapitulation of this extended phrase allows Osbourne the opportunity of penning a brief suicide threat of sorts before the song is enveloped in the relentless black fug of the emphatic C sharp riff first encountered at 4:30. The fade-out works cinematically, pulling the camera higher and further back, leaving the ever-diminishing, strait-jacketed patient occupying centre-screen.

The album closes with a bit of tomfoolery: Osbourne extemporising

---

* C sharp/G sharp – D sharp7/G – F sharp – C sharp. The peculiar D sharp7/G can be approximated 345343 on guitar. Alice Cooper's 'Only Women Bleed', which also came out in 1975, shares a similar, if slightly less elaborate, sequence for its verse structure; both pieces owe a debt to Spirit's 'It Shall Be', from their 1968 album *The Family That Plays Together*.

lyrics on the notion of blowing on a jug whilst Ward hammers away at a piano. Just as The Beatles followed the medley on side two of *Abbey Road* with the light-hearted and totally unnecessary 'Her Majesty', so Sabbath close the monumental *Sabotage* with a similar tribute – only theirs is to Mungo Jerry.*

* The story, recounted by Ward in Stark (p. 27) and referenced in Tangye and Wright (pp. 43–4), concerns the Hollywood Festival held in Stoke-on-Trent, Staffordshire, in 1970. Mungo Jerry and Sabbath – along with Colosseum, The Grateful Dead, Screaming Lord Sutch, Free, Traffic and others – played this weekend festival together, and Mungo Jerry managed to capture the audience's interest whilst on stage by blowing into a jug.

Afterword

Thrill of It All

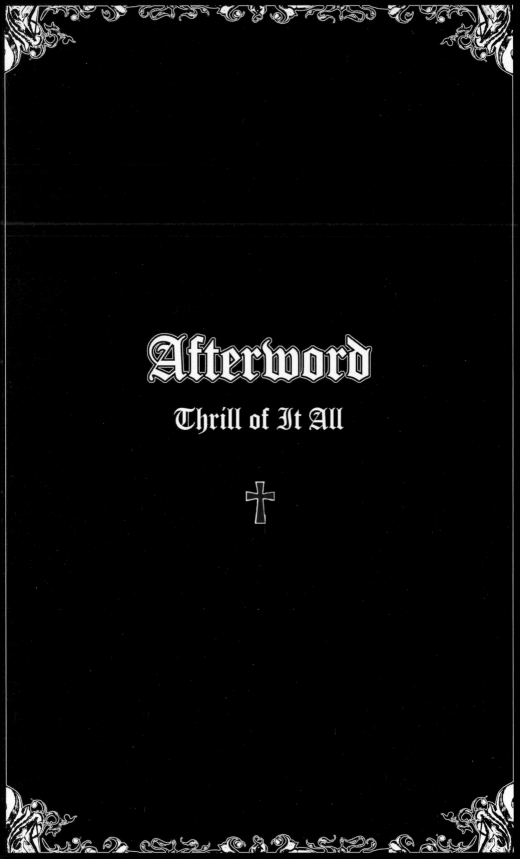

As far as future recorded material goes, well next we want to do a real rock album. *Sabotage* was a bit laid-back by our standards. We want to get back to the roughness and rawness of our first album. We feel we should be able to do exactly what we do in the studio on stage. We're not going to do any more of this fucking about like brain surgeons with hundred-track machines.*

Technical Ecstasy could be described as Iommi's overdub baby.*

I bought *Sabotage* the week it came out. It was the first album they released while I was a fan. I cradled it in my arms riding the bus home. Several times during the long and bumpy journey I removed the vinyl from its sleeve and stared at the grooves, hoping I'd get some kind of foresight into what they might be holding. And when I got home and placed the thing on my stereo, I felt the privilege of being let into the world's most closely guarded secrets. Of course, I do realise how precious this must seem now, but that's really how it felt at the time. No one I knew had heard this music before; it felt like I was the first in the world.

We can all recall defining moments in our development: instances where our lives seemed either to take on some new aspect or else be changed forever. This was not one of those. This was not some sort of epiphany where I came to the belief that my future and the future of Black Sabbath were to be inextricably linked. No door opened for me, no great sense of realisation overwhelmed me, but there was, nevertheless, a certain feeling of

* Osbourne speaking to Geoff Barton, 1975. Hoskyns (pp. 64–5).
* Hoskyns, *Creem* magazine, 1982.

 223

communion with the band – or, at least, of my catching up with them – and, in telling this story, both mine and theirs, this sudden confluence seems somehow significant.

I didn't realise then – as I know now in retrospect – that the years immediately following this moment would place a tremendous burden on my idolatry. I wasn't to know that the next Sabbath album was to be a stinker, the one after that even worse, and when Osbourne and Sabbath parted company acrimoniously in May 1979, it felt like death had arrived after a long illness: heartbreaking, certainly, but, nevertheless, something of a relief. I didn't buy Sabbath albums for a while. I couldn't conceive of a Sabbath without Ozzy – or an Ozzy without Sabbath. I heard *Heaven and Hell* and it wasn't Sabbath; I heard *Blizzard of Ozz* and that wasn't Sabbath either. I didn't know where to turn in the eighties for music; I didn't know where to go to get my customary fix of dark, heavy sounds and unremitting melancholy. I couldn't believe in all that goth drivel or any of its professed misery when its perpetrators evidently spent such meticulous effort on their appearances. So I kept turning back to the seventies, and I kept listening to those first six records – somewhat morosely like a child looking at photos of a pet that has since died – and I knew that, as far as music went, I'd never love anything as much as I had loved those albums. And, although I've tried to write this book as a critical analysis of Black Sabbath's music, I am all too aware that it is also something of a love letter.

I first saw them at Sheffield City Hall on 16 May 1978 – our first date, if you like. Like a lot of first dates, it ended disastrously: the PA broke down after an hour, following periodic blips throughout the earlier part of the set. Bill Ward manfully treated us to an un-amplified and spontaneous drum solo, while the other members sheepishly trudged offstage. I was right at the front, and I could hear Bill shout 'Fuck it!' as he dumped his sticks and trounced off to join them. There was a long pause, and then the house lights came up; someone made an apologetic announcement, and two thousand disappointed Sabbath fans were left to make their way dejectedly home. Some said Van Halen

– who were supporting Sabbath on the tour – had sabotaged the PA. Most of us realised that such a step was hardly necessary: Van Halen were incandescent; Sabbath were merely in decline.

The tour had originally been scheduled to promote the *Never Say Die* album. However, the record's release was delayed, and there was accordingly nothing to promote. So someone had the bright idea of making it the tenth anniversary tour. The programme notes were celebratory – valedictory, even – but the perspective was concentrated firmly on the past. We all knew that Osbourne wasn't going to stay with Sabbath for long, and, once we'd heard Van Halen, we knew that rock itself was about to undergo a sea change. Long hair was going out; big hair was coming in. Guitarists started to play faster and lost touch with everything remotely connected with feeling. As punk's vivid, ephemeral and ugly spectacle was sanitised and corseted under the austere, be-suited, monochrome banner of 'new wave', rock parodied itself in leather-bound, coke-feasting, cock-thrusting caricature. Elvis had been dead for the better part of a year; Margaret Thatcher was beating at the door of Downing Street and Ronald Reagan well on his way to the White House. Nat King Cole, Frank Sinatra and Johnny Mathis all had albums in the Top Ten;* Boney M did battle with selections from *Saturday Night Fever* and *Grease* for the singles' crown. Punk may have killed off a dinosaur, but in this crucible Lester Bangs was to term 'a society of cannibals and suicides',* it created a monster.

But whereas punk had stripped rock of its finesse, it was disco which, kicking in a couple of years earlier, had robbed it of its feeling. Embraced from many perspectives – rock, soul, funk, euro-pop, power-pop and, later, reggae and new wave – disco represented not only the 'cult of self', laying down the predominant social ethos for the ensuing eighties, but also the embodiment of insincerity. Disco really *was*

---

* Cole's and Sinatra's albums – both entitled *20 Golden Greats* – and Mathis's *You Light Up My Life* were placed at four, seven and five respectively in the 20 May, 1978 album chart. Additionally, The Platters, Buddy Holly, Manhattan Transfer and no fewer than four soundtrack albums all featured in that week's top thirty.
* Writing in *NME*, 17 December 1977. Reprinted in *Psychotic Reactions and Carburetor Dung*, Serpent's Tail, 1996.

product, accessible from almost anywhere musically. Marketed ruthlessly across cultures and age groups, it subverted artistry in music and replaced it with artifice.

Disco may well have died years ago – its bubblegum fatuousness now strikes us upon revisiting its most celebrated output as something almost endearing – but its bastard progeny is with us still. And although an unhealthily copious surfeit of good-looking ladies and bad-tasting bottled beer might get me shaking my tired limbs to, say, Chic's 'Good Times' at some cheesy discotheque, I know that the rest of me – the bits that aren't directly fired by sex and alcohol – would rather be splashed out on the floor of some godforsaken community hall, listening to 1970 Sabbath with my greatcoat, crushed packet of Players No. 6 and a pint.

More recently, on a freezing cold night in December 1999, I caught up with them again. I took my sister to London's Astoria on Charing Cross Road to see them play a warm-up for their brief tour of Europe, which culminated in two nights at Birmingham's NEC – later commemorated on *The Last Supper* DVD and video. They hadn't played a venue this small for nearly thirty years – almost certainly never would again – and it was magical. I didn't feel at all ridiculous punching my peace signs in the air while Osbourne struggled with the melody in 'War Pigs' – because everyone else was doing the same; and I didn't mind one bit paying well over three quid for a pint of gassy bitter and then spilling most of it on my way back to the stage – because everyone else had done that, too.

The incongruity of Osbourne taking frequent, lengthy sips from a steaming mug of herbal tea didn't register at the time; neither did the alarming unfamiliarity of Bill Ward's hair, shockingly grey and antithetically short – or Butler's well-fed paunch, only partially obscured by his gunslinger bass. They perhaps didn't register because, although I certainly saw them, I was completely transfixed by Iommi. I was sufficiently near to him that, had he suddenly taken ill and fallen forward, we'd have cracked heads. He looked both magnificent and proud, like some ancient patriarch whose errant sons have just returned

home. Remaining conspicuously aloof, without once breaking sweat, he caressed his guitar strings (he was never the kind of guitarist who would embellish his playing by cavorting about or striking bizarre facial contortions) and those riffs just radiated out of him. That night, dressed top to toe in his customary black, he was a god. He was Vulcan, Vishnu and Vegas rolled into one, and he never once stopped smiling.

Walking to the Tube station afterwards, my sister said something about the years melting away – something about her being a child again, my borrowing her Clearasil, the hairdrier fights, arguing over who was to get the tear-out bits from Alice Cooper's *Billion Dollar Babies*. And it's easy and inviting for us to look at our lives that way: as an indeterminate length of elastic which stretches forever ahead of us – increasing the strain as it does so – and which occasionally snaps back to some point years ago before you even realised that life, or the recollection of it, *was* elastic.

Someone once said that life is a cemetery of retrospective lucidities* – that the things we do in life, the decisions and mistakes we make, seem as obvious to us in their remembrance as they are imperceptible at the time; however, such words give too great a credit to hindsight. There are some moments in life whose significance we recognise as they're happening, and which don't rely on the perspective of adult commemoration in order for them to make sense, and which we absorb – rather than their absorbing us. Madeleine Morgan's liquorice kiss, shelling peas whilst hearing my grandfather's last confession, the rise and fall of the baby-sitter's breasts, the first time I heard Black Sabbath: these things haven't become important to me with the passage of time – they're not flashbacks that I recognise *now* as being somehow significant, character-forming or life-changing – they've *always* been that way. And neither do these memories require any sort of recollective key in order for me to access them – they're not locked away in some long-buried subconsciousness – I carry them around with me. They've shaped me and formed me; in ways I am almost too embarrassed to acknowledge, they *are* me.

* Jean-François Revel in his *La Connaissance Inutile* – in case you're interested.

So, that night, after seeing Sabbath at the Astoria, when my sister asked whether the years had melted away for me too, I didn't even have to check: I could still feel them there, weighing my pockets down and straining their seams, with all the cold, time-worn familiarity of beach stones.

Glossary

(This is by no means a comprehensive list of musical terms, but it does cover all the fancy technical nomenclature used in this book.)

accelerando	An acceleration in tempo: the end of 'War Pigs', for example.
adagio	A slow section; in slow time. See also **andante, largo** and **lento**.
Aeolian	See **modes**.
agitato	A piece played in a jerky, agitated manner.
andante	A slow section; in moderately slow time. See also **adagio, largo** and **lento**.
arpeggio	A chord played note by note rather than all at once. This may be plucked by the fingers ('Orchid') or picked with a plectrum ('Sleeping Village').
carillon	A piece of music redolent of the pealing of church bells. Such extracts will usually feature the tonic, mediant and dominant quite heavily. See also **voluntary**.
chorus	Other than the obvious meaning, chorus is the name given to an effect created by a slight desynchronising of multi-tracked sound. For example, a vocal track can be recorded, and then duplicated with a slight delay. This gives the sound a peculiar and 'spacey' exotic lushness.
chromatic	The name given to a scale comprising every note within it. The **scale** chromatic scale consists of twelve notes separated by semitonal intervals: C, C sharp, D, D sharp, E, F, F sharp, G, G sharp, A, A sharp and B.
coda	The final section of a song or piece of music; the opposite of a **prelude**.

diatonic scale   The name given to the traditional seven-note scale prevalent in 'Western' music. This may be either major or minor. It comprises the **tonic** (first note); the **supertonic** (second note); **mediant** (third); **subdominant** (fourth); **dominant** (fifth); **submediant** (sixth) and **subtonic** (seventh). In minor scales, the mediant, submediant and subtonic are a semitone lower than in the major scale.

diminuendo   Strictly speaking, this would be an orchestrated (i.e. written and played) fading out of a piece of music. Virtually all fade-outs in popular music in the modern recording age are achieved through a gradual lowering of the recording volume, rather than a lowering of playing volume by the ensemble.

divertimento   A musical passage of no fixed form.

dominant   The fifth note of any given scale or chord, located between the **subdominant** and the **submediant**. In major and minor scales, it is located seven semitones above the **tonic**.

Dorian   See **modes**.

exotic chords   A generic term covering chords comprising more than three notes. The additional notes (which augment the **tonic, mediant** and **dominant**) may be the **submediant** (major/minor sixth); **supertonic** (ninth or suspended second); **subdominant** (suspended fourth); the **subtonic** (seventh/major seventh) or any combination of these.

flat   A note dropped by a **semitone**; e.g. B flat is located a semitone beneath B.

flattened fifth   See **tritone**.

glissando   The sliding of the fretting fingers up or down the neck of the guitar, as at the very start of 'Into The Void'.

interval	The gap between two notes (either played in sequence or together), e.g. the interval between a natural E and a natural G is a minor third (three semitones); the interval between a C and an E is a major third (four semitones).
key	The location (in terms of pitch) of a given piece of music and its corresponding arrangement of sharps or flattened notes.
largo	A piece of music played slowly and broadly. See **andante**, **adagio** and **lento**.
lento	A slow section. See also **andante**, **largo** and **adagio**.
major chord	A group of three (or more) notes, comprising the **tonic**, the (major) **mediant** and the **dominant**.
mediant	The note located between the **supertonic** and the **subdominant** - (the third note) of any scale or chord. In a major scale, it is located four semitones above the **tonic**; in a minor scale, it is three semitones above.
melisma	In singing, the extension of a single syllable over two or more different notes. In 'Changes', the final syllable of the word 'changes' encompasses three notes.
minor chord	A group of three (or more) notes, comprising the **tonic**, the (minor) **mediant** and the **dominant**.
Mixolydian	See **modes**.
modes	Scales using only natural notes (i.e. the white keys on a piano). The scale from C to C (the Western 'major' scale) and the scale from A to A (the Western 'minor' scale) are by far the most predominant and are referred to modally as the Ionian and **Aeolian** respectively. The **Mixolydian** (from G to G) and the **Dorian** (D to D) are perhaps the next most prevalent in popular music. The remainder, the **Phrygian** (E to E), **Lydian** (F to F) and **Locrian** (B to B), are much more obscure and feature only rarely in contemporary music.
modulation	A change in key. A piece may modulate up or down; i.e. it may move to a higher or lower key.

octave An interval of twelve semitones – or six full tones. The term 'octave' is, therefore, rather an odd one, and it can be confusing. The octave is the most elementary of harmonic constructions: when a man and a woman sing the same song, the chances are they will be singing the melody an octave apart from one another. Where Osbourne sings the same tune as the song's riff ('Electric Funeral', 'Iron Man'), he does so an octave above the guitar.

pastorale A piece of music evoking the countryside or rural scenes.

pentatonic scale A scale (neither major nor minor) comprising five notes and often used as the basis of rock/blues composition. In the key of E, the five notes would be E/G/A/B/D; in A, A/C/D/E/G.

pitch How high or low a given piece of music is.

power chord A chord consisting of just two notes: the **tonic** and the **dominant** (the fifth). This is neither major nor minor, as it is missing the **mediant** (third), which would give the chord a major or minor identity. Most rock riffing is played in power chords.

prelude An introductory section.

recapitulation A fancy musical term for a repeat of any given musical theme or phrase.

rallentando A slowing down of the tempo; also called 'ritardando'.

relative major/minor Each major key has its relative minor; i.e. a key that shares all the same notes as itself. Similarly, each minor key has its own relative major. The relative minor is located three semitones beneath its parent major; e.g. A is the relative minor of C (A is three semitones beneath C). Not to be confused with the term 'parallel major/minor': A major's parallel minor is A minor and vice versa.

semitone A half-tone; the smallest interval in standard musical notation (one fret on a guitar).

sforzando	Played loudly and with great attack.
sharp	A note raised by a **semitone**, e.g. C sharp is located a semitone above a natural C.
staccato	Where notes are played with emphasised separation, rather than looped together: the final guitar attack in 'Children Of The Grave', for example.
subdominant	The fourth note of any given scale or chord, located between the **mediant** and the **dominant**. In major and minor scales, it is located five semitones above the **tonic**.
submediant	The sixth note of any given scale or chord, located between the **dominant** and the **subtonic**. In major scales, it is located three semitones beneath the **tonic**; in minor scales, four semitones beneath.
subtonic	The note located beneath the **tonic** (the seventh note) of any scale or chord. In a major scale, this is a **semitone** beneath the **tonic**; in a minor scale, a full tone.
supertonic	The note located two semitones above the **tonic**; the second note of the **diatonic** scale.
suspended chord	(e.g. suspended fourth, second etc.) A chord that contains a note (usually indicated in the name of the chord – e.g. the fourth in a Dsus4) that keeps the chord in suspense: it does not suggest finality or resolution.
tonic	The first (or home) note of any scale or chord.
triplets	Three notes of equal length played in a time value (tempo) of, usually, two or four: there is a sequence of triplets in the 'fast' riff in 'Black Sabbath'.

tritone Referred to exhaustively throughout this book – usually as the 'flattened fifth' – this is a musical term for an **interval** of three full tones. Known affectionately as the 'diabolus in musica' (translation unnecessary) since the Middle Ages, this rarely-used interval can be made to sound strangely beautiful: Leonard Bernstein used it all over his musical *West Side Story*, with particular effect on the painfully earnest torch-ballad 'Maria', where he features it in the notes of the two syllables Ma-ree, before resolving on the **semitone** shift up to the **dominant**. This **interval** features heavily in the Sabbath canon from 'Black Sabbath' onwards.

voluntary In the musical sense, a fanfare-like piece of music often used in church to initiate a religious ceremony. See also **carillon**.

Credits

For permission to reproduce illustrations the author and the publishers wish to thank the following:

DACS (15)
Mark Gerson (6)
Jane McCarthy (10)
National Portrait Gallery, London (7)
Redferns Music Picture Library (3, 5, 11–14, 17–19)

Grateful acknowledgement is made to Onward Music Ltd for kind permission to quote from the song lyrics of 'After Forever', 'Black Sabbath', 'Changes', 'Children Of The Grave', 'Cornucopia', 'Killing Yourself To Live', 'Lord Of This World', 'Planet Caravan', 'Sabbath Bloody Sabbath' and 'The Wizard'.

Every effort has been made to trace and contact copyright holders. The publishers will be pleased to correct any mistakes or omissions in future editions.

Index of Songs

(Emboldened entries represent detailed analyses; italicised entries represent mentions in footnotes.)

After Forever	47, 59, **107–9**, 115
Am I Going Insane	185, 196, *198*, **216–17**
Behind The Wall Of Sleep	43, **46–7**, 116
Black Sabbath	23, **44-5**, 117, 137, 144, *151*, 151, 207, 208, 210
Changes	6, *6*, 137, **141-3**, 153
Children Of The Grave	**110–12**, 113, 115, 137, 183, *194*, 208.
Cornucopia	131, *131*, 137, **147-8**, 149, 161
Don't Start (Too Late)	**207–8**
Electric Funeral	69, **82–3**, 88, 111, 151, 175, 213, 215
Embryo	1, *107*, **109-10**, 113, 148, 175, 208
Evil Woman (Don't Play Your Games With Me)	37, **48–9**, 51, 52, 117
F.X.	**143**, 149
Fairies Wear Boots	47, 69, 70, 83-4, **87-8**, *112*, 146, 206, 210, *210*
Fluff	149, 153, **176–7**, 181
Hand Of Doom	47, *70*, **83–6**, 87, 88, 106, 137, 145, 183, 210, 217
Hole In The Sky	198, **206–7**, 212, *217*

Into The Void	113, **117–19**, 141, 175, 207, 208
Iron Man	69, 70, **80-82**, 111, 115, 118, 213
Killing Yourself To Live	153, **179–81**, 205-6
Laguna Sunrise	130, **148-9**, 153, 207
Looking For Today	153, **183–5**, 207, 209, *213*
Lord Of This World	**113–15**, 115, *210*
Megalomania	*53*, 137, **209–11**, 212
N.I.B.	43, **47-8**, 49, 69
National Acrobat, A	**172–6**, 209
Orchid	*107*, **113**, 148, 185, 207
Paranoid	69, 70, **76-8**, 94, 115, 137, 140-1, 142, 195, 208
Planet Caravan	69, *70*, **79-80**, 82, 116, 117, 175
Rat Salad	69, *70*, **86-7**, 148
Sabbath Bloody Sabbath	144, 163, **170–2**, 179, *184*, *185*, 195, 206
Sabbra Cadabra	168, 170, *177*, **177–9**, 206
Sleeping Village	**50-1**, 113
Snowblind	106, 130, **145-7**, 208
Solitude	**115–17**
Spiral Architect	153, 170, **185–6**, 219
St Vitus Dance	130, 149, **149-151**
Supernaut	130, **143-4**, 153, 183
Supertzar	196, **214–15**
Sweet Leaf	47, 104, **106-7**, 180, 210

Symptom Of The Universe   196, 198, 207, **208–9**

Thrill Of It All   137, **211–14**
Tomorrow's Dream   130, **140-1**, 145, 153

Under The Sun   *131*, 137, **151-3**, 208

War Pigs   69, 70, 71, **72–76**, 83-4, *112*, 115, 183, 208
Warning   50, **51-2**, 148
Wheels Of Confusion   137, **138-40**, 146, 153, 175
Who Are You   164, 168, **181–3**, 195, 217
Wicked World   37, **52-3**, 49
Wizard, The   43, **45-6**
Writ, The   196, 198, **217-20**